Pragmatics and Emotion

It has long been received wisdom in semantics and pragmatics that 'the head' and 'the heart' are two opposing forces, a view that has led scholars, until now, to explore the mental processes behind cognition, and the mental processes behind emotion, as two separate entities. This bold, innovative book challenges this view and provides an original study of how we communicate our emotions through language, drawing on both pragmatic theory and affective science. It begins with the assumption that emotional or expressive meaning plays such a central role in human interaction that any pragmatic theory worth its salt must account for it. It meets the associated challenges head-on and strives to integrate affect within one theory of utterance interpretation, showing that emotional meaning and rationality/reasoning can be analysed within one framework. Written in a clear and concise style, it is essential reading for anyone interested in communication and emotion.

TIM WHARTON is a linguist based at the University of Brighton. His research explores territories beyond those regarded as the 'traditional' fields of linguists and as a result, he has worked with poets, artists, clinicians, designers and even mathematicians to expand the boundaries of linguistic pragmatics.

LOUIS DE SAUSSURE is Professor of Linguistics at the University of Neuchâtel where he co-founded the Cognitive Science Centre. He has published extensively in semantics, in pragmatics and in discourse analysis.

Pragmatics and Emotion

Tim Wharton
University of Brighton

Louis de Saussure
University of Neuchâtel

CAMBRIDGE
UNIVERSITY PRESS

Shaftesbury Road, Cambridge CB2 8EA, United Kingdom

One Liberty Plaza, 20th Floor, New York, NY 10006, USA

477 Williamstown Road, Port Melbourne, VIC 3207, Australia

314–321, 3rd Floor, Plot 3, Splendor Forum, Jasola District Centre, New Delhi – 110025, India

103 Penang Road, #05–06/07, Visioncrest Commercial, Singapore 238467

Cambridge University Press is part of Cambridge University Press & Assessment, a department of the University of Cambridge.

We share the University's mission to contribute to society through the pursuit of education, learning and research at the highest international levels of excellence.

www.cambridge.org
Information on this title: www.cambridge.org/9781108799034

DOI: 10.1017/9781108869867

© Tim Wharton and Louis de Saussure 2023

This publication is in copyright. Subject to statutory exception and to the provisions of relevant collective licensing agreements, no reproduction of any part may take place without the written permission of Cambridge University Press & Assessment.

First published 2024
First paperback edition 2026

A catalogue record for this publication is available from the British Library

ISBN 978-1-108-83596-1 Hardback
ISBN 978-1-108-79903-4 Paperback

Cambridge University Press & Assessment has no responsibility for the persistence or accuracy of URLs for external or third-party internet websites referred to in this publication and does not guarantee that any content on such websites is, or will remain, accurate or appropriate.

For our fathers

Contents

Acknowledgements		*page* ix
1	Introduction	1
	1.1 Prolegomena	1
	1.2 Clocks and Clouds	3
	1.3 Overview	6
2	Pragmatics and Emotion: The Challenges	13
	2.1 Introduction	13
	2.2 Two Challenges	14
	2.3 Pragmatics	26
3	What Is Emotion?	29
	3.1 Introduction	29
	3.2 The Early History of Emotion Studies	33
	3.3 Affective Science	38
4	From Proto-pragmatics to Pragmatics	52
	4.1 Introduction	52
	4.2 Towards Expressive Meaning	54
	4.3 Bally's *Parole*	59
	4.4 Speech Acts: How to Do Things with Words (and Emotional Expressions)	63
	4.5 Alternatives	70
5	Relevance Theory, Non-propositional Content and Ineffability	72
	5.1 Introduction	72
	5.2 Relevance	74
	5.3 Two Notions of Relevance?	98
6	Beyond Propositions	104
	6.1 Introduction	104
	6.2 Affective Effects	106
7	Emotion and Evolution	126
	7.1 Introduction	126
	7.2 Creature Construction	130

8	Pragmatics and Emotion: The Challenges Revisited	144
	8.1 Introduction	144
	8.2 Two Challenges	144
	8.3 The Challenges: Our Response	145
	8.4 Pragmatics and Emotion: Closing Remarks	148

References 149
Index 167

Acknowledgements

The authors would like to thank the following colleagues for cognitive and affective effects, past, present and future: Tamlyn Adatto, Nick Allott, Stavros Assimakopoulos, Constant Bonard, Myriam Bras, Billy Clark, Anne le Draoulec, Danny Dukes, Jean-Pierre van Elslande, Chengying Gao, Alex Golding, Elly Ifantidou, Caroline Jagoe, Pauline Madella, Didier Maillat, Misha Müller, Steve Oswald, Katerina Panoutsou, Anna Piata, Ismaël Pozner, Mengyang Qiu, Andrea Rocci, David Sander, Ryoko Sasamoto, Kate Scott, Mat Smith, Jonathan Steimer, Claudia Strey, Marianna Traka, Lemonia Tsavdaridou, Nathalie Vincent-Arnaud, Chara Vlachaki and last, but by no means least, Deirdre Wilson.

Thank you also to everyone at Cambridge University Press. In particular, we would like to give a special mention to Helen Barton and Izzie Collins, for their seemingly limitless, good-natured patience, and Frances Tye, for her hard work, intelligence and keen eye.

Finally, we would both like to express our love and thanks to our families. To Alice de Saussure, Arielle de Saussure, Cyril de Saussure, Marina de Saussure, Laura Evans, Luna Evans-Wharton, Xanthe Wharton and Zoë Wharton, thank you for everything.

1 Introduction

> Reason is like a map ... If you know where you want to go, it can tell you how to get there, but it can't tell you where to go. It can't stop you wanting something either. What people want has nothing to do with reason. You can't reason your way out of a passion: all you can do is oppose it with a stronger passion.
>
> Grace Ritchie, in *Slave of the Passions*[1]

1.1 Prolegomena

In the above epigraph, Grace is drawing on a view of the relationship between rationality and emotion first articulated by Scottish Enlightenment philosopher David Hume. 'Reason is, and ought only to be the slave of the passions, and can never pretend to any other office than to serve and obey them', he famously wrote (1739 Book II. 3.3.4: 414–15). It is not rationality that motivates humans to engage in acts of reasoning. That motivation comes only from the passions, and even though we often feel them to be opposing forces, reason and passion, cognition and affect or – in Hume's terms – *ideas* and *impressions*, work together in complex ways (see Radcliffe 1999).

Fast forward 300-or-so years, and Patricia Greenspan (2002: 206) is making a related point when she writes:

[Emotional] states are commonly thought of as antithetical to reason, disorienting and distorting practical thought. However, there is also a sense in which emotions are factors in practical reasoning, understood broadly as reasoning that issues in action. At the very least emotions can function as 'enabling' causes of rational decision-making ... insofar as they direct attention toward certain objects of thought and away from others. They serve to heighten memory and to limit the set of salient practical options to a manageable set, suitable for 'quick-and-dirty' decision-making.

Given the relationship between emotions and reasoning and given the fact that among humans the communication of information about emotional states is ubiquitous, the reader of this book might be forgiven for assuming that

---

[1] Wilson (1991). This quote appears with the permission of the author.

pragmatic accounts of linguistic communication (which, after all, are based on reasoning), would include quite well-developed views of not only the role of emotion in reasoning described in the quote from Greenspan but also how information about emotional states is communicated. However, for a range of reasons, those working in pragmatics have tended to persist in the view that the mental processes behind reason and passions exist in somehow separate domains, and as a result, the emotional dimension to linguistic communication has tended to play very much a subordinate role to the rational or cognitive one. Indeed, in many accounts it plays no role at all.

One of the authors remembers during our undergraduate years asking a now eminent professor of linguistics where emotion might fit into the kind of pragmatic theories of communication we were discussing. 'It doesn't, and we don't talk about it', came the response.

It would be easy, but wrong, to suggest that this reflects some kind of lazy, anti-affect bias by pragmatists. The view that emotion is antithetical to cognition in fact has its roots in ancient rationalist philosophy, in which emotion was assumed to be of minor importance, a property of the 'soul' rather than the body. For Socrates, the mind was limited by emotions. Plato believed that they were not to be trusted and had to be skilfully harnessed and reined in. Emotional responses required careful reflection and action was to be taken only once this reflection had been completed. The Stoics took an even harsher view: the ultimate state to which humans could ever aspire – *apathea* – called for a total absence of emotion. For Cicero, the appropriate word with which to best represent the Greek word for 'emotions' – *pathē* – was 'diseases'.

This view persists and perhaps still permeates the way we think about the role of emotion in our everyday interactions with other people. Faced with a difficult professional decision, imagine a friend asks your advice. You might try to help by offering a few general thoughts. In making the decision, you might suggest, they should try to be level-headed, that is, rational and logical. At the same time, you might add that they should avoid being led too far astray by their feelings or emotions. When it comes to making difficult decisions, feelings and emotions are best left firmly in the background. Emotion, which must have served humans so well as a biological adaptation in order that it continues to play a role in our mental lives, is still viewed as something of which we need to be wary.

While modern-day pragmatics has inherited aspects of these ancient traditions, historically it was not always the case. As Foolen (1997: 17) notes that in the early 1900s, linguists such as Erdman (1900), Bally (1905, 1910), van Ginneken (1907) and Sperber (1914) criticised the 'strongly ideational orientation' of semantics that dominated at the time, suggesting instead that the expressive, emotional side of semantics might be at least as important a field of study as the cognitive, rational one. In fact, van Ginneken went further, proposing that rational meaning had its roots in emotional meaning. In *Het Mysterie der Menschelijke taal* he wrote:

Modern signifies is wrong if it wants to fix all content words in definitions, ignoring metaphorical language use, and wants to oblige intellectuals to apply only these definitions. Intuition and loving empathy in human conversation will certainly bring us nearer to shared understanding than algebraic formulae. After all, language is much better and deeper than algebra or a signal code.[2]

The idea had indeed had already been suggested in the eighteenth century by Rousseau, but it still failed to gain in popularity. As Foolen also notes, Edward Sapir took severe exception to it: '[I]deation reigns supreme in language ... Volition and emotion come in as distinctly secondary factors' (in Foolen 1997: 40). Of van Ginneken's work, Sapir went on (in Foolen 1997: 40): 'There are, it is true, certain writers on the psychology of language who deny its prevailingly cognitive character but attempt, on the contrary, to demonstrate the origin of most linguistic elements within the domain of feeling. I confess that I am utterly unable to follow.'

In what remains of this chapter, we provide an overview of the issues discussed in this book. These all point towards our principal motivation: our belief that emotional or expressive meaning, along with other affect-related, ineffable dimensions of communication, play such a huge role in human interaction that any pragmatic theory worth its salt *must* account for them. We have personal as well as professional reasons for believing this: one of us is also a songwriter and musician; the other a published poet. The expression and communication of emotions needs to be put right back at the centre of research into pragmatics.

1.2 Clocks and Clouds

Imagine two very different physical systems. We might model the differences between these systems in terms of Karl Popper's famous distinction between clocks and clouds.[3] The first system is like a pendulum clock. It is precise, regular and orderly: it is predictable. The second resembles a physical system which, like a gas cloud, is imprecise and irregular: in contrast to the clock-like system, it is largely unpredictable.

---

[2] Quote from and translation by Elffers (2020). 'Significs' is the movement in which van Ginneken, for a short while, was heavily involved. Its creator was Lady Victoria Welby, whom we discuss in Chapter 4.

[3] Popper's paper was the inspiration for Ligeti's haunting musical dreamscape *Clocks and Clouds*. According to Ligeti: 'I liked Popper's title and it awakened in me musical associations of a kind of form in which rhythmically and harmonically precise shapes gradually change into diffuse sound textures and vice-versa, whereby then, the musical happening consists primarily of processes of the dissolution of the *clocks* to *clouds* and the condensation and materialisation of *clouds* to *clocks*' (www.laphil.com/musicdb/pieces/1313/clocks-and-clouds). One of the authors finds listening to this piece to be one of the most emotive musical experiences there is.

According to what I may call the common-sense view of things, some natural phenomena, such as the weather, or the coming and going of clouds, are hard to predict: we speak of the 'vagaries of the weather'. On the other hand, we speak of 'clockwork precision' if we wish to describe a highly regular and predictable phenomenon. (Popper 1973: 208)

Popper points out that the distinction is far from clear-cut. The changing seasons, he remarks, are like 'somewhat unreliable clocks' (1973: 208) and would be positioned somewhere between the two systems. Indeed, the main point in the 1973 paper is to point out the two ends of predictability in modern scientific thinking and to argue for an alternative to the kind of physical determinism that Popper felt had plagued scientific thought since the advent of Newtonian theory: the idea that, ultimately, *all clouds are clocks*. Popper argued that the reverse was true: 'all clocks are clouds, to some considerable degree – even the most precise of clocks' (1973: 215).[4] Our aims in introducing Popper's distinction are more prosaic. We use the distinction between clocks and clouds as a metaphor with which to reflect two key distinctions. The metaphor is not perfect in either case, but serves our purpose.

The first distinction is one that we, and many others, draw between two different types of *content* that humans communicate to one another. The first type of content is precise and, consequently, easily described: in that respect it is clock-like. Thus, when a speaker says to a hearer 'The train for *Abondance* leaves from platform three in ten minutes precisely', they express a clear proposition to the effect that some particular train leaves from a particular location to a particular location at a particular time. Language allows us to communicate such content with perfect precision.

The second type of content is imprecise, indistinct and nebulous (this is no etymological accident): it is cloud-like. It is content that is extremely difficult, if not impossible, to capture adequately in words. To use a term that is currently in vogue, it is 'descriptively ineffable'. Having arrived at their destination, our two travellers disembark from their train in the early evening. The view from the station is beautiful: snow-topped mountains, clear, dark-blue skies and a small, picturesque town – nestled in the orange glow of street lighting – which stretches out below them. One of them surveys the landscape, smiles and glances back at the other, urging him to look also. What is it that she is drawing attention to? Is it one thing, many things, or everything in her line of sight?

---

[4] Chomsky, we believe, was making a related point in a 2014 talk delivered at the Vatican: 'It is commonly believed that Newton showed that the world is a machine, following mechanical principles, and that we can therefore dismiss "the ghost in the machine", the mind, with appropriate ridicule. The facts are the opposite: Newton exorcised the machine, leaving the ghost intact. The mind/body problem in its scientific form did indeed vanish as unformulable, because one of its terms, body, does not exist in any intelligible form.' It could be countered (as it is by our colleague Nick Allott [personal communication TW]), that Popper and Chomsky are talking about different things – Popper is talking about determinism, while Chomsky is talking about matter. But there are definitely links between the two positions.

1.2 Clocks and Clouds

He does not, nor indeed could he, reply 'What do you mean?' He acknowledges her and smiles back because he understands. Everything that he can perceive is somehow reinforced by her smile and her glance. They share something. *This* is what she intended to convey. But this something is nothing precise; it is merely a cloud-like impression. She did not mean any one single thing and her intention in behaving the way she did cannot be pinned down to one specific proposition, a small set of propositions or even, we will argue, an array of propositions.

The distinction between clock-like and cloud-like content is as clearly seen in the written word as it is in everyday communicative exchanges. In June 2000 the MV *Treasure*, a Panamanian-registered cargo ship transporting 140,000 tonnes of iron ore from China to Brazil, sank some 10 kilometres off the South African coast. Four hundred of the thirteen hundred tonnes of bunker oil also being transported by the ship spilled into the sea. Crawford et al. (2000: 157) reported the tragic wreck of the oil tanker as follows:

> On 23 June 2000, the bulk ore carrier *MV Treasure* sank off western South Africa between Dassen and Robben islands, which individually currently support the largest and third largest colonies of African penguins *Spheniscus demersus*.

The information is precise, explicit. A particular vessel sank in a particular location at a particular time. The sentence even makes reference to two specific colonies of a precise species of penguin.

Contrast this with this stanza from Susan Richardson's 'African Villanelle', in which she describes the emergent environmental disaster (2007: 53):[5]

> A swollen tongue of oil invades the sea
> Its kiss is one of death, not of pleasure
> The coast's the throat it probes so ruthlessly[.]

The metaphors of the swollen tongue invading the sea with its kiss, ruthlessly probing the throat that is the coast, are pregnant with emotion. The words paint an endlessly evolving picture, which goes well beyond anything we might realistically claim that the words themselves say. It is unparaphrasable. This is what metaphors do, and as a consequence, to try to describe precisely what the words conjure in our mind is impossible. As Davidson (1978: 47) famously put it: 'Words are the wrong currency to exchange for a picture.' The feelings, sensations and emotions metaphors elicit cannot be pinned down in terms of words or propositions.[6]

The *second* distinction is the one we mention in our introductory paragraphs. It is not a distinction relating to communicated content, or information, but one

---

[5] This quote appears with the author's permission.
[6] Despite the fact that ineffability was central to his work, we won't speak much about Wittgenstein in this book. While his genius is beyond question, his work was only peripheral to the circles responsible for the development of pragmatics that we discuss in Chapters 2 and 5.

that relates to two different kinds of mental activity: the distinction traditionally drawn between, on the one hand, rationality or reasoning and, on the other, emotions or Humean 'passions'. When we advise our friend to be rational, logical and precise we are, in effect, advising them to think in a clock-like manner. Emotions and feelings are shapeless, amorphous, nebulous things: emotional thinking is cloudy, imprecise thinking.

1.3 Overview

1.3.1 Chapter 2

Chapter 2 is entitled 'Pragmatics and Emotion: The Challenges'. In this chapter we describe what we regard as the two essential challenges in accommodating emotional communication within a theory of utterance interpretation. These are closely related and are, to an interesting extent, historical in origin. The first of these we call the challenge of *description versus expression*. One of the principal concepts in the analysis of the meaning of language is its 'aboutness', sometimes called 'intentionality'. Language can be used to describe things in the world. In that sense sentences and utterances are about the world, and in the sense that they are about the world they can be judged true or false. Emotions can be described too: an individual might utter 'I am angry', for example, or 'I am frightened' and those utterances can be judged true or false. However, this is because those utterances describe an emotional state rather than express it.[7] It could be argued that, in a way, utterances of 'I am angry' or 'I am frightened' *rationalise* the emotions they describe.

But emotions, of course, can also be expressed directly in such a way that they are not really *about* anything at all (and are most certainly not being rationalised): so by shouting 'Aaaaaargh!', an angry person might express their anger, rather than describe it, and by sitting quaking in a corner with a terrified facial expression, a frightened person might express their fear rather than

---

We will, however, quote briefly Lars Furberg – a student at Oxford of Austin, Grice, Urmson and Warnock in 1956/1957 – who writes intriguingly of Wittgenstein's well-known pessimism in the *Tractatus*: the view that there exist mystical unsayables (Furberg 2010: 85). 'Can't a so-called pessimist', Furberg asks, 'see and recognize that *belles-lettres* sometimes bring about an understanding deeper than any brought about by other wordings? Can't he think that different art-genres are engaged in something essentially communicative but "beyond" words? ... The poem's words are in their surroundings filled with new meaning, perhaps in the vein of Gricean implicature, or perhaps with music, a suggestion which would take this essay too far afield. This is vague but hardly mystic.' The omitted section contains a quote which, to Furberg at least, suggests Wittgenstein thought the unsayable was not 'transcendent', but 'immanent', real rather than mystical.

[7] It goes without saying that with the addition of appropriate prosody, facial expression and so on, utterances such as these could express as well as describe the emotional states being communicated.

1.3 Overview

describe it. Note also that communicative acts such as these cannot be true or false. This direct nature of the expression of emotion is a big problem for any attempt to integrate the communication of emotions into a theory of utterance interpretation, whether in everyday human interaction, such as screaming in anger or quaking in fear, or in trying to analyse tropes, such as metaphor in the Richardson poem, which expresses the poet's feelings as well as (or instead of) describing them. The difficulty is, if not an accident of history, certainly a consequence of the way research into language generally has developed and evolved through the years. And it is the second challenge – that of *propositions and ineffability* – which underlies this approach.

With this in mind, we continue this chapter with a sketch of the prehistory of philosophical thought and show how the sidelining of emotional communication in modern linguistic pragmatics is very much a consequence of the propositional foundations on which modern theories of semantics and pragmatics are built, and the consequent problems theories have in accounting for ineffability. Until the nineteenth century, language was almost exclusively studied from either a grammatical or a philosophical perspective, and theorists developed theories on how the structure of language reflected the structure of thought, where thought was understood as propositions. Many of the current grammatical and pragmatic notions we have are manifestations of this perspective, which originated in ancient philosophy and continued through to the Port-Royal Grammar. As a result of this, the vaguer aspects of communication, those descriptively ineffable emotional meanings that are too nebulous to be paraphrased in propositional terms, are not merely overlooked; they are singled out as being unworthy of attention. In this section (§2.2) we also lay the foundations for our concepts of descriptive ineffability and propositional vs. nonpropositional knowledge, aspects of which we also develop in Chapter 4.

There are two further challenges also, though these are different in nature and concern how we define the two content words from the title of this book. The first of these concerns the e nature of the term 'pragmatics': we conclude Chapter 2 with some background on what we mean by 'pragmatics' in this book. The second concerns the nature of emotion itself: what is emotion? We turn to that problem in Chapter 3.

1.3.2   Chapter 3

It is not our aim to provide a definitive account of emotion from all possible perspectives, but our project is not possible without at least sketching an answer to the fundamental question we posed in the previous chapter as our third challenge: what is emotion? Answering this question is the goal of Chapter 3. We begin by presenting a brief overview of the early history of emotion studies and provide some substance to our claims at the beginning of this chapter about how the way emotions were viewed by the early rationalists might have influenced modern-day thinking. We chart a trajectory from the study of emotions from Aristotle in Classical times through to the work of St. Augustine and Thomas Aquinas; from Descartes to Hume; and then move on to those thinkers who were, arguably, responsible for the very beginnings of modern enquiry into emotion study: Charles Darwin (1872/1998) and William James (1884; Lange and James 1922).

To follow, we offer a summary of the three main theoretical approaches to affective science that exist today. The first is the so-called basic emotion view (Ekman 1992, 1994, 1999), in which theorists posit a certain limited number (between seven and fourteen) of basic emotions that are universal across humankind. The second is the psychological-constructionist view, the central tenet of which is the claim that the main ingredient of a specific emotional experience is to be found in a kind of free-floating blend of positive versus negative responses to stimuli: what we call an emotion is then constructed on an ad hoc basis according to linguistic and cultural considerations (Feldman Barrett 2011, 2017a, 2017b Russell 1994; Russell and Feldman Barrett 1999). The third and final approach is the appraisal theory view, under which it is subjective evaluations that are made concerning an object in question that are responsible for the elicitation of emotional events (Ellsworth 2013; Ellsworth and Scherer 2003; Moors et al. 2013; Scherer and Moors 2019).

We will claim that there are good reasons to favour the appraisal theory account, though – as we also point out – we are presenting something of an oversimplified triumvirate of views. One of the principal reasons, which we will develop across the book, is that there are good reasons to suggest it is the one that marries most successfully with relevance theory (Sperber and Wilson 1986/1995), the pragmatic framework we adopt. As such, it offers a route ahead for genuinely interdisciplinary research involving those working in pragmatics and those working in affective science.

1.3.3 Chapter 4

In Chapter 2 we pointed out that until the nineteenth century, language was almost exclusively studied from a grammatical perspective. The kind of theories that were developed were developed around claims about how the structure of language reflected the structure of thought, where thought was understood as propositions. Chapter 4 begins where that chapter left off and opens with more historical discussion, in which we sketch the prehistory of the study of the pragmatics and trace a route in development of expressive meaning from Thomas Reid and Jean-Jacques Rousseau in the eighteenth century to the work of Michel Bréal, Ferdinand de Saussure and Charles Bally in the nineteenth and twentieth. Bally, a member of the Geneva

1.3 Overview

school, was motivated to explore *parole* largely by Saussure's focus on *langue*. Since his contributions seem to us to have been somewhat overlooked, we devote a few pages to presenting them. For many of our readers, we suspect this will be the first time they have seen them.

Following an expression coined by Nerlich and Clark (1996), we use the term 'proto-pragmatics' to refer to those thinkers who were the first to take the role of context, emotion and non-propositionality in communicated meaning seriously. We should point out that it is not our aim here to construct a full history of the development of modern pragmatics. Rather, we merely attempt to demonstrate some of the ways in which our own focus on the importance of non-propositional information, and indeed affect, is reflected in the historical literature.[8] Our attempt to introduce affect into the centre of theories of utterance interpretation is, we claim, an act of *re*introduction, rather than an original move. The sidelining of affect by theories of communication has not happened in the absence of opposition, and we are simply the latest in a long line of researchers in that field who have argued that the role of emotion in communication is deserving of more serious attention.

Whether or not they were directly influenced by Bally, we also suggest that there are parallels between his work and that of those involved in the so-called 'ordinary language approach to philosophy' going on the 1940s at Oxford,[9] who committed themselves to the study of natural language use rather than the logical formulae of formal languages (even though their focus was still largely on propositional meaning). Among the most important achievements of this work was Grice's proposal of an inferential model of communication, the model on which much modern pragmatics is based. In this chapter we also introduce Austin's speech-act approach to emotional expression and a modern version of the theory, presented under the name of theory of affective pragmatics (TAP), as well as describing a few more modern attempts at developing a pragmatics of emotional communication. Again, our situating the ordinary language philosophers at the fulcrum of the development of modern pragmatics in this way is in no way to overlook the value of contributions by others.

---

[8] For more on proto-pragmatics and the prehistory and *history* of pragmatics (which Nerlich and Clark regard as beginning with Charles Morris and John Austin), see Nerlich and Clark (1996), which provides a wonderfully comprehensive survey. A further useful resource is Recanati (2004).

[9] While the term has become widely accepted, Grice himself appears not to have recognised it as particularly relevant to his work: 'The other day a philosopher of science in a university quite a long way from Oxford asked me whether I thought that "The Ordinary Language Approach to Philosophy" had anything to contribute to the philosophy of science. Finding this question difficult to handle for more than one reason, I eventually asked him what he meant by "The Ordinary Language Approach to Philosophy"' (1989: 171).

1.3.4 Chapter 5

As we pointed out in Chapter 2, there are good historical reasons why many linguists, philosophers and pragmatists have tended to stay close to those areas of meaning illuminated by semantics and logic (Sperber and Wilson 2015). The view is common in the contemporary literature – see Gazdar (1979), Davidson (1978) and, more recently, Levinson (2000) and Lepore and Stone (2010). We propose in Chapter 5 that relevance theory offers a solution to this limiting view. In this chapter we say a little about the context in which the framework was devised, and how it follows on historically from the ideas presented in Chapter 4, and present the main tenets of the theory itself. We then explain the two theoretical advances which form the basis of our belief that it is uniquely positioned to accommodate the communication of affect and emotion.

The first of these is the notion of non-conceptual or *procedural* meaning (Blakemore 1987, 2002). This, we believe, can deal with the problems associated with the challenge of describing versus expressing presented in Chapter 2. The second involves two key innovations in relevance theory which result in theoretical divergences from the work of both Grice himself, and other post-Gricean and neo-Gricean approaches. In the first of these, and in contrast to broadly Gricean approaches, the relevance-theoretic informative intention is not characterised as an intention to modify the hearer's thoughts directly. This move sheds new light on how better to analyse some of the weaker, vaguer aspects of communication, including the communication of impressions, emotions, attitudes, feelings and sensations. In the second, and again in contrast with Gricean approaches, relevance theory does not attempt to draw the line Grice drew between showing and meaning$_{NN}$ and recognises both as instances of overt intentional communication. These two innovations result in the theory being able to accommodate extremely vague types of communication and, further, demonstrate that communicated information – whether clock-like or cloud-like – can be *shown* rather than merely meant$_{NN}$, in the Gricean sense. It offers a unique opportunity to respond to the challenge of propositions and ineffability presented in Chapter 2 and also reflect insights about emotion and non-propositionality discussed in Chapter 4. Just as the two challenges are inextricably intertwined, so are these two theoretical developments closely linked.

As well as this, we show how the concept of relevance used in relevance theory bears interesting comparisons to the notion of goal relevance as used by those working in appraisal theory, a framework we described in Chapter 3.

1.3.5 Chapter 6

In Chapter 6, we develop our proposals further and suggest that the next step in addressing the challenges we raised in Chapter 2 is to suggest that the relevance theory notion of cognitive effect – relevant contextual implications, strengthenings or contradictions of existing cognitive assumptions – be supplemented with the new notion of *affective effect*. Affective effects involve processes that are not adequately described by the representation and management of conceptual information; rather, they involve a kind of mental processing which is best described, in Sperber and Wilson's words (2015: 139), as 'patterns of activation, none of which might be properly described as the fixation of a belief'. Affective effects generate cognitive processing by constraining the construction of the context within which communicative acts are understood (see also Maillat and Oswald 2013; Saussure 2005).

We propose that there are two different types of affective effect: *primary affective effects*, which typically act as input to inferential processes, and *secondary affective effects*, which are typically the output of inferential processes. Primary affective effects come in two flavours: *anticipatory* effects and *transfer* effects. The first of these are those effects which prepare an individual for a course of action; the latter are communicative, and inextricably linked with the interpretation of *natural codes*, inherently communicative behaviours which are 'natural' in the sense of Grice 1957 (Wharton 2009): affective prosody, facial expression and gesticulations, to name a few. Natural codes can be contrasted with natural *signs*, which carry information but are not inherently communicative (the fact that they carry information owes nothing to their continued propagation within our species), but which may nonetheless, as we point out, lead to the development of their own proprietary cognitive mechanisms.

In the case of secondary affective effects, propositional descriptions give rise to affective effects which rest on the imaginative abilities of the hearer/reader. This happens typically with literature and poetry. Emotions, after all, are key to the interpretation of poetry, art works and even music, which, we argue, are not about communicating contents but rather expressing mental states of a non-propositional nature. As for narrative literature, we suggest that it involves affective effects related to the way readers project perspectives on situations in such a way that it leads them to experience mental replicas of the experiences lived by characters or imaginary witnesses (Saussure 2021). In what remains of this chapter we discuss the role of free indirect speech in the interpretation of literary effects linked to emotion, as well as the role of emotion in argumentation and persuasion. Emotions, we argue, appear to be a central contributor to persuasion (Plantin 2004) and we suggest that this is so because of the special relationship that exists between affective and cognitive effects within the domain of achieving relevance.

1.3.6   Chapter 7

In Chapter 7 we broaden the discussion by looking at pragmatics and emotion from an evolutionary perspective (see Cornell and Wharton 2021). We suggest that in modern-day humans, two systems of processing and communication coexist: one evolutionarily ancient, to which *affective effects* are more closely related, the other evolutionarily more recent, in which conceptual, propositional processes – and *cognitive effects* – tend to dominate. The classic reference for this idea, that emotion and cognition are – in a sense – mediated by different systems, is LeDoux 1989: 'Emotion and cognition are mediated by separate but interacting systems of the brain' (1989: 267). The existence of these two systems, we suggest, goes at least some way to explaining why emotional and cognitive effects are so intertwined in human communication. It also reflects the so-called 'dual-route' system to the amygdala, the brain area that plays a central role in the evaluation and appraisal of sensory information. Evolution has equipped humans with both a faster, (mostly) subcortical 'low' route to this part of the brain, and a slower one (Garrido et al. 2012) which involves the cortex. We illustrate how two such systems work with reference to an underexplored paper by Paul Grice (1975) in which he outlines his 'creature-construction' thought experiment. One of the main claims of this book is that in focusing exclusively on high, slow propositional inference, those studying pragmatics have ignored the low, fast route. The existence of these two routes might shed light on how emotional vigilance presented in Dezecache et al. (2013) may make use of both the specialised inferential and coding–decoding mechanisms discussed in Chapter 5 and may even represent a precursor to those strategies that underlie epistemic vigilance (Sperber et al., 2010).

1.3.7   Chapter 8

Chapter 2 was entitled 'Pragmatics and Emotion: The Challenges'. We described what we regard as the four essential challenges in accommodating emotional communication within a theory of utterance interpretation: the challenge of *description versus expression,* of *propositions and ineffability* and the two further challenges of providing satisfactory, and mutually complementary, notions of 'emotion' and 'pragmatics'. We conclude our book with brief summaries of our responses to those challenges. We argue that the account we offer here shows promise and that the evidence is clear that, of all theories of utterance interpretation, relevance theory is uniquely positioned to accommodate emotion and affect.

None of which is to suggest that we believe the presentation, argumentation and discussion offered in the forthcoming pages provide any definitive answers. We do, however, hope that, here and there, they will make it possible to ask important new questions.

2 Pragmatics and Emotion
The Challenges

2.1 Introduction

In this chapter, we present what we regard as the main challenges associated with any attempt to accommodate emotional communication within a theory of utterance interpretation. These challenges form the context around which the whole book is structured. The first two are, essentially, two sides of the same coin: the solution to both is to be found in the same place. However, for ease of exposition, we keep them separate. We address both in this chapter. The third and fourth challenges are of a different nature and concern the two content words in the title of this book. The third concerns what we mean by the term 'pragmatics', and we turn to it at the end of this chapter (§2.3). The fourth concerns the nature of 'emotion' itself. Perhaps reflecting our anecdote in the previous chapter, many linguists have paid very little attention to what emotion is, let alone how it has been studied. We turn to that in the next chapter.

Challenge number one we call the challenge of *description versus expression*. Many people have noticed that when it comes to the communication of emotions, the descriptive power of language is often not enough. Describing our emotional states is not enough. We feel the need somehow to express them directly and spontaneously. Expressive utterances are not only less measured than those that contain little or no emotional content; they are also vaguer and harder to pin down. As we saw in the previous chapter, they are nebulous, ineffable. This creates massive problems for theories of meaning. Why?

It does so because of the challenges of *propositions and ineffability*. As well as reflecting the ancient history of rationalist philosophical thought, the sidelining of emotional communication in linguistic studies is very much a consequence of the foundations on which modern theories of semantics and pragmatics are built. We sketch the prehistory of the study of language and show that well before the formal, the so-called idealised language philosophy of, for example, Frege (1948), Russell (1903) and Tarski (1941) – which we address in more detail in Chapter 4 – the study of language was dominated by propositions. Even the ordinary language philosophy of Austin (1962), Searle (1969) and Grice (1989) tended to regard the only kind of meaning worthy of attention as that which can be rendered as propositional (whether as one proposition or a few closely related propositions). For this reason, linguists, philosophers and pragmatists have tended to stay close to those areas of meaning illuminated by semantics and logic, and as a result attention has been almost entirely focused on propositional meaning (Sperber and Wilson 2015). The vaguer, emotional aspects of communication are descriptively ineffable: too nebulous to be paraphrased in propositional terms – cloud-like rather than clock-like. We begin here discussion on the concept of descriptive ineffability and the notions of expressive meaning and non-propositional content, which we also develop in Chapter 4. We address the third challenge towards the end of this chapter, and the fourth – the nature of emotion – in the next.

2.2 Two Challenges

2.2.1 Description versus Expression

In the previous chapter we gave an example of a poetic metaphor in an excerpt from a poem by Susan Richardson. Our aim was to show the extent to which language can be used to communicate things that are, in one way at least, impossible to paraphrase satisfactorily in words. Instead of conveying a precise, clock-like message, the metaphor paints what we called 'an endlessly evolving picture': a cloud of sensations, feelings and emotions. Such sensations, feelings and emotions do not depend on complex, grandiloquent words. Japanese *haiku* are, after all, often very simple, linguistically speaking, but they are powerful expressive tools nonetheless.[1] The poignancy of the famous six-word flash fiction attributed to Ernest Hemingway is testament to this: 'For sale: Baby shoes, never worn', the story goes. (The attribution is probably mistaken – see Budanovic 2017.)

But poetic metaphor and art generally are, of course, just two of the many ways that artists express themselves. After the death of his close friend Casagemas, Picasso famously spent the next four years pouring out his desolation, anguish and torment in paintings composed entirely in shades of blue. 'Colours, like features ...', he once mused, 'follow the changes of the emotions'. We will touch later in the book on the synaesthetic strategies people adopt to try and describe the ineffable: emotions can be rendered as sounds, as colours or as temperatures, to provide just three examples. Conversely, sensations such as how temperatures are felt – the sensation of coldness or warmth – and perceptions such as colours are ineffable too: there's no possible way to describe the impression of 'red' to someone who can't see it. We suggest that

---

[1] We are indebted to Ryoko Sasamoto (personal communication TW) for making this point.

2.2 Two Challenges

emotions are not only ineffable, but they can't be described to an interlocutor who has never felt anything similar.

But there are far more prosaic examples of the ways in which the communication of emotion is non-paraphrasable. We therefore begin our discussion of description versus expression here. Consider (1a–c):

(1a) I'm happy!

(1b) I'm surprised!

(1c) I'm disgusted!

One of the leading protagonists in work on emotion over the past thirty years or so, Paul Ekman, includes the three emotions being expressed here – joy, surprise and disgust – as among his six universal basic emotions. (The other three are fear, contempt and anger.[2]) In each of these utterances, a speaker communicates their emotional state as well as any number of other things. The reader's response to reading these examples may well be that, actually, there is nothing remotely cloud-like about what is being conveyed here at all. The utterances 'I'm happy', 'I'm surprised' and 'I'm disgusted' are far from being vague and imprecise. So, what is left of the distinction we made in §1.2 between clouds and clocks?

We would argue that the speakers of (1a–c) are not *expressing* their emotional state at all: they are *describing* them (even rationalising them). The three utterances in (1a–c) are propositions, where – as we have said – a proposition is a statement that is capable of being true or false. Someone who is experiencing overwhelming joy, or fear, or disgust, may indeed report their condition by uttering (1a–c), but it is unlikely that is all they would say. The utterances in (1a–c) are hardly spontaneous expressions of 'emotion' in the sense that most of us use that word. Rather, or at least additionally, they would probably express their emotion (in English at least) by comparable utterances of, for example, (2a–c):

(2a) *Yay*!

(2b) *Wow*!

(2c) *Yugh*!

The linguistic items in the single-word utterances in (2a–c) are known as interjections. We have argued extensively in the past (see Saussure and Wharton 2020; Wharton 2003a, 2009, 2015) that using an interjection to

---

[2] In Ekman's original work (Ekman 1972) there was a seventh basic emotion: interest. We are grateful to David Sander for pointing this out in conversation and suggest that, since finding an object or activity 'interesting' is largely an exercise in finding aspects of that object or activity 'relevant', there is much interesting (and relevant) work to do in this area.

express an emotion directly, as is happening in these examples, is very different to describing it (see also Padilla Cruz 2009a, 2009b; Wałaszeska 2004).[3] This simple intuition lies at the heart of the notion of the phenomenon of expressive meaning, which has received a great deal of attention (see also Kaplan[4]; Blakemore 2011; Potts 2005, 2007).

Having said that, the most straightforward way to analyse the meaning of (2a–c) – a temptation to which many have yielded – would be simply to say that, actually, what they communicate is their propositional equivalents in (1a–c). So *yay*! simply means 'I am happy', *wow*! means 'I'm surprised' and *yugh*! means 'I am disgusted'. But there are a number of reasons to think this kind of analysis cannot work. The opening section of Wharton (2003a) proposes a range of arguments against claims made in previous work by proponents of what we have referred to as the 'conceptualist' view (Ameka 1992; Wierzbicka 1992, 1996, 2000; Wilkins 1992). This is a view under which interjections encode decompositional conceptual structures such as the one in (3):

(3) 'ow!'
I suddenly feel a pain (in this part of my body) right now that I
    wouldn't have expected to feel.
I say '[*au*]' because I want to show that I am feeling pain right
now [and because I know that this is how speakers of English can
show (other speakers of English) that they are in pain (in a situation
like the situation here)].

Before we move on it is worth remarking here that, contrary to the idea implicit in (3), it is far from clear that the main function of interjections such as *ow*! or *ouch*! is actually to 'show (other speakers of English) that they are in pain'. Empirical evidence suggests that this kind of spontaneous expression is related as much to the regulation of the degree of pain felt as it is to any desire to communicate information regarding that pain. Swee and Schirmer (2015) demonstrate that individuals in their experiments could tolerate a noxious stimulus longer when allowed to vocalise spontaneously than those who were forced to be silent. Moreover, the analgesic effect the individual notices only occurs when that individual produces the sound. Hearing their own utterances, or someone else's, has no analgesic effect.

---

[3] Bernd Heine (2023: n.p.) proposes the existence of two different modes of communication: one controlled by a sentence grammar, which involves the communication of propositions, the other by an 'interactive' grammar, responsible for social, interactional communication. The latter, he suggests, has a 'holophrastic' organisation and 'is shaped by the indexical nature of the situation of discourse' (n.p.). In many ways, we are arguing for the same kind of distinction, but building it around affective rather than sociocultural concerns.

[4] The ideas presented in this unpublished manuscript, dating from 1997, were delivered at the UC Berkeley, Howison Lecture in Philosophy, August 2004. Notes from the lecture, transcribed by Elizabeth Coppock, are available at https://eecoppock.info/PragmaticsSoSe2012/kaplan.pdf.

2.2 Two Challenges

The conceptual structure sketched in (3) is obviously much more complex than the kind of conceptual representations in (1a–c) (which we recycle aspects of below), but we think our arguments still obtain. Firstly, as can be seen in (4), utterances of *ouch!* are non-truth-conditional (see Kleiber 2016 for similar cases in French):

(4) A: *Ouch!*
     B: – *That's false! / *That's not true!
     A: It hurts.
     B: – That's false / That's not true.
     A: *Ouch!*
     B: – *I know.
     A: It hurts.
     B: – I know.
     A: Does it hurt?
     B: – Yes / *Ouch!*

Secondly, consider (5) and (6):

(5) I'm in pain! That hit me!

(6) *Ouch!* That hit me!

The speaker of (5) is expressing two propositions; and these are true when the speaker is in pain and when they have been hit by something (and false otherwise). By contrast, the speaker of (6) is only expressing a single proposition: it is true if they have been hit by something. A person hearing (6) could not object: 'You're lying! You're not in pain'. Given the discussion so far, this much is not surprising. Interjections such as *ouch!* express pain (to the extent they communicate it) rather than describe it.

If *ouch!* does encode a concept, and one that forms part of the proposition expressed by an utterance, one would expect intuitions of a synonymy between (7) and (8) below:

(7) I'm in pain! I'm in pain!

(8) *Ouch!* I'm in pain!

But while (7) intuitively involves a conceptual repetition, (8) does not (and also overlooks the distinction we have just made between describing something – in this case pain – and expressing it). In summary, interjections seem to function in a way that is separate to the related conceptual structures which, it has been argued, communicate something similar to them.

As well as this, what is conveyed by an interjection is highly context dependent. This suggests a substantial pragmatic contribution to their comprehension, one that is not captured by the rigid structure in (3). Utterances of *yay!*

or *wow*! might convey a vast range of different emotional states, each of which is hard to describe independently of their context of use. To return to a term we used in the previous chapter, the meaning they convey is descriptively ineffable: impossible to paraphrase in words. It's very easy to say what (1a–c) mean. In contrast, it's very hard to say with any precision what (2a–c) mean at all. The phenomenon known in linguistics as expressive meaning is very hard to capture and that has been one of the reasons associated with the difficulties of providing a satisfactory analysis.

While we argue in the next section that the historical tendency towards propositions and formality has meant that expressivity has been largely overlooked, some formalists have, for example, addressed the linguistic difference between 'I feel pain' and *ouch* (see Kaplan).[5] Well known for his work on indexicals, Kaplan remarks on the similarities between indexicals on the one hand and expressives (interjections – *ouch*, *oops*) and epithets on the other: all these expressions, he claims, are better analysed in terms of a *Semantics of Use* rather than (or as well as) a *Semantics of Meaning*. To account for the difference between 'I feel pain' and *ouch*, he introduces his distinction between descriptive (truth-conditional/propositional) and content and expressive (non-truth-conditional/non-propositional) content. This distinction is similar to the distinction drawn by speech-act theorists between describing and indicating that we discuss in Chapter 5, and elements of it inform the account we offer here. For Kaplan, one of the reasons that *ouch* and 'I feel pain' are not synonymous is that while 'I feel pain' has descriptive meaning, *ouch* has expressive meaning. In Kaplan's terms, the *modes* of expression are different.

Like Kaplan's, the main aim of Christopher Potts' work on expressivity is to integrate it within a formal semantic framework. Indeed, his 2007 paper begins with an epigraph from Kaplan: '[I]t seems to me quite possible to extend semantic methods ... to a range of expressions that have been regarded as falling outside semantics, and perhaps even as being insusceptible to formalization.'[6] Potts (2005) formulates a 'descriptive logic' for Gricean conventional implicatures (so, in other words, a semantic rather than pragmatic account) and then shows how his framework can deal with, among other phenomena, expressive meaning. The effect of an utterance of *the damn dog* leads to the propositional entailment 'bad (*the dog*)' in a separate dimension 'the expressive dimension'). While in subsequent work the account offered by Potts is subtly changed, the formalist approach remains. So, according to Potts (2007), an utterance of *the damn dog* does not lead to any propositional entailment, but instead contributes to an expressive 'index', itself part of the

---

[5] Notes from Kaplan's 1997 lecture, transcribed by Elizabeth Coppock, are available at https://eecoppock.info/PragmaticsSoSe2012/kaplan.pdf.
[6] See https://eecoppock.info/PragmaticsSoSe2012/kaplan.pdf, p. 18.

2.2 Two Challenges

'context', emphasising the role played by expressives in 'pragmatic inference and discourse structure'.

In a series of papers, Diane Blakemore provides a sustained challenge to this formal approach to expressive meaning: 'While the approach offers some interesting insights, we find this a rather one-dimensional approach to the range of emotional attitudes and states which can be communicated by an expressive' (Blakemore 2011: 3543). Perhaps instead of analysing expressives as contributing to expressive 'indices' or 'contexts', we might be better advised to reinterpret his work in cognitive terms and explore what kinds of processes they actually activate. This type of interpretation is much more directly relevant to the notion of pragmatics adopted in this book. Blakemore's solution is to invoke her own notion of non-conceptual or procedural meaning (Blakemore 1987, 2002) and offer that as part of the solution to dealing with this, the challenge of description versus expression. Our account makes related proposals and, indeed, utilises Blakemore's notion (though it should be noted that procedural meaning has evolved a great deal since it was first proposed (see Wilson 2011a)).

The importance of the expressive dimension in communication certainly needs no justification, but a taste of it is given by this remark by the famous French lawyer and former Minister of Justice Robert Badinter (known for making an address to the French parliament that led to the eventual abolition of the death penalty). While later summarising his defence of the final six criminals facing that penalty, a defence which ultimately led the jury to reject that penalty, he said:

If, unfortunately, you read, then you are lost. ... The reason I was able to save them ... was not because the language or the argumentation was perfect. The reason is different. It's that I addressed them, as the Italians say, 'naked face'. They must feel that I am a man warning them against the trap set up for them, and in which they are about to fall. That here is a man who is telling them: 'Don't do that'.[7]

Badinter's argumentation owes its success to his direct appeal to emotion, rather than to reasoning over propositions. This is perhaps one version of the so-called *amygdala hijack* from popular psychological work on emotional intelligence (Goleman 1995), where the fast, low subcortical route takes over from slower neocortical processing (to put this more accurately, before it even gets underway). As Grace says in our epigraph to Chapter 1: 'You can't reason your way out of a passion: all you can do is oppose it with a stronger passion' (Wilson 1991: 29).

---

[7] Robert Badinter, Episode 22, *La Grande Librairie*, TV5 Monde, October 2018. Our translation. https://europe.tv5monde.com/en/tv-guide/entertainment/la-grande-librairie/robert-badinter-invite-exceptionnel-460053.

There are many other facets of cognitive activity that are hard to explain in terms of the propositional content of slow conscious processing. Lieberman asks us to consider '"intuition"[, which] seems to lack the logical structure of information processing' (2000: 109), and *Eureka!* moments (Schooler and Melcher 1994), during which sudden insights are gained in the absence of any conscious thought. Building on work by Stanley (2011), Fridland (2015) considers the case of embodied skills, such as knowing how to play a musical instrument. Is the system of knowledge needed to *know how* to play the trumpet propositional? Indeed, it could be argued that a player has only truly mastered their instrument when they can stop thinking about it when they are playing. As Miles Davis is widely credited with saying: Anybody can play; the note is only 20 per cent - the attitude of the motherf****er who plays it is 80%. Wharton (2022) is a sustained search for this 'something else', which Davis calls attitude but most musicians generally call 'feel'.

Does 'feel' rely on propositions? We think not.

In terms of the aims of this book, what is needed is some machinery through which we can account for the differences between cases where emotions are described and those in which they are expressed. This machinery will also need to somehow capture the ineffability of emotional communication. We will suggest solutions to these problems in the chapters that follow. However, for now we turn to the second of the problems we identify. As it is, this second problem goes a long way towards explaining why it is that linguists have had such problems dealing with emotions. Focusing too much on the kind of meaning conveyed in (1a–c) has left linguists thoroughly under-equipped to accommodate expressive meaning within theories of utterance interpretation. To explain fully how this situation has arisen, a little historical perspective is required.

2.2.2 Propositions and Ineffability

> Propositions are the bricks out of which a logical system is built.
>
> R. M. Hare (1949: 1)

Until the nineteenth century, language was almost exclusively studied from either a grammatical or philosophical perspective. This is not to say that particular languages were left unstudied. Latin and Greek, for example, were explored by all manner of intellectuals and scholars interested in philology. However, rather than reflecting an interest in the nature and properties of language, these studies were essentially philological, with the sole aim of achieving a better understanding of classical texts. With few exceptions, those theorists who were interested in language *per se* developed theories on how the structure of language reflected the structure of thought, where

2.2 Two Challenges

'thought' was understood – as indeed it still is in mainstream philosophy – as 'propositions'. The grammatical notion of the proposition as well as many other grammatical concepts we still have – 'substantive noun', 'adjective noun' and so on – are manifestations of this perspective, which originated in Ancient Stoicist philosophy and continued through work such as Augustine's *De Dialectica* up to philosophical grammars such as Arnauld and Lancelot's *Grammaire Générale* of 1665. This famous work is also known as the 'Port-Royal' grammar (1665/1966).

To the extent that classical philosophers were interested in the communication of emotion at all, it was a concern for the kind of epistemic effects emotions were capable of producing, and whether it was fair or unfair, or sound or unsound, to appeal to πάθοσ (*pathos*) in order to persuade (see, for example, Plato's *Gorgias*). In his *Rhetoric*, Aristotle developed a theory of emotions in which *pathē* are organised into opposing pairs (love–hate, anger–calm, etc.).[8] But he famously also framed a theory of how emotions might be passed from one individual to the other. He explained that the manifestation of an emotion by a speaker triggers a sympathetic response in which the hearer is affected in a similar manner to the speaker (or at least pretends to be). According to this view, individuals align their emotions with those displayed by others, and thinkers who subsequently explored the notion of *sympathy* (*compassio* in the Middle Ages) stuck, broadly speaking, to the Aristotelian assumption that displayed emotions are 'shared' in some sense. Apart from these quite general claims within the study of rhetoric, emotions were generally considered to be of little interest to those scholars specifically interested in language. It is true that a few lines were written about interjections (see the discussion of Jean Buridan in Kneepkens 2015), and some claims made about language originating in emotions, but most scholars showed a complete disdain for the topic.

This view, which dominated scholarly work on language for centuries, took it that thought is organised by the principles of logic. Since thoughts were private, permanently out of the range of the world offered to perception, language was viewed as a means of making them publicly available: public signs signify private thoughts. Consider the following from Locke's *Essay Concerning Human Understanding* (Locke and Bennett 1689/2004):

If society is to flourish, thoughts must be communicated; so people had to devise some external perceptible signs through which they could let one another know of those

---

[8] Aristotle defines emotions in terms of notions such as 'desire' and 'pain' or 'state of mind', together with 'dispositions', 'persons' and 'things'. These combinations lead to the conclusion that some emotions are compatible, or not, with others. Viano (2018) mentions the following examples: fear excludes compassion because of its intensity; anger and assurance exclude fear because they don't take the future into account, and so on. These incompatibilities lead ultimately to opposing couples.

invisible ideas of which their thoughts are made up. For this purpose nothing was so suitable – because plentiful and quickly available – as those articulate sounds they found they could make so easily and in such variety. That is presumably how men came to use spoken words as the signs of their ideas. (Locke and Bennett 1689/2004: Book III, chapter ii: 147)

The Port-Royal view, that linguistic expressions are 'signs', was more than a merely superficial observation.

Perhaps the clearest illustration of a semiotic relation is to be found in so-called natural signs. We discuss what Grice called 'natural meaning' (meaning$_N$) in more depth later in the book, but essentially the notion involves a particular piece of evidence, which activates a plausible causal relation that gives access to an imperceivable, or at least not currently perceivable, fact. So, in a now-classic example from Grice (1957), black clouds are a natural sign of rain and (in English at least) might be said to 'mean naturally' (or mean$_N$) rain. Parallel examples are that a shiver means$_N$ that someone is cold, smoke means$_N$ fire, and so on (or even that a smile means something about someone's internal state – more of which later.)

This kind of relationship is often described as 'direct' in the sense that the causal relation is so strong that it appears not to require any inferential reasoning for it to arise: A means$_N$ B, in this sense, is more a fact than an inference. Grice described natural meaning as 'factive': a true statement of A means$_N$ B entails B. If, for example, the black clouds a speaker is pointing out are, say, fumes rising from a factory chimney in the distance, an observer might simply counter that, in this case, those black clouds didn't mean$_N$ rain at all. Grice's famous 1957 paper begins by exploiting the fact that in English the word 'mean' is apparently ambiguous between the natural and the non-natural sense of the word. Later in his work he attempted to show that the non-natural sense had its roots in the natural one. This is also something we address later.

There is, however, a serious problem to resolve if the relationship between a word and its referent is to be analysed as a semiotic relationship, in the sense of activating a non-perceptible thought on the basis of a perceptible linguistic expression. The problem is this. If signs are bound by natural, typically causal relations of the kind we have mentioned in this section, words and sentences *cannot* be perceptible signs of a thought. The relation between an element of language and an element of thought is not natural at all, and neither is it direct or causal. It is, to use Grice's term, *non*-natural. The English word 'rain' (or the Hungarian word *eső*) means rain irrespective of the presence, or any expectation anyone may have, of rain. This observation lies at the heart of one of Hockett's famous design features of language (1960): displacement. Language affords humans the ability to communicate about matters that are neither physically nor temporarily present. And while we don't subscribe to his

2.2 Two Challenges

account, Derek Bickerton (2009: 217) singles out the need to talk about things that exist neither in the here or the now as the single more important evolutionary pressure behind the evolution of language: 'It's only when you fully appreciate what displacement means, how the absence of displacement is not just a casual feature of [animal communication systems] but a crucial defining feature of pre-human minds, that you can start getting the complete picture'.

In Chapter 7 we turn to evolutionary issues and discuss in some detail Grice's approach to one iteration of the relationship between these two notions, and how causal natural meanings might evolve into non-natural meanings. But while Grice attempted to solve the conundrum through recourse to the evolutionary development of metacognitive strategies, the solution envisaged by ancient scholars was that there must exist a direct parallelism between the logic of thought and the grammar of language: the laws of grammar are nothing other than linguistic – or *bijective* – correspondents of the laws of logic. For each element of logical thought, there is exactly one corresponding grammatical element in language; and for each grammatical element in language there is a corresponding element of logical thought.

The Port-Royal grammar, perhaps the paradigmatic example of this type of theory, was built around a central assumption that for each grammatical item in language there is an unambiguous corresponding instance of thought. Speakers understand this rigid correspondence and automatically match instances of language with the mental instances they stand for. As a few examples: the category of substantive nouns corresponds to the mental operation of conceptualisation of substances; the grammatical notion of adjective nouns corresponds to the logical notion of accidental properties; the grammatical notion of 'sentence' corresponds to propositions, and so on.

This approach, in which elements of language mirror their counterparts in thought, is commonly referred to as the theory of 'logic–grammar parallelism': as the authors of the grammar say: 'the knowledge of what happens in our mind is necessary in order to understand the foundations of grammar; and this is where the diversity of words, that form the speech, depend from [our translation]' (Arnauld and Lancelot 1966/1665: 26, epigraph of Part II, chapter 1).

It is important to note that notions of expressive meaning and, indeed, any manifestation of an emotional dimension to language use of the kind we have referred to so far are pretty much totally left aside in such traditions. The Port-Royal grammar, for example, dedicates exactly five lines to interjections, suggesting they are 'more natural than artificial voices' which 'mark the movements of our soul' (Arnauld and Lancelot 1665/1966: XXII). In the context of an approach which regards language as an apparatus of rationality, which is itself perhaps the feature which distinguishes humans from so-called 'lower' animals, this is not remotely surprising. Rationality and logic were elevated human capacities that were induced by God. And according to a long trend of thought, which dated back to Thomas Aquinas, anyone who opposed this view – as, indeed, Rousseau would a century later – was considered a danger: such thinking would threaten the natural order of things.

Another reason classical scholars were not equipped to study closely the manifestation of affect in language is that such manifestations are intimately bound to the pragmatic circumstances of the utterance. Focusing on the metaphysics and ontology of language as an abstract apparatus in the mind does not help much us to understand the elements of language that are bound to its real-life usage, by real individuals in particular circumstances, with all the attendant feelings and sensations.

A possible exception to this view was the study of deictics or indexicals. For this trend of research – which ultimately led to Frege's philosophy of language and formal semantics – the status of deictics (which are context-dependent items of language par excellence) is an issue that cannot be ignored. Such words seem only to derive their meaning by means of an access to the particular circumstances of speech. In antique, medieval and classical grammar and philosophy of language, there is indeed ample theorising of deictics, which relate language to pragmatic contexts and operations that require more than abstract thinking. Scholars such as Aulus Gellius and Apollonius, not to mention Aristotle, had already explored the processes by which deictics point to referents in the situation of speech. But even though such theorisation might ideally have led thinkers to explore notions such as subjectivity and affect in language, and – who knows – perhaps even begin to regard interjections as a special subclass of deictics (as Kaplan famously would in the 1990s), the vast majority of scholars preferred to keep deictics as a marginal class of significations, operating in a very specific way. They then treated interjections as a subclass of adverbs or even verbs, arguing that they are related to action in a way deictics are not.

The nature of interjections, either natural or conventional, and the relative part played by these two dimensions in their 'meaning', is historically disputed, but their connection to affects is obviously recognised by all authors. The Roman grammarian Varonus treats *interjecta* as items that 'generate a strong emotion' (see Buridant 2006). In Plato's *Cratylus*, Hermogenes argues that some names are natural rather than conventional (translated quote from Jowett n.d.):

I should explain to you, Socrates, that our friend Cratylus has been arguing about names; he says that they are natural and not conventional; not a portion of the human voice which men agree to use; but that there is a truth or correctness in them, which is the same for Hellenes as for barbarians.

One twelfth-century grammar suggests that interjections are later manifestations of the 'primal cry' of infants (Buridant 2006: 4), an idea that will

2.2 Two Challenges

reappear occasionally, notably in Rousseau's *Essay sur l'Origine des Langues*. In the 1960s Erving Goffman popularised an account of interjections as 'response cries' (see Goffman 1964).

The situation would only really begin to change when linguistics, a science primarily interested in cross-linguistic comparison and reconstruction of the history of languages, came into view. Linguists proper were concerned with the origins of language, a question that was a natural continuation of their concerns about their history.[9] Wilhelm von Humboldt, an early prominent Indo-Europeanist, assumed (with Rousseau) that some 'movement of the soul' that cannot be analysed in terms of propositions preceded the emergence of language as we know it. In his book *On Language*, published in 1836, he also suggests that language is not a 'product', as it was in Stoic thought. Rather, he argues, it is a force of action (*energeia*) which has a bearing on people's thinking:

Words well up freely from the breast, without necessity or intent, and there may well have been no wandering horde in any desert that did not already have its own songs. For man, as a species, is a singing creature, though the notes, in his case, are also coupled with thought. Humboldt (1836/1999: 62)[10]

Influenced no doubt by Humboldt, Anton Marty published his book *On the Origins of Language* in 1875 and, in the early years of the twentieth century, made a distinction between emotional and *emotive* language, where the latter was intentionally used to convey emotional states. His notions formed the basis for Buhler's (1933) distinction between the *Ausdruck* and *Appel* functions of language in the 1930s and, indeed, Caffi and Janney's proposals years later in 1994.

But in many ways there was still a lack of consideration of what has come to be known as the *context* of an utterance, which has persisted in the work on the philosophy of language in the modern era. Frege, Russell and Tarski, for example, were logicians, interested in how insights from logical languages might be applied to the study of language in a very general sense. They were not concerned at all with language as a tool for communication. Indeed, Carnap's

---

[9] That question ended up attracting so much interest and speculation that in 1865, the Société de Linguistique de Paris, probably the most important scholarly venue for linguists, decided to ban communications on the matter entirely. Since then, a high degree of wanton speculation remains and the quality of the debate has barely improved.

[10] Von Humboldt's remarks were probably at least partly behind Otto Jespersen's *La-La Theory*, according to which language evolved from song. They also no doubt influenced some of the more outlandish accounts of language origins. *The Ding-Dong Theory* has it that 'there is an apparently mysterious harmony between sound and sense in a language ... Every sensory impression was like the striking of a bell, producing a corresponding utterance'. The *Yo-He-Ho Theory* 'envisages language arising from the noises made by a group of men engaged in joint labour or effort – moving a tree-trunk, lifting a rock'. In *The Pooh-Pooh Theory*, language began with interjections, and so on and so forth (Barber 1972: 30)

logical positivists took the approach to surprising extremes, with unfortunate sociocultural consequences. Karl Popper, the man behind the distinction in the previous chapter between clocks and clouds, fiercely opposed the idea that science might be reduced to a formal, logical system or method. Good science is not just creative or inventive. It is (to use his word) 'speculative'.

We agree.

2.3   Pragmatics

Before moving on to the fourth challenge, which we point out in the next chapter – the challenge of unpicking the nature of emotion itself – there is one further issue to mention. We do not devote a whole chapter to this, but this is because it is something to which we return at various times during the book. It concerns the other word in the title of this book – 'pragmatics' – which is equally open to a whole constellation of interpretations. Since we are going to take the time to say precisely what we mean by 'emotion', it seems only fair that we offer an account of what we mean by 'pragmatics' and why we take the view we do.

Pragmatics is many things to many people. A quick glance though any of the numerous encyclopaedias or handbooks of pragmatics now available will reveal hundreds of different approaches, within as many traditions. We are aware that our take on pragmatics may not be to everyone's taste, but we ourselves have learned a lot from work that has taken place within other traditions and hope the same may be true for others reading our work for the first time. The tradition of linguistics from which both of us come has its roots very much in the cognitive revolution of the late twentieth century. Broadly speaking, the view of language we adopt is a cognitive one. Language is an individual, intensional object. Humans have a dedicated mental 'organ' or 'faculty of language' (Chomsky 2000: 168) – potentially a module (or set of modules). In a typically developing individual, and given exposure to an appropriate environment, this will mature from an initial genetically determined state to a steady state that can be said to represent knowledge of language. Our view of pragmatics is one that complements this approach to language. For this reason, and others, we adopt the framework of relevance theory (Sperber and Wilson 1986/1995), which was inspired by Chomskyan (and Fodorian) insights into language and mind, and much of which is in the same spirit as their work.

Relevance theory combines Gricean intention-based pragmatics with aspects of modern research in psychology and cognitive science to provide a cognitive-inferential pragmatic framework. Relevance theory has a relatively narrowly delimited domain. It is not even a general theory of communication but focuses on a subtype of human communicative behaviour: behaviour by which a communicator provides evidence of an intention to communicate something – or, as they call it, ostensive behaviour. As noted above, language itself is seen as

2.3 Pragmatics

governed by a code which relates phonetic representations to semantic representations (or 'logical forms'). However, utterance interpretation is a two-phase process. The linguistically encoded logical form which is the output of the mental grammar is simply a starting point for rich inferential processes guided by the expectation that speakers will conform to certain standards of communication. In (highly) intuitive terms, an audience faced with a piece of ostensive behaviour is entitled to assume that the communicator has a good reason for producing this particular stimulus as evidence not only of their intention to communicate, but of what they want to communicate. Adopting a relevance-theoretic framework has a number of advantages. As we have shown, it marries uniquely with aspects of affective science – something that initially came as a surprise to the small team of pragmatists and affective scientists we are part of. But also, the very fact that we adopt this position has allowed us to engage in the kind of genuinely interdisciplinary work we feel the future of pragmatics depends on.

Interdisciplinary study is crucial (and funding bodies demand it more and more), but it is much easier to talk about than it is to undertake. And for those working within the arts and humanities – where much work on language and linguistics takes place – the problem is made doubly difficult by the kind of approach to language and communication which seems to have become even more popular in recent years. In direct contrast to the paradigm we adopt, which sees the study of language as a matter for naturalistic scientific enquiry, more and more people favour a view of language study rooted in social constructivism or ethnomethodology: in other words, a matter for the social, rather than the natural sciences.[11]

But much work in the arts and humanities has remained totally unaffected by the cognitive revolution that influenced relevance theory so. There is no clearer example of this than in the realm of poetics and literary theory. In 1992, David Trotter remarked (1992: 11):

Literary theorists have hardly paid any attention at all to Relevance Theory. This seems to me a mistake. Relevance Theory is not only the most elegant version of pragmatics currently available, but the most uncompromising in its view that inference cannot be assimilated to a code model of communication. It asks questions which literary criticism has never been able to ask, let alone answer.

Alastair Fowler (1989: n.p.) was of the same view:

[I]f the theory of communication sketched in *Relevance* is as significant as I take it to be ... contemporary methods of criticism all need to be thought through afresh.

Even if academics working in literature finally do get round to taking this body of work seriously, they may well be too late. A recent target article in *Nature Human Behaviour* asked whether it was time to ask whether we are now in an

---

[11] Kolaiti and Wharton (in press) is devoted to a robust defence of the position that pragmatics must be situated in the natural sciences.

age, not of behaviourism or even, any longer, cognitivism, but affectivism (Dukes et al. 2021). The article outlines a number of ways in which the study of affect has become more and more central in various field: affective neuroscience, comparative affective science, affective computing and many more.

At this point, a reader based in the arts and humanities may well protest and point out that in recent years there has been an important 'affective' or 'emotional' turn in those disciplines also (Clough and Halley 2007; Hoggett and Thompson 2012). Our response would be to ask what, precisely, this putative affective turn is a response *to*. In most of the arts and humanities there never *has* been a cognitive turn and academics in those areas have become entrenched in a kind of theorising which is a long way from the kind of theorising typical of work in the natural sciences, and a long way from the kind of theorising offered by those whose work language and communication was seriously influenced by the cognitive turn.

> The belief that theorising in the humanities is intrinsically incapable of making truth claims – the only way in which it could articulate theory in any robust or adequate sense of the term – has become so deeply entrenched in the post-modern literary mentality that some literary scholars seem to have given up the ambition of actually forming or pursuing such claims. I take it as self-evident that nothing can be a theory of something unless it can make at least one truth claim about this something. Thus, theorising in the humanities, like theorising in the psychological and cognitive sciences, is committed to the pursuit of truth. (Kolaiti 2019: 6)

But different disciplines evolve along different timescales, and this fact, as well as the physical divisions set up by departmental buildings, departmental doors and (crucially) the signs on those buildings and doors, give rise to virtual intellectual divisions that are so hard to overcome that they soon seem insurmountable.

We raise this issue because in this book we seek to demonstrate that relevance theory, the pragmatic theory adopted here, is uniquely positioned to solve the problems associated with accommodating emotion into a pragmatic theory. In the study of linguistic communication it has largely replaced the kind of discourse that so typifies constructionist approaches with testable theoretical principles and empirical hypotheses. It has, we argue, done for the study of utterance interpretation what Chomsky did for the study of language.

3 What Is Emotion?

> Everyone knows what an emotion is, until asked to give a definition.
>
> Fehr and Russell (1984: 464)[1]

3.1 Introduction

Whatever emotion is, the epigraph to this chapter perfectly encapsulates the observation that it is hard to pin down. In terms of the distinction we drew earlier in this book, while thought can sometimes be clock-like, emotions never can. But before we begin this chapter in earnest, it is worth pointing out that there are many different ways in which humans have tried to gain a better understanding of emotions, and many more ways than we can realistically attempt to cover in one short book. It is, for example, much, much harder to think of one or two disciplines where emotions are *not* directly involved – pure mathematics, particle physics? – than it is to draw up a list of those in which they are.

Keltner et al. (2019) present a comprehensive overview of the various different facets of emotion research, and indeed, some facets of emotional investigation that might not even be considered 'research' at all. After all, the work of poets and novelists often seeks to explore emotions, as does that of musicians, and work in the performing arts generally. Yet for some reason we are often reluctant to call their explorations 'research'.[2] The interested reader is directed to Oatley et al.'s excellent volume (2006). (As, indeed, are they directed to as much literature as they can read and as much music as they can listen to!) Our aims here are much more straightforward. We are looking to articulate a view of emotion that is comprehensive enough, that is, one that fits

---

[1] We are grateful to colleague Danny Dukes for sharing this quote with us (and he is grateful to David Sander for sharing it with him).

[2] The 2015 *Frascati Manual*, which defines what kind of work counts as research and development, explains this is because artistic performance represents the search for new forms of expression rather than new forms of knowledge. This is not the place to dwell on such matters, but this seems to us to be the challenge of description versus expression applied across human activity generally: www.oecd.org/sti/frascati-manual-2015-9789264239012-en.htm.

the requirements of this book, and remain all too aware that in this short chapter we are only barely touching the surface of a topic that is vanishingly vast (see Dennett 1995).

So, what is an emotion? Is experiencing an emotion the same thing as, say, having a feeling? Perhaps. In English, if you have hurt someone's feelings, then it follows that you have had some kind of negative impact on their emotional well-being. Presumably, then, feelings and emotions are interlinked. But does it follow that emotions and feelings are the same thing? What about the physiological sensations that are characteristic of excitement, or fear, or anxiety? Are *they* emotions? Again, perhaps. Emotions certainly involve physical sensations. Indeed, for Plato, that was what emotions were: a particular class of sensations or feelings (Scarantino and de Sousa 2021).

This much is not only anecdotally obvious to anyone who experiences such sensations and feelings (and we all do), but is reflected in language use. In English, for example, a person who acts rationally in a crisis is someone who stays 'cool'. A person who easily loses their composure might be described as getting 'hot under the collar' and, if they do so regularly, they might gain a reputation for being something of a 'hothead', with a 'fiery temper'. French speakers warn that during an argument it is important to *garder la tête froide*: *s'échauffer* is not recommended.

And there is more to this than simply a coincidence to be found in English and French – two, after all, related languages. While we do not subscribe to embodied views of emotion such as those proposed by Escobar at al. (2021), the cross-linguistic evidence that speakers of all languages tend to equate words for 'hot' with high emotional arousal and words for 'cold' with low emotional arousal is compelling (Levinson 2003; Salazar-López et al. 2015; see also Jackson et al. 2019 for a more nuanced view). Physiological evidence suggests that behind these idiomatic expressions there lurks a degree of truth. When affective scientists speak of so-called 'hot' emotions, they are describing emotions linked with high levels of interest and emotional activity. They are so named because when we experience such a state, the release of adrenaline and increased blood flow to the muscles makes us feel physically hotter.[3]

In a tangentially related set of experiments, Williams and Bargh (2008) hypothesised that physical experiences of higher temperatures might subconsciously increase feelings of interpersonal warmth (as in friendliness) among individuals. In one of their studies, those participants who had briefly held a hot cup of coffee judged others to have warm personalities more often than those who had held a cup of iced coffee. In another study, they found that participants

---

[3] Danny Dukes reminds us (personal communication) that this is a link between arousal and language, and not necessarily about emotion and language. He points out that Karl Scherer distinguishes between anger that is 'hot' and anger that is 'cold'. This matches the kind of common sense distinction reflected in expressions such as French *colère froide*.

3.1 Introduction

who had been given a heated, rather than a cold, massage pad to lean on were more likely to exhibit signs of generosity towards others.

This kind of discussion, about the relative uses of words in different languages and how they relate to emotional states, is often as far as linguists get when talking about the relationship between language and emotion. Since we are linguists, and work with the assumption that many of our readers will also be linguists, we believe it is important to clarify that when we ask the question 'what is emotion?' our primary interest is not in how languages across the world label such things. We don't believe there is much of particular interest in the fact that, say, a particular language does not have a word for 'sadness' (any more than we believe there is much of particular interest in the fact that a particular language does not have a word for 'blue' – see §3.3.3). Thought and perception depend only marginally on whether particular concepts are lexicalised: English speakers, for example, are as perfectly capable of experiencing and recognising *Schadenfreude* as are speakers of German.

Of course, whether a particular concept is lexicalised may have some influence on thought, but this influence lies in matters of categorisation, conceptual links, facility to activate the representations, and so on. However, it has no significant impact on whether one is capable or not of representing them at all. This issue, known as the problem of linguistic relativity and linguistic determinism (the Sapir–Whorf hypothesis – see Bohnemeyer 2020), has been largely overestimated. See, for example, the response to the claims by Boroditsky (2006) about the different ways speakers of Mandarin and English visualise and process time relations in January and Kako (2007) and also the contradictions exposed by Adger (2015a, 2015b) within the extreme version of linguistic relativity put forward by Evans (2014). On the limited accuracy of experimental research in relativity studies on the influence of gender, we also recommend Samuel et al. (2019).

In any case, whether affective mental states are labelled differently in various languages has no impact on the existence of these mental states themselves, even when the boundaries of the lexical items may vary from one language to another. Indeed, later in this chapter we will argue that there is a trap here that some modern affective scientists have fallen into (just as many linguists have).

We are not, then, discussing the semantics of words like 'emotions', 'feelings', 'affect' and the like, or even 'happiness', 'sadness' and 'fear', but seeking to identify precisely what emotional states themselves are and, more importantly, seeking to distinguish between a number of specific categories of mental states, only some of which belong to the domain of the affective or the emotional. Of course, it may turn out that emotional states exist along some sort of continuum, and as a result are not divisible into neatly discrete elements, but nothing much follows from that for us. We are simply seeking a useful working definition.

In *The Ontology of Emotions*, Naar and Teroni (2018: i) begin their answer to the question 'what is emotion?' as follows:

> No-one will seriously doubt that [an emotion] is a psychological state of some sort. Rich and lively philosophical debates have failed to generate any stable picture regarding the nature of emotions that extends much beyond this platitude, however. At most, a bare majority of philosophers would agree that emotions exemplify the following features. First, emotions are characterised by a certain phenomenology: they are felt. Second, they are intentional phenomena, ... directed to various sorts of entities in the world (one is amused by the joke, sad at the death of a dear friend). ... Third they are closely connected with evaluations of those entities – amusement connects with a positive evaluation of the joke, sadness with a negative evaluation of the death. Fourth, emotions are relatively short-lived: unlike other phenomena that are closely related to them, such as character traits and sentiments that may endure for substantial stretches of time, emotions endure at most for some hours.

We find little to disagree with here, and as a first attempt at answering our question we offer the following key features in lieu of a definition. An emotion is a psychological state (or process or event, see Soteriou 2018) and, moreover, a state typified by a particular kind of felt experience. This experience is directed towards objects or events in the world and connected with evaluations or appraisals of those objects or events. Finally, in contrast with, say, a mood, which is a chronic rather than an acute episode of affect, an emotion is temporary or transient.[4]

In §3.2.1 we present a summary of the early history of emotions studies and attempt to provide some substance to the claims made at the beginning of Chapter 1 regarding the views of emotions held by classical and early philosophers. We chart a trajectory from Plato to Thomas Aquinas, from Spinoza to Hume, and end at the point where, arguably, modern enquiry into emotional states began: the evolutionary approach of Darwin (1872/1998) and the somatic approach of William James (1884; Lange and James 1922). The work of these key thinkers is the subject of §3.2.2.

In §3.3 we present the three leading current views of the study of emotion which exist at the present time. §3.3.1 provides a brief introduction and in §3.3.2 we introduce Paul Ekman's basic emotion view (Ekman 1992), in which a certain limited number of basic emotions (between seven and fourteen) are proposed: since Ekman's approach presupposes a uniquely human evolved set of emotions, we also discuss those objectors to aspects of Ekman's approach whom, nonetheless, broadly accept an evolutionary account. In this subsection we also present the view from evolutionary psychology. In §3.3.3 we introduce the view of the psychological constructionists, who take issue with Ekman's

---

[4] Keltner et al. (2019) add that in addition to this, what we might call emotional disorders can last weeks, months or years, and personality traits might last years or even a lifetime.

approach on very different grounds and argue that emotions are socially constructed. In §3.3.4 we discuss the view from appraisal theory, a theory which takes as its focus those subjective evaluations made by an individual concerning the object deemed responsible for the elicitation of an emotional event.

3.2 The Early History of Emotion Studies

3.2.1 Aristotle to Hume

Among the many ways Plato followed Socrates was by adopting a view that, with only a few exceptions, *pathē* (emotions) were negative reactions with their origins in the lower part of the human soul. As such, his interest lay not in attempting to characterise or taxonomise emotions, but in exploring how the spirited part of the soul (*thumoeides*) might be tamed and educated in order to serve an ideal state (see *The Republic*, Book IV). Both positive and negative responses were wayward stallions, requiring careful guidance from reason and rationality. In *Phaedrus* he personified reason as a charioteer, attentively reining in potentially damaging emotional impulses. Aristotle's subsequent approach to emotions was more systematic insofar as he did begin to propose a type of taxonomy, as well as which, so it has been argued, he began to develop a view in which emotions were to be seen as componential in nature (Cooper 1999, Knuuttila 2004). Elements of this account, which included evaluative, phenomenological and physiological components, have remained influential to this day. Indeed, aspects of the James–Lange model (see §3.2.2) are reminiscent of it. Nonetheless, as we pointed out in the previous chapter, Aristotle was concerned less with accounting for the nature of emotions themselves and more with the soundness (or lack of soundness) of a rhetorical strategy which appealed to them in order to persuade others. In *Nichomachean Ethics* (Book IV) he turned to the role of pathos in the moderation of reason.

The Stoics owed a great deal to Plato and Aristotle, but, if anything, took an even dimmer view of the value of emotions. The Greek word *stöikos* has provided the etymological root for a great many words in numerous of the modern European languages which describe a person who remains indifferent to emotion ('stoic', 'stoïque', 'stoicki', 'stoico', 'estóico', etc.). Cicero was heavily influenced by the Stoics and indicates the kind of disregard afforded to emotions by describing the process of how best to represent the Greek word *pathē* as follows:

I might have rendered this literally, styled them 'diseases', but the word 'disease' would not suit all instances; for example, no one speaks of pity, nor yet anger, as a disease, though the Greeks term these pathos. Let us then accept the word 'emotion' [*perturbatio*], the very sound of which seems to denote something vicious and these emotions are not excited by any natural influence. (*De Finibus Bonorum et Malorum*[5])

Reflecting this negativity, the word *pathos* was replaced by the Roman word *perturbatio*, and much of the bad press emotions have continued to endure through history probably stems back to this time. According to the Stoics, the state of being to which all people should aspire, yet few could ever reach, was called *tranquillitas*. This could only be attained once a person had shed themselves entirely of the emotion – the 'excessive impulses' of *perturbatio* – which belonged to the 'irrational mind' (Graver 2002: 134).

By the time of St Augustine, some 500 years later, Christianity had begun to exert a powerful influence. St Augustine replaced the Stoic translations of *pathē* with the Latin word *passio* (perhaps influenced by his work on early Christian doctrine) and reserved the word *perturbatio* for those instances in which emotion had a negative influence. Living a good Christian life, he argued, was not about living a life in which all emotions were abandoned at the expense of reason but, rather, about achieving some kind of balance between the two (Knuuttila 2004). The word *tranquillitas* (or *apathea*, from which the English word 'apathy' has evolved, but which then meant something more akin to perfect happiness)[6] did not, as it had for the Stoics, mean the absence of all emotion. It simply meant freedom from negative emotional states:

It may, indeed, reasonably be maintained that the perfect blessedness we hope for shall be free from all sting of fear or sadness; but who that is not quite lost to truth would say that neither love nor joy shall be experienced there? (*City of God* 14.9[7])

Following the Platonic/Aristotelian traditions, but practically a millennium later, Thomas Aquinas wrote that the intellectual soul should indeed seek to control the emotions (by now translated as *passiones animae*). However, he was also critical of the Stoic notion of *apathea*. What he added to the philosophy of emotion was a still more developed taxonomy of at least eleven emotions, divided between two broad types: on the one hand, delight and distress, love and hate, which he termed *concupiscible* passions – those emotions directed towards objects evaluated as either good or evil, and, on the other, hope and despair, fear and confidence – *irascible* passions – those passions directed at objects evaluated as something from which something good or evil may be possible or difficult to achieve. Aquinas' views are notoriously difficult to untangle. He seems, for example, to have believed

---

[5] Reference to Rackham's 1914 Harvard University Press edition (Cicero 1914: 255).
[6] The term is still used in the Orthodox church, and the freedom from ungodly urges is one of the aims of Orthodox monastic life.
[7] Reference to 1922 edition, edited by F. Hitchcock (Hitchcock 1922).

there was a sense in which individuals were responsible for their emotions (see Murphy 1999). As well as this, while the group of phenomena he included within the term *passiones* included those we would today call emotions, his term probably included phenomena we would not regard as emotions proper.

In the seventeenth century, first Descartes and later Spinoza both wrote widely on the passions. If anything, during that period the terminology becomes even more confusing. Descartes did use the term 'emotion', but typically used it to signify 'motion of the soul'. More favoured terms included 'affect', 'sentiment' and 'perturbation', and in 1670 Pascal introduced the term 'feelings' into the mix (Schmitter 2014). Accounts of around this time were littered with new attempts at taxonomies. While Descartes listed six basic passions, Spinoza listed around forty affects. Locke worked with a taxonomy of eleven and Hume ten, though the latter were divided into numerous subtypes and he, famously, treated sentiments separately.

What made Descartes' treatment of emotions so different to anything that had gone before, and ultimately so revolutionary, was that with his detailed discussion of nerves, memory and reflexes, his work in many ways presaged modern neurobiology (Keltner et al. 2019). As well as that, he regarded emotions as very different to other types of perception. While vision, for example, gives us information about the outside world, emotional states tell us about what is happening in regard to our concerns, our goals, even our identities. While he still regarded these activities as taking place in the human soul, his work, along with that of his contemporaries (such as William Harvey), began to move thinking about human biology and neurology away from Galen and Hippocrates' balance of humours. As Keltner et al. put it (2019: 14): 'His saying "I think therefore I am" takes us into the modern world. In the new physiology to which he contributed, emotions arise in the mind, enable our plans, and affect our bodies.'

Despite these advances, the suspicion with which early thinkers such as Socrates, Plato and Aristotle had regarded emotions remained. Not until the work of Hume was it suggested that without emotion, reason was powerless. As we saw in the epigraph to Chapter 1, Hume believed that reason alone was not capable of producing actions: what motivates us to act is our passions. And more than that; it is our emotions that facilitate decision-making by enabling us to filter out objects and stimuli that are not relevant to us. In this, he arguably prefigured work on heuristics and biases in cognitive science and, also, on relevance itself. After all, only information that is relevant is worth attending to.

3.2.2 *Charles Darwin and William James*

There are two nineteenth-century thinkers on emotion whose work is immediately relevant to the concerns of this book: Charles Darwin, whose *The Expression of the Emotions in Man and Animals* (1872/1998) is arguably the finest and most important book ever written on emotions and develops the evolutionary ideas first presented in *The Origin of Species*; and William James, whose 1,000-page *Principles of Psychology* remains hugely influential, assuring James his position as one of the founding fathers of modern psychology.

A central theme of Darwin's work was, of course, that humans are descended from other animals. Of course, there are still people who deny this, but we accept it as the most plausible evolutionary hypothesis. With this in mind, he began observing the expression of emotion in both human and non-human animals. Essentially, *The Expression of the Emotions in Man and Animals* is an attempt to answer two questions. The first of these is concerned with *how* human and non-human animals express their emotions: which somatic systems are responsible for those visible expressions of emotion we see, and which emotions do they serve to express? The second is concerned with the question of where these emotional expressions come from in the first place.

Turning to the first question, Darwin provides a comprehensive overview of how humans express many emotions: fear, anger, sadness, pain, shame and many others. As far as the second goes, his view was that these expressions are largely vestigial: evolutionary accidents, if you like, which persist as features of modern humans but no longer serve their original purpose. As a non-expressive example, consider Darwin's tubercle: this is that visibly 'pointed' part many humans have on their ears, roughly two thirds of the way around inside of the helix of the ear close to its apex. This point serves no purpose in modern humans but is an extant human vestige of a homologue we see in modern-day macaques, for whom it reflects essential musculature (no longer working in humans) which gives the ear greater mobility, allowing it to be turned towards a particular source of sound. The human appendix is also vestigial, as are wisdom teeth.

As an expressive corollary, Darwin asks us to consider the human emotion of contempt. This, he argued, is typically expressed with a sneer. Why? Darwin argues it is because the facial expression of sneering is a vestige of the physical act of snarling, which, in many mammals, is that partial uncovering of the teeth which precedes the act of biting. In early humans the sneer may indeed have preceded a snarl, which – as in non-human animals – may have indicated that an individual was preparing to bite. However, it no longer does. Darwin (1872/1998) is full of examples like this.

This is not to say that Darwin regarded emotions as having no function. His claims about the universality of facial expression persist in whole swathes of experimental work, but also lie at the heart of one of the main bones of contention in modern affective science: whether there do exist basic, underlying and universal emotions in humans and whether expressions reliably correlate with them. This is a debate that is very much alive.

William James was born some forty years or so after Darwin. He published on a broad range of topics, including philosophy and the nature of religious experience. Arguably, however, his most lasting legacy has been in his work on psychology. James' interest in emotion lay principally in the physical nature of affective episodes, which he argued lay at the core of emotions. He argued against the prevailing view that emotions caused bodily responses. Rather, he argued, emotional episodes are responses to feelings and sensations.

> Common-sense says, we lose our fortune, are sorry and weep; we meet a bear, are frightened and run; we are insulted by a rival, are angry and strike. The hypothesis here to be defended says that this order of sequence is incorrect ... that we feel sorry because we cry, angry because we strike, afraid because we tremble ... [.] (1890: 1065–6)

The Jamesian view chimes harmoniously with a view of emotion that has influenced us greatly: the functionalist view of emotion presented in Rey (1980). For Rey, full-fledged emotional states are distinguished from 'sensations' or 'feelings' by the fact that they involve an interaction between several elements: cognitive, qualitative and physiological. So the emotion we call 'fear' is characterised as involving an interaction between a cognitive element – a belief that you are in danger, or knowledge that you are in a situation you would prefer not to be in; a qualitative element – the physical feeling of being afraid, which is typically accompanied by a tendency to behave in a certain way (the 'action tendencies' of appraisal theory), and behaviours consistent with feeling this way (wanting to escape); and a physiological element – among which are the secretion of epinephrine, a neurotransmitter associated with changes in heart rate and respiration rate, and cortisol, which heightens awareness and short-term memory. (Interestingly, cortisol also *hinders* reasoning abilities, a point we return to later in the book.) While emotional states crucially involve cognitive as well as qualitative and physiological elements, 'feelings' or 'sensations' need not.[8]

Around the same time that James was writing, a similar view of emotions was also proposed by the physiologist Carl Lange, and this view is commonly

---

[8] A question we have been asked is whether a bipartite distinction, which ignores Rey's 'qualitative' dimension, might suffice in place of the tripartite one he proposes. We don't believe it would and suggest the following two tests to sharpen intuitions. Both concern pain which, whilst not an emotion, is nonetheless intrinsically linked with affective episodes. The first test involves the case of when you are woken up from your sleep by, say, a pain in your back. Before waking, the physiological and qualitative dimensions are presumably present (otherwise you wouldn't have been woken up), but the cognitive element is missing (that is, until you wake and are conscious of that pain). A bipartite distinction could not explain this as easily. The second test is the case of when hypnosis is used, as it sometimes is, to control pain. It seems clear that such cases involve neither the suppression of the physiological components of pain (no anaesthetic is used), nor a suppression of cognition in the sense Rey means it, since patients are conscious. Anecdotally, we add that those under hypnosis acknowledge that they are cognisant of the presence of the physiological elements, but simply cannot 'feel' them. Again, Rey's qualitative dimension appears to be necessary.

referred to as the James–Lange theory of emotion. Emotions are built around groups of bodily responses. James (1884: 193–4) asks:

What kind of an emotion of fear would be left, if neither of quickened heartbeats, nor of shallow breathing, neither of trembling lips nor of weakened limbs, neither of goose-flesh nor of visceral stirrings, were present, it is quite impossible to think. Can one fancy the state of rage and picture no ebullition of it in the chest, no flushing of the face, no dilatation of the nostrils, no clenching of the teeth, no impulse to vigorous action, but in their stead limp muscles, calm breathing, and a placid face? The present writer, for one, certainly cannot. ... In like manner of grief: what would it be without its tears, its sobs, its suffocation of the heart, its pang in the breastbone? A feelingless cognition that certain circumstances are deplorable, and nothing more.

To return to the characterisation offered above by Naar and Teroni, emotions are complex physical, psychological states which are felt by those experiencing them. Darwin and James differ in terms of the aspects of emotion they choose to focus on, but that much is agreed. Their work (and the work of others – psychoanalysts such as Freud (1915/1957), sociologists such as Goffman (1964), early neuroscientists such as Hess and Akert (1965)) has spawned a huge amount of research into human emotion. In the next section we turn to the three main views of modern affective science.

3.3 Affective Science

3.3.1 Three Views

Modern affective science is built around three principal approaches. This is also something of a generalisation but, again, seems to us to be the best way of summarising a complex and still evolving field. The first theory is basic emotion theory. Proponents of this theory propose a certain limited number of basic emotions – between seven and fourteen – and make three claims: emotions, they claim, have a particular expressive pattern, are universal across humankind and have specialised neurobiological origins. Probably the most widely known proponent of this view is Paul Ekman (1989, 1992, 1994, 1999) who, like Darwin, focuses on the range of spontaneous facial expressions which have evolved in humans to reflect a signaller's internal state. The second view is the psychological-constructionist view. Proponents of this view believe the main ingredients of a particular emotional experience are to be found in a free-floating core affect – a blend of (positive and negative) valence and arousal – and that this core affect is contextually categorised according to linguistic and cultural factors (Russell 2003; Feldman Barrett 2017a, 2017b). The third view, appraisal theory, proposes that emotions are elicited and unfold as subjective evaluations are made concerning the object in question.

Before moving on to summaries of the three approaches, we should perhaps point out that what we have here is something of a false trichotomy. The differences between the first two are very real (and, indeed, have caused considerable rancour between opposing theorists). However, the third view, appraisal theory, is so closely concentrated on the psychological processes of evaluation and appraisal which it regards as responsible for the elicitation of emotional episodes, that one can imagine an appraisal theorist remaining quite agnostic on the whole nature/nurture debate.

3.3.2 Basic Emotions

The work of Paul Ekman and colleagues suggests that there is a whole range of spontaneous facial expressions that have evolved in humans to reflect a signaller's internal state: 'these expressions these expressions have been selected and refined over the course of evolution for their role in social communication' (Ekman 1999: 51; see also Izard 1971; Tomkins 1962). Ekman's claim is that these facial expressions are universal and reflect the existence of a set of underlying basic emotions which are part of our human biological inheritance.

In order to confirm (or disconfirm) the claims that Darwin makes in *The Expression of the Emotions in Man and Animals*, Ekman and Friesen began by taking thousands of photographs of individuals performing facial expressions that expressed anger, disgust, fear, happiness, sadness and surprise. These expressions were carefully correlated with the patterns of musculature described by Darwin. The photos were then shown to participants from across the world (specifically Argentina, Brazil, Chile, Japan and the United States), who were then asked to select emotion terms which they felt correlated most closely with the facial expressions. Ekman et al. (1969) presented results which confirmed that participants were between 80 and 90 per cent accurate in identifying the correct emotion.

Critics of the study pointed out that the cultures from which participants had chosen hardly represented a sample on the basis of which claims of universality could realistically be made. With the exception of Japan, the cultures chosen were all, broadly speaking, Western. Moreover, as a result of increased exposure to US media, films and television, Japan was becoming increasingly Westernised. To meet the challenges these critics raised, Ekman decided to undertake follow-up work with the Fore people of Papua New Guinea. These people lived in fairly primitive conditions and had had little-to-no contact with Westerners. Using a specially devised judgement paradigm which involved separate stories for each emotion (Ekman and Friesen 1971), participants (even Fore children) were also between 80 and 90 per cent accurate (i.e., over 60 per cent better than chance). Indeed, US college students scored highly when it came to recognising the posed facial expressions of Fore subjects.

As we remarked earlier, the nature–nurture debate which surrounds the expression of emotion is one that has generated at least as much heat as it has shed light, possibly more. Alan Fridlund (1992, 1994) and James Russell (1994) were, historically, the most notable detractors of the universalist paradigm, arguing against Ekman's claims on several grounds. Firstly, they point out that Ekman overlooks the fact that, actually, there is evidence suggesting that cross-cultural recognition of facial expression varies greatly depending on whichever particular facial expression and emotion are under consideration. So while it may be true that the facial expression for happiness is universally recognised, the same may not be true for expressions of disgust, fear and surprise. If facial expressions truly are universal, we would surely expect them all to be equally recognisable? Secondly, much has been said about the kind of 'forced-choice' dimension inherent in Ekman's work. If participants had been able to use their own words, rather than the ones forced on them in the task, we cannot be sure that the results would be the same. As we say above, we don't believe there is much to learn about the true nature of emotions from the kinds of words people use to describe them, a point we develop in the next subsection, but we agree that the forced-choice element inherent in Ekman's tasks is a potential weakness.

A further, subtle, objection raised by Fridlund revolves around Ekman's assumption that particular facial expressions are reliably correlated with underlying emotions. He prefers to stress the social and manipulative communicative function of such expressions. Among the evidence he cites are data from experiments on 'audience effects' in human smiling (Kraut and Johnson 1979). Researchers monitoring the smiles of people involved in various sporting activities noticed that people tend to smile more for the benefit of others than for themselves. In a more recent set of observation-based experiments, Fernández-Dols and Ruiz-Belda (1995) noticed that the swimming gold medallists at the Barcelona Olympics smiled a great deal when actually being awarded their medals and considerably less during the rest of the ceremony. Their delight at having won the medal was presumably stable throughout the whole period. (The men's and women's Wimbledon final presentations are good places to observe this phenomenon.)

Of course (and as argued by Hauser 1996: 495–6), there are elements of Ekman's and Fridlund's accounts that are not mutually exclusive. Both, for example, acknowledge the communicative role of facial expression in signalling internal states (whatever those states may be), and both also acknowledge a broadly Darwinian account of the evolution of both the expressions and the states they signal. In the next subsection we present a view which denies even that, but before that we turn briefly to the view of emotion taken in evolutionary psychology, which – like the work of Ekman and his colleagues – is influenced greatly by Darwin (1872/1998).

3.3 Affective Science

Evolutionary psychology is not a subdiscipline of psychology (in the same way as, say, developmental psychology, behavioural psychology or, for that matter, affective science). It is an approach to the psychological sciences in which data, observations and results from disciplines such as evolutionary biology, cognitive science and anthropology are drawn together in order to map what, for want of a better phrase, might be called human 'instinct'. Evolutionary psychologists are effectively charting the evolved, neural architecture of the human mind and brain that constitute human nature.

For cognitive scientists such as Leda Cosmides and John Tooby, 'mind' and 'brain' are terms that refer to precisely the same thing. The mind is 'a set of information processing procedures (cognitive programmes or evolved mental organs) that are physically embodied in the neural circuitry of the brain' (2000: 97). Put differently, 'the mind is what the brain does' (2000: 97). According to this view, the mind – like every other human organ – is seen as a set of responses (a so-called adaptive toolkit) to the numerous adaptive problems faced by our human ancestors. Evolutionary pressures ensured that these adaptive problems were successfully addressed and, like the bills of Darwin's finches, or the wing-colour of Darwin's moths, the mind has been shaped according to the principles of natural selection (for more discussion, see Cosmides and Tooby 1987; Tooby and Cosmides 1992). There are numerous sources of evidence that a given cognitive ability is an adaptation: there will be precursors of the ability in other species, the ability arises spontaneously in children and independently of other abilities, and the ability is not acquired via slow, domain-general learning mechanisms:

An evolutionary perspective leads one to view the mind as a crowded zoo of evolved domain-specific programs. Each is functionally specialized for solving a different adaptive problem that arose during hominid evolutionary history, such as face recognition, foraging, mate choice, heart rate regulation, sleep management, or predator vigilance, and each is activated by a different set of cues from the environment. (Cosmides and Tooby 2000: 91–2)

However, they point out that a mind that has evolved as a 'crowded zoo' would have brought with it its own challenges, the principal one being that many of these domain-specific programmes are designed to produce responses which would potentially conflict with each other if simultaneously activated. They provide an example:

Sleep and flight from a predator require mutually inconsistent actions, computations, and physiological states. It is difficult to sleep when your heart and mind are racing with fear, and this is no accident: disastrous consequences would ensue if proprioceptive cues were activating sleep programs at the same time that the sight of a stalking lion was activating programs designed for predator evasion. (Cosmides and Tooby 2000: 91–2)

In order that these disastrous consequences are avoided, the mind has evolved what Cosmides and Tooby (2000: 92) call 'superordinate programs'. These programs override certain programs at the expense of others. So when those programs responsible for the avoidance of predators are activated, those responsible for sleep will be cancelled. Emotions, they propose, are one type of superordinate program. They function to regulate or mobilise cognitive subprograms responsible for perception and attention, goal choice, information-gathering, specialised types of inference, physiological changes and so on. They give the example of fear. When experiencing the emotion of fear, an individual is automatically put into a state of hyper-alertness (and of being unable to sleep), in which they pay a high degree of attention to perceptual inputs they may not normally even notice. They will be equipped with a newly defined set of goals, in which safety is suddenly the most important of a range of new informational priorities – *Where is my baby? Where are others that can protect me?* (2000: 93); they will be subconsciously directed to different, prioritised inferential processes which are activated to aid the making of valuable inferences; and they will be subject to the kind of physiological changes summarised in the discussion of Rey's notion of sensations.

Evolutionary psychologists have been responsible for making huge advances in how we understand the mind and it origins. There is now a good deal of evidence supporting claims that, rather than being born *tabula rasa*, children are born with a rich system of innate expectations and biases: for the early acquisition of concepts in agency (Leslie 1994), naïve physics (Baillargeon 1987, Premack 1990, Spelke 1990), the moral and social sphere (Cosmides 1989, Premack and Premack 1994) and various other areas, in all of which conceptual development takes place independently of the acquisition of language (Fodor 1998, Margolis 1998).

3.3.3 *Constructed Emotion*

> The Tahitians have no concept of 'Sadness'. This last item is very difficult for Westerners to accept ... life without sadness? Really?
>
> Feldman Barrett (2017b: 148)

Social constructionism is a theoretical approach based on the assumption that there are certain facts which, rather than depending on some kind of metaphysical reality, depend on shared ways in which people think or talk about them. In its most radical form, the claim is that reality itself is a social construct. Needless to say, the notion of 'reality' in such a claim is at odds with any claims people have about a metaphysical reality, and this leads to various (in our opinion, insurmountable) issues when it comes to articulating constructionism as an objective, or – for that matter – even common-sense approach. Conceptions of reality are, of course, influenced by social factors, but the claims that form the tenets of social constructionism are more radical than

3.3 Affective Science

that. Emotions are no exception: for social constructionists, emotions are social constructs.

Social constructionism entails a commitment to cultural and linguistic relativity: conceptions of reality are nothing other than social constructs provided by language. It includes a solipsistic, often nominalist stance. A central claim is that reality exists only by virtue of the mind's conceptualisation. This is conventional and arbitrary and reflects the language of the person whose mind is in question.

The origins of this approach, closely related to other forms of denial of objective and metaphysical reality, are shrouded in the mists of antiquity and hark back to the famous claim by Gorgias that either nothing exists or that whatever might exist cannot be stated objectively. Historical figures in the development of cultural relativity include Montaigne in the sixteenth century. However, his claims were about axiological – moral – values, in the context of religious wars in France, and his conception of relativity was essentially a normative one. In the eighteenth century, Bishop Berkeley was, on the contrary, a major thinker in the history of the tenets of relativity and solipsism: for him nothing existed except perception and mental projections. In the mid-nineteenth century Nietzsche asserted: 'There are no facts, only interpretations'.

In the 1960s the whole constructionist movement really took off with the publication in 1967 of Berger and Luckman's *The Social Construction of Reality*. Since then, this approach has become hugely popular in sociology, educational psychology and a wide range of other fields. It connected with the development of continental philosophy and postmodernism, which were developing similar ideas on the basis of politicised (and highly disputable) interpretations of structuralism. The locus of much of this work was in France.

In affective science, constructionism has had a huge influence. Proponents of this type of view, rather than considering emotions as natural kinds, propose that the main component of an emotional experience is to be found in a free-floating core affect, which is a mixture of positive and negative valence and arousal. This core affect is contextualised by a given individual's knowledge of their own language and culture (Feldman Barrett 2006, 2011; Russell 1991, 2003).

Lisa Feldman Barrett, certainly one of the most lauded affective scientists of modern times, acknowledges that her account of constructed emotion incorporates various 'flavours' of social construction (2017b: 70):

One flavor of ... social construction, studies the role of social values and interests in determining how we perceive and act in the world. ... Where emotion is concerned, social construction theories ask how feelings and perceptions are influenced by our social roles or beliefs. For example, my perceptions are influenced by the fact that I am a woman, a mother, an atheist who is culturally Jewish, and a rather pale person living in a country that once enslaved people for having more melanin in their skin than I do.

Social construction tends to ignore biology, however, as irrelevant to emotion. Instead, the theories suggest that emotions are triggered differently depending on your social role. Social constructionist theories, then, are primarily concerned with social circumstances in the world outside you, without considering how those circumstances affect the brain's wiring. Another flavor of construction, known as psychological construction, turns this focus inward. It proposes that your perceptions, thoughts, and feelings are themselves constructed from more basic parts.

Feldman Barrett ties up emotion with language (and the way in which words encode concepts) to the extent that she claims an individual cannot experience an emotion unless they have a word for it in their language. We are not affective scientists and do not pretend to be, but what we can bring to the debate on affect is our knowledge of how language works and, in particular, the interplay between words and concepts. To us, tying up the existence of emotions in a culture with the existence of words in a culture for those emotions is an unrealistic way of exploring the relationship between language and thought (see our earlier discussion of the Sapir–Whorf hypothesis in §3). In human phylogeny and ontogeny, thoughts and emotions come before mere words, and there is a wealth of evidence to support this (Byrne and Whiten 1988, Cornell and Wharton 2021, Cosmides and Tooby 2000, Sperber 2000).

As just one example, consider the following. In the Russian novel *Oblomov* by Ivan Gonsharov, the main character – Oblomov – has a particular feeling that can only be translated by a quite complicated paraphrase: a feeling of being useless, tired, overwhelmed by his own superfluousness and the nonsense associated with life and decision-making. This is a feeling that anyone can not only feel but represent, and all the more so when looking at the example of how the character acts and reasons in the novel and how that kind of experience may mirror the reader's own memories of having felt in a related way at some time in their own life. That rather common feeling – in fact the property of having that feeling during a certain time, or at a certain frequency, which resembles being depressed – received a label which became incorporated into the Russian lexicon, directly inspired by the novel itself: *oblomovshina* (something like 'oblomovism'). The word emerged only after the feeling had been identified as having a form of existence, but one which had not been captured in detail by the Russian lexicon, thus – of course – existing before the word to name it.

Words do not create our meanings. The meanings come first, and we try to explain how in Chapter 7. As Suppes puts it (1996: 113):

…language must have begun from attempts at communication between a few individuals. At first these efforts at communication did not have very much stability of literal meaning. Only slowly and after much time did a stable community of users lead to the abstract concept of literal meaning ... There is no hard and fast platonic literal meaning

3.3 Affective Science

that utterers' meanings attach themselves to ... The story surely is exactly the other way round.

A natural extension of the claim that a person cannot experience fear unless they have a word for it is the claim that humans only began to experience emotions when the word 'emotion' came into being.

According to Feldman Barrett: 'In every waking moment, your brain uses past experience, organized as concepts, to guide your actions and give your sensations meaning. When the concepts involved are emotion concepts, your brain constructs instances of emotion' (2017b: 31). A useful analogy with which to illustrate Feldman Barrett's analysis of emotion is the way in which many scholars have viewed human perception of colour. Indeed, this is an analogy she herself uses (2017b: 84):

When you look at a rainbow, you see discrete stripes of color ... But in nature, a rainbow has no stripes – it's a continuous spectrum of light, with wavelengths that range from approximately 400 to 750 nanometers. This spectrum has no borders or bands of any kind. Why do you and I see stripes? Because we have mental concepts for colors like 'Red', 'Orange', and 'Yellow'. Your brain automatically uses these concepts to group together the wavelengths in certain ranges of the spectrum, categorizing them as the same color. Your brain downplays the variations within each color category and magnifies the differences between the categories, causing you to perceive bands of color. We experience colors as belonging to discrete categories – blue, red, yellow, and so on – and the names of these categories vary according to the language you speak. But the physics of color is continuous rather than discrete and the wavelengths we perceive as discrete colors can be accurately measured in nanometers along a scale incorporating, at one end, ultraviolet and, at the other, infrared. When someone experiences an object as 'blue' they are sub-consciously using their color concepts to categorize this wavelength.

In a manner analogous to this, so the claim goes, we tend to feel that emotions are discrete and distinct – fear, anger, happiness – while affect (which we sense internally through a process called 'interoception') is continuous. Feldman Barrett's theory of constructed emotion suggests that at any given moment, the brain is predicting and categorising the present moment (of continuous affect) via interoceptive predictions and the emotion concepts present in your language and culture and constructing an instance of emotion.

We suggest that there are two grave misconceptions in the approach. The first of these is that it confuses the way people *experience* colours with the way they categorise them in the mind. These two things, which are completely conflated here, are situated on completely different levels. The raw truth is that humans *do indeed* experience colours as a continuum (click on 'colour gradient' on any image-related software to see this). So the *experience* of colour is something distinct from the *categorisation* of colours. It is true that the manner in which colours are categorised in the mind is reflected in how basic colour terms are lexicalised in a given language. And yes, it is also true that, retroactively, the manner in which they are categorised in the lexicon induces some superficial effect on their perception – some experiments, for example, have shown an interaction between the left hemisphere (where the lexicon is stored) and the right visual field. But this effect is highly marginal. Native speakers of Russian, for example, who have two basic terms for *blue* (one light and one dark blue), identify the passage from light to dark blue 124 milliseconds quicker than speakers of languages where there is only one basic term for *blue* (see Martinovic et al. 2020). And it could be argued that this 124-millisecond effect has nothing to do with a social construct and more to do with the ease of facilitation that arises with the process of identifying something common or, usually, lexicalised. All this is a matter of cognition, not of social conventions.

Consider also Feldman Barrett's answer to the question 'Why do we see stripes?' 'Because we have mental concepts for colors like "Red", "Orange" and "Yellow".' But people do not unconsciously use their colour concepts to categorise the wavelength: there is no such thing as experiencing an object *as a word* or even as a concept. We experience percepts; we don't experience concepts, or at least not in a sense where concepts would be equivalent to percepts. When Feldman Barrett writes 'Everything you perceive around you is represented by concepts in your brain' (2017b: 85) she is wrong. And this is *very* important. It is clear evidence that in theories such as this the world of the conceptual and the world of the non-conceptual are entirely conflated. The confusion between words, concepts and perceptive experience is massive here, as it often is in such romantic claims about the objective being the product of sociocultural phenomena.

Second, the claim about the lexicon of colours being discrete in face of a physical continuum, and varying across cultures and languages, is the common *locus* of relativist theories which were prevalent in linguistics until that claim was revealed as a misconception by Berlin and Kay's (1969) world-famous book, *Basic Colour Terms*. It was further corrected by decades of subsequent research and refinements within the *World Colour Survey* in 2011 (Kay et al. 2011) and countless articles about the universality of colour perception and naming, despite a superficial variation in the numbers and extensions of the colour categories in a given language.

Barrett's claim about emotions is in exactly the same vein. The idea that humans resort to names of emotions, or emotion concepts from their culture in order to construct an instance of emotion, is the same as to say that in order to experience the taste of chocolate, one needs to know the word 'chocolate'. Of course, if one *describes* one's emotion, the labels available in the language will be used, but this is trivial and does not in any way play a role in the emotion experienced by the individuals (or, perhaps, only very marginally, as with the colours).[9]

That events conventionally viewed as positive deliver positive emotions, and the reverse does not mean that these emotions themselves are social constructs. That some particular action in the social world – for example offering a reward to a sportsperson – drives a positive emotion to the recipient but a negative one to the jealous other has nothing to do with the nature of emotions themselves. Their *triggers* may be socially determined, depending on the particular context, but the emotions themselves are not: the activation in the brain that they correspond to are not social constructs.

The theory of constructed emotion is confused throughout. One such confusion is particularly evident in the sentence we chose to put in the epigraph of this section (§3.3.3). The fact that there is no word exactly corresponding to 'sadness' in Tahitian (or any given language) plays no role in the fact that an individual can experience the reality that the English speaker calls 'sadness', just as the English speaker can – of course – experience what German speakers call *Schadenfreude* and what French speakers call *accablement*. This is not to deny that these labels cover slightly different stretches of reality – they do, and these fine differences are often what the linguist is most interested in. They may, for example, activate relations and connotations foreign to the other language. However, the realities themselves are untouched by these variations. That a wooden table is a table made of a tree in many languages may perhaps have some consequences in aspects of the conceptions one has about wood and trees and wooden tables. But it has no impact on the actual matter of the table.

It is common to see examples in the popular press of words in one language that are 'untranslatable' into another. One such word that has received recent attention is the Norwegian word *hygge*. But the problem with this is not only that *hygge* is actually quite easily translatable (it's a fusion of 'cosiness' and 'togetherness' – what the popular press actually mean is that there is no corresponding *single word* in English) but that if you take this debate to extremes it turns out that pretty much every word in a given language cannot be translated completely into another. Few people would deny that the English word 'river' and the French word 'rivière' encode the same thing. But while English rivers can happily flow into the sea, French ones cannot. Only French *fleuves* can do that … . Linguists could produce whole dictionaries here, making claims of non-translatability for just about every word in every language. But one conclusion that can never be drawn is that it is mentally

---

[9] Of course, it may happen that if we experience fear, and at some point realise that what we are experiencing is fear, then the emotion itself is reinforced: we can be afraid because we realise that we are afraid. However, this kind of effect has nothing to do with what Feldman Barrett is claiming.

impossible for a person to represent the concepts accessed by words delimiting other categories than the words of one's own language.

That some emotion might be called 'sadness' in English, designated by some other word in a given language, or by no particular, specific word in Tahitian, doesn't affect the actual emotion itself: mental configurations and processes are realities independent from the words you choose to use to describe them.

3.3.4 The View from Appraisal Theory

In the previous chapter we discussed the central role played by the cognitive revolution of the late 1950s and 1960s in the development of linguistics. Other disciplines – cognitive science, anthropology, computer science – were equally influenced. Affective science was no exception and in the 1960s Magda Arnold (1960a, 1960b) and Richard Lazarus (1966) began to notice that research into the emotions tended to ignore the question of how emotions were elicited, that is, the nature of the type of cognitive processing that caused emotional episodes. It had been proposed before this time that some form of evaluative process needed to take place before an emotion was elicited. The intuition behind this is that, plainly, the same stimulus can elicit different emotions in different people: a remark that I consider inappropriate and highly offensive might, for example, amuse someone else. But it was Arnold (1960a, 1960b) who subjected the claim to systematic examination.

Appraisal theory (Ellsworth 2013, Frijda 2007, Lazarus 1991, Roseman 2013, Scherer 2009) takes it that emotions are episodes that are triggered by a stimulus. The episodes themselves are componential and comprise bodily symptoms (Rey's physiological sensations), subjective feelings (Rey's quantitative dimension) and action tendencies. Crucially, however, this 'triggering' is the result of the final component: subjective evaluations, or 'appraisals', made concerning the stimulus in question (Rey's cognitive dimension). In her comprehensive overview of the various 'flavours' of appraisal theory, Moors (2014: 5) adds three additional criteria: firstly, that the stimulus is appraised as relevant to a particular goal or concern (so-called 'goal relevance' or 'goal congruence'); secondly, that it gives rise to an action tendency which has priority over other goals or concerns; and, thirdly, that these episodes have what Moors (2014: 3), following Scherer 2009) calls 'strongly synchronizing components'.

Early approaches to appraisal theory proposed that a stimulus is appraised along three separate dimensions: whether the stimulus is positive or negative; whether it is present or not present and whether it is easily attainable or easily avoidable (Arnold 1960a, 1960b). The reason a particular stimulus causes happiness would be that it is appraised as positive, present and easily maintained. Fear, on the other hand, would be the result of a stimulus appraised as negative, currently not present (but potentially present) and difficult to avoid.

3.3 Affective Science

Over the years, the dimensions along which appraisals take place have been augmented and finessed. Lazarus (1991) proposes six dimensions, adding moral considerations, whether the self will be subject to credit or blame, to the two central criteria of goal relevance or congruence. Scherer et al. (2001) distinguish sixteen, termed *stimulus evaluation checks*.

As we remarked at the beginning of this chapter, the trichotomy we present here is something of a false one. While we do not personally know an appraisal theorist who is entirely agnostic on the nature/nurture debate that lies at the heart of the disagreement between the first two approaches introduced in this chapter, it is nonetheless possible to imagine that one exists. However, it is, we submit, impossible to imagine a person committed to the view presented in §3.3.2 who is agnostic about the one presented in §3.3.3, and vice versa.

Having said that, appraisal theorists do not commit to the kind of position adopted by Barrett concerning the centrality of the labelling of emotional episodes with words to the whole experience of having the episode. According to Moors (2014: 305), the experience or feeling of an emotion:

can, but does not have to be labeled with an emotion word. If it does get labeled, the label also enters consciousness where it also colours the emotional experience. Crucially, appraisal theories accept that there can be emotional experience without categorisation or labelling of the experience as emotional (or as angry, sad, and fearful). In this respect, they differ from [Feldman] Barrett's psychological theory.[10]

A final point to note concerns the precise nature of the role of appraisals in emotional episodes. The aim of appraisal theories is to demonstrate that this role is a causal one, but causality is notoriously difficult to evidence. So, while subjective evaluations may well be the cause of emotion elicitation, it is equally possible that they are merely components of emotions or even consequences rather than causes. This issue presents a very real challenge for appraisal theory.

---

[10] Following Feldman Barrett herself, we call her approach 'constructionism' rather than (as Moors does) 'constructivism'. The two concepts are closely related (Papert (1970) developed the former from the latter, which was developed by Piaget (1957)), but they essentially refer to knowledge acquisition in developmental psychology and in education respectively. The version known as 'social constructionism', still quite widespread in the social sciences, assumes in its strong version that the physical world has little or even no impact on knowledge; rather, this is 'constructed' through social interaction by integrating notions that are socially prevalent in a certain culture. Since these notions are categories encapsulated in a language, words are assumed to constitute the basis for knowledge, taken as a convention. It's in that sense that Barrett's claim is constructionist: in her view, humans grasp the division of colours in the rainbow not primarily because they perceive differences or because the brain is equipped so as to analyse the wavelengths in a particular way, but because of how words in a given language cut them up into a particular set of categories. It is this perspective that makes her claim compatible with Whorfian linguistic determinism and leaves it susceptible to all the associated issues such radical claims raise.

As far this book goes, whichever flavour of the theory you adhere to, the term relevance (or a related one) is likely to be found at its core: Scherer (1994a) includes the detection of relevance as the first process in his component model of emotion; Sander et al. 2003 characterise the amygdala as a relevance detector. In appraisal theory, for an object to elicit an emotion that object must in some way be relevant to the person experiencing the emotion (for discussion, see Sander et al. 2003). Because of this, we believe there are good reasons to suggest that aspects of appraisal theory marry particularly successfully with the pragmatic theory we build our account around later in this book. Indeed, we propose that there exist untapped similarities between the two approaches which suggest a route ahead for genuinely interdisciplinary research involving pragmatists and affective scientists (see also Wharton et al. 2021).

The question of what precisely emotion theorists mean by 'relevance' is an interesting one. Typically, they mean concern relevance or goal relevance, but as far as we know, no formal definition has been provided. As early as the 1950s, Lazarus was developing a notion of motivational relevance, and in formalising and developing his theory of emotion he continued, with the notion of primary appraisal, to consider motivational significance as key to understanding elicitation conditions of stress and emotion. The appraisal of goal relevance was a key mechanism for emotion elicitation in Scherer's work also. Scherer (1982: 559) defines the evaluation of the goal relevance of a stimulus as 'the appraisal of the extent to which the introduction of that particular stimulus or event will further or hinder the attainment of a goal high in priority at that particular point'. This definition, which is very similar to Lazarus' motivational relevance or Frijda's concern relevance, highlights the role of goals in emotion, advocating that cognitive processes are critical in the elicitation of emotions (see also Oatley and Johnson-Laird 1987).

Relevance can be conceptually linked to other constructs in motivation research – for example, the wanting component in reward processing (Pool et al. 2016a) – and operationalised to study the effects of relevance not only on the emotional response (Scherer 2013) but also on cognitive mechanisms such as attention (Pool et al. 2016b; Maratos and Pessoa 2019), learning (Stussi et al. 2018) and memory (Montagrin et al. 2018). As an operational definition of relevance, Sander et al. (2003: 22) suggest that an 'object or situation is appraised as relevant for an individual if it increases the probability of satisfaction or dissatisfaction toward a major concern of the individual'. This is consistent with recent work that links relevance to how much a stimulus is informative (Olteanu et al. 2019).

The idea of 'relevance', then, is central to very different theories of emotion. Whether, moving forward, it will be possible to define it in the same terms as the way it has been in pragmatics remains to be seen, and we will explore that issue in Chapter 5 and in our final chapter, when we suggest further directions research might take. Ultimately, though, that is as much a question for affective scientists as it is for pragmatists, and in these pages our main goal is to see what affective science can teach us about pragmatics rather than the other way round.

4 From Proto-pragmatics to Pragmatics

4.1 Introduction

Emotions, then, are complex phenomena, formed of a number of different components. In a way the idea that cognition and affect are antithetical, a possibility raised on the opening page of Chapter 1, is turned on its head. After all, the single component that seems crucial to an event being an emotional event or episode – as opposed to merely a sensation or feeling – is the presence of a cognitive dimension: in appraisal theory terms, an appraisal. As Hume rightly proposed, cognition and affect (or reason and passion) work together. In the next chapter, and in later chapters also, we develop a theoretical framework which accounts for how this interaction takes place.

In this chapter, however, we return to more traditionally linguistic issues. We explore various threads in the development of pragmatics as we know it today, focusing particularly on what we – following Nerlich and Clark (1996) – call 'proto-pragmatics'. As it happens, much of the work in this area has paid very close attention to the communication of affect and is therefore important to our concerns. Our attempt to introduce affect into the centre of theories of utterance interpretation is by no means the first: the sidelining of affect by theories of communication has not happened in the absence of opposition. We trace a route from Thomas Reid and Rousseau in the eighteenth century to Ferdinand de Saussure and Charles Bally in the nineteenth and twentieth. Bally, of the Geneva school, was motivated to explore *parole* largely by Saussure's focus on *langue*. Since his contributions seem to us to have been somewhat overlooked, we devote a few pages to presenting them. As we said earlier, for many of our readers we suspect this will be the first time they have seen them.

A further reason for dwelling a little on Bally's work is to draw attention to parallels between it and the work of the so-called ordinary-language philosophers of Oxford (see Chapter 1, fn. 5), who committed themselves to the study of natural language *use* rather than the logical formulae of formal languages (more about this later in this chapter). We will try to keep our route as direct as possible, and tracing the origin of the historical parallels is not easy (and nor is exegesis our principal aim), but it is worth pointing out that

4.1 Introduction

one of Bally's influences, Michel Bréal, was a regular correspondent of English semiotician Lady Victoria Welby, and her work certainly influenced the Oxford group (see Petrilli 2009) and, indeed, the work of Jacques van Ginneken, a member (though a member who entertained with reservations) of the little known 'Significs' movement in the Netherlands (Elffers 2020). This was a movement which evolved from meetings Welby had originally held with Frederik van Eeden, a Dutch psychotherapist/poet.

A list of Welby's regular correspondents reads like a *Who's Who* of intellectuals and personalities of the day. Among the 500-or-so people she regularly corresponded with were: James M. Baldwin, Henri Bergson, Mary Boole, Rudolf Carnap, Thomas Huxley, William James, Max Müller, Violet Paget, Charles Sanders Peirce (who praised her work effusively), Bertrand Russell, Julia Wedgwood and H. G. Wells, to name but a few. Welby was an astonishing figure – a self-educated philosopher, theologian, musician, traveller and watercolourist. She had no institutional affiliation (though she had been maid of honour to Queen Victoria) and the only honour she is said to have valued was 'that of being treated by workers as a serious worker' (Hardwick 1977).

Welby clearly had some influence on Grice's view on the connection between meaning and intentions (see also Wharton 2009). And as well as this, there is no doubt that Welby was a huge influence on another person whose work certainly played a role in Grice's intellectual development: Charles Ogden. Welby and Ogden met at Cambridge before World War I and Ogden mentions her, though only briefly, in the famous book *The Meaning of Meaning* (Ogden and Richards 1923). Though her influence is hardly acknowledged, Welby's pragmatic conception of language is writ large throughout the book.[1]

Contemporaneous with work that was principally influenced by Welby, there were two other circles of thought within the United Kingdom, each of which was developing largely independently. These were the Oxford group, which we have already mentioned, and the Cambridge circle, which comprised Frege, Russell and Moore. The former was popularised in the United States by first Austin, then Grice and then Searle. By Grice's time at least, the movement had become known as Anglo-American pragmatics.

Another person deserving of mention here is philologist and Egyptologist Alan Gardiner, who influenced Austin greatly and was another of those people who believed that the correct way to analyse language was as one sphere of human social activity (see Furberg 1970). If Gardiner *did* influence Austin, and as far as we can tell he probably did, Austin's reaction was to denigrate his contribution completely. The philosophers who worked with Gardiner in the 1940s and 1950s at both Oxford and Cambridge virtually ignored him,

---

[1] McElvenny 2014 suggests that this was one reason for Russell's largely negative response to it.

although Chomsky later read his book and regarded it as one that would 'live in the annals of linguistic history' (Nerlich and Clark 1996: 356).[2]

The ordinary language philosophers inherited the more pragmatic conception of language study propounded by Welby, Ogden, Richards and so on and argued that the formalist approach adopted by those working at Cambridge and, also, the logical positivists, which in effect equated the study of linguistic meaning with logic and truth, obscured the crucial features of language use rather than illuminated them. They maintained that the truth conditions of sentences exist only in virtue of the linguistic act, or *speech act*, a given sentence is used to perform. Indeed, among the most important achievements of the latter part of the movement was Grice's proposal of an inferential model of communication, the model on which most modern pragmatics is based. We turn to a discussion of this group in §4.4 but leave discussion of Grice and his broader programme to the next chapter, and Chapter 8 also.

4.2 Towards Expressive Meaning

While most people in the eighteenth century accepted one version of the Aristotelian or Stoic tendency towards formality and propositions outlined in §2.2, there were occasional dissenters. Scottish philosopher Thomas Reid wrote in 1787:

I believe the principles of the art of language are to be found in a just analysis of the various species of sentences. Aristotle and the logicians have analysed one species – to wit, the proposition. To enumerate and analyse the other species must, I think, be the foundation of a just theory of language. (Works, 72[3])

Reid thus became interested in sentences that could not be analysed using the notion of propositional meaning (see Schuhmann and Smith 1990 for a comprehensive overview). As one example of what he had in mind when he used the term 'other species', he wrote in his 1774 account of Aristotelian logic that:

[Aristotle] observes justly that besides that kind of speech called a proposition, which is always either true or false, there are other kinds which are neither true nor false, such as a prayer or a wish; to which we may add, a question, a command, a promise, a contract, and many others. (Works, 692[4])

---

[2] Together with Malinowski and Firth, Gardiner was a member of 'The London Group', whose interest in linguistics grew out of their interest in functionalism and contextualism. Indeed, Gardiner 'found' linguistics because of his job as an Egyptologist and used it to better understand Egyptian grammar. Arguably, both the London School and Welby's Significs movement were overshadowed by ordinary-language philosophy.
[3] Quoted in Schumann and Smith (1990: 47).
[4] Quoted in Schumann and Smith (1990: 53).

4.2 Towards Expressive Meaning

Reid's words are highly prescient of John Austin's work on speech acts at Oxford nearly two centuries later in which a distinction was made between constative utterances, or descriptive propositions, and performative ones, which indicate the performance of illocutionary acts. Indeed, Schuhmann and Smith (1990) point out that Bühler's *Theorie der Sprechhandlungen* (literally, speech-act theory), outlined in 1933, is also conceived as the theory of concrete uses of language in the sense of Saussurean *parole*. There are parallels with the work of Bally here, as we shall see.

While Reid's acknowledgement of a dimension of meaning that exists beyond propositions is quite startling to the modern reader, Nerlich and Clark (1996: 111) quote a warning provided by Stephen Land (1986: 235): 'Reid still works in the eighteenth-century mode, seeing language as the reflection of underlying thought, which is for him the true object of study'. The Port-Royal logic–grammar parallelism was still vital to the view Reid was presenting, no matter how modern his ideas might seem to us with the benefit of hindsight.

Another person who challenged the classical Stoic view, but on the other side of *la Manche*, was Jean-Jacques Rousseau, who objected to the tradition that the structure of language reflected the structure of thought (where thought was understood as propositions). His thinking was subversive, separating itself from – as it did – the theological view that humans were the only rational creatures and therefore superior to any other member of the natural world. As we saw in Chapter 2, rationality and logic were regarded as elevated human capacities, induced by God. It was the fate of humans to reign sovereign over all of nature and, in particular, over the irrational beast. Rousseau's views, naïve as they may appear to the modern reader, were dangerous to the monarchic power of the times, not to say heretical, and presaged a completely different way of conceiving human language and thought. According to Rousseau, both originated in nature, and in claiming that, he was addressing what would one day be called 'evolutionary' issues.

Rousseau's views on non-propositionality stemmed not so much from an interest in speech acts but, rather, from his belief that the sophistication of language had its origins not in the need to describe and convey rational judgements, but rather what he called moral needs, even Humean 'passions'. It is hardly surprising that his views are redolent of those of Hume, for the two were good friends. When Rousseau came under physical attack from the mob at his house in Geneva, he sought refuge with Hume in the UK:

Where might this origin [of language] come from? From moral needs, passions. All passions. All the passions tend to bring people back together again, but the necessity of seeking a livelihood forces them apart. It is neither hunger nor thirst but love, hatred, pity, anger, which drew from them the first words . . . One can take nourishment without speaking . . . But for moving a young heart, or repelling an unjust aggressor, nature dictates accents, cries, lamentations. There we have the invention of the most ancient words; and that is why the first languages were singable and passionate before they became simple and methodical. (Rousseau, Essay 12[5])

Here, the invocation of 'nature' rather than God-given reason as a primary force was revolutionary, and the first signs emerge of a division that would soon appear between religious Creationism and more naturalistic, evolutionary approaches to human phylogeny. Rousseau's approach had little apparent effect on contemporary grammarians and philosophers of language of the time, but slowly his ideas found favour. And at the beginning of the twentieth century aspects of the logical approach to language described in Chapter 2 finally came under sustained criticism through the work of Ferdinand de Saussure.

It is impossible to underestimate Saussure's influence on the study of language and no exaggeration to say his work instigated a completely new approach. While most philosophers remained interested in the relationship between language and thought, paying virtually no attention to the subtle differences between actual spoken languages, the influence of Saussure led many scholars to begin work on comparative grammars. They were quick to notice that the differences between languages were more profound than had previously been thought and uncovered subtle ways – other than Lockean arbitrariness – in which languages might be said to be different. The Port-Royal logic–grammar parallelism had no place in Saussure's theory and as a result language came to be seen as an object that dwelt in the minds of humans, rather than in some realm of abstract logic. As we shall see, while Saussure paid no attention to emotion at all, his ideas nonetheless opened the door to new ways of exploring human mental activity.

Michel Bréal was another important figure. He was the main founder of the Paris School of Comparative Linguistics and advocate (to-be) of Saussure. In 1863, greatly influenced by Welby, he began applying the methods of comparative grammar to culture and published a comparative study of the mythologies of the Indo-European world. Bréal was clearly one of those with whom Rousseau's thoughts on language, affect and thought resonated. Language, he affirmed, was bound to action, and the grammar of sentences reflected not an underlying logic but an essential notion of the action to which language was bound. In this he was arguably following Welby's pragmatic considerations, proposing that humans were initially concerned with practical needs and that human conceptions were therefore naturally oriented towards attitudes which bear on what is required for practical benefit.[6] Bréal linked action with

---

[5] From *On the Origins of Language*, first published 1781 (Rousseau 1986: 12).
[6] In this they were also, to an extent, following Reid and, hence, prefiguring Austin. Writing in the 1969 edition of Reid's *Essays on the Intellectual Powers of Man* (1785/1969: xxvi). Baruch Brody states: 'Reid's remarks about ordinary language are parallel to a remarkable degree in the writings of J. L. Austin.' The same can be said of Bally, as we develop later in the chapter. (Though we should be wary of Land's warning.)

4.2 Towards Expressive Meaning

imagination and, crucial to the argument in this book, with emotion. His conclusion was that language was essentially poetic, emotional, narrative; a view that reflected the views of Rousseau.

Bréal was also hugely influenced by Henri Weil, whose book he edited and popularised.[7] Weil's baton was ultimately passed on to Swedish linguist Carl Svedelius, but Bréal certainly read him. So as well as the line that can be traced from Bréal to Bally to Emile Benveniste, which led to the development of the French theory of *enunciation* – a counterpart to Anglo-American pragmatics – another can be traced from Weil to Bréal to Svedelius (Nerlich and Clark 1996: 246). Like Bréal, Charles Bally drew on Saussurean linguistics and considered orientation to action as a central driver of language use. But before we can sketch Bally's contribution in more detail, some context is required. In order to provide that, we must dwell a little on the work of Ferdinand de Saussure.

Saussure was, without question, *the* major figure in Indo-European linguistics. After decades of studying the history of languages and their relations, he ended up forming his theory of 'general linguistics', a philosophy of language that was unique. The theory focused on the nature of language, not language use. It also all but disregarded the role of affect in language. Many of the questions he asked and the answers he provided now seem obvious to linguists everywhere. But his work needs to be taken in the spirit of the time. The intellectual *Zeitgeist* at the time was one in which the fundamental nature of language was barely considered. Everyone knew what language was. (This, incidentally, is a view that persists and is reflected in the lack of characterisations offered of language in contemporary work that purports to be about it.)

Saussure was arguably the first to address the ontology of language in claiming that it is on the one hand mental, all languages sharing fundamental, natural properties (every language is a mental system of signs), and on the other, conventional (the mental system is tied to conventions in a given linguistic community). More precisely, Saussure's theory held that a language is not a list of items corresponding to mental elements but rather a system of interrelated elements, which Roman Jakobson later termed a 'structure'. These interrelated elements are 'signs', bound together to form a system where the categorisation of reality can be different from one language to another. Having said that, the fundamental abstract apparatus itself remains the same: every language is a system of signs and thus obeys the same general laws (language is a 'faculty', an 'instinct').

But the Saussurean 'sign' is not the classical sign of previous studies. Saussure's notion is entirely mental: it is the association of an acoustic

---

[7] *De l'Ordre des Mots dans les Langues Anciennes Comparées aux Langues Modernes* (Weil 1844).

memorial trace, which he calls *le signifiant* – the signifier – with another 'psychic' element, the concept, or *le signifié* – the signified. Since signs are associations involving a concept, and are the atoms of languages, concepts themselves are delineated by language (in fact, by the specific structure which is core to language and that he calls *langue*). We add that this idea led to a number of erroneous interpretations of Saussure's approach which took it as being relativistic, but in fact all that really mattered to him was that there might exist different categorisations of reality in different languages. This is hardly disputable and does not at all involve anything like Sapir–Whorfian worldviews.

Central to the concerns of this book is the fact that the perspective Saussure introduced rid linguistics of the view under which logic was the only way in which language could be properly addressed. Also, Saussure was a Protestant and largely unfettered by the old influence of Thomism and Catholic theology. Perhaps for this reason, he was able to deal more comfortably with matters that scholars working in earlier eras had necessarily regarded with suspicion: the human brain and specifically Broca's and Wernicke's areas (discovered in 1861 and 1874, respectively). For Saussure this was where language resided: in the minds of humans.

While Saussure affirmed that language was an instinct, a faculty that resides in the brain (see his *Third Course in Linguistics* 1993), he did not develop anything like a theory of how it is that language became externalised. For Saussure, this externalisation, or *parole*, was the mere verbalisation of language structures, which is a very different thing to offering a theory of actual language usage. Chomsky's famous distinction between competence and performance was at least partly inspired by Saussure's focus on *langue* and his dismissal of *parole*. Chomsky became interested in Saussure's work largely due to an encounter with Jakobson at the Massachusetts Institute of Technology in the early 1950s (it was Jakobson who helped Chomsky gain a position there as Associate Professor in 1955). However, Saussurean distinctions were to some extent also incorporated into what would come to be known as American structuralism. (Bloomfield signed a review of Saussure's course in 1929 in which he wrote: 'Saussure gave us the means to a theory of language' (see Koerner 1989)).

The field was now open for Charles Bally, who developed a theory of language use *including affect* within a broadly Saussurean framework. Bally's theory of 'stylistics' (1905) not only marks the first comprehensive theory of affect in language use but also, we argue, anticipates contemporary cognitive pragmatics in many ways. For this reason, we dwell for a short while on his contribution to the debate, without intending to underplay the valuable contributions of others.

4.3 Bally's *Parole*

Bally's theory of *parole* was essentially the view that language use was better articulated along two dimensions: abstract ideas and affect (or feelings). His 1909 *Traité de stylistique française* presented this distinction on its very first page:

> Language expresses the contents of our thought, that is, our *ideas* and our *feelings*: since intellectual and affective elements are almost always united to various degrees in the formation of thought, the same composition is reproduced in [linguistic] expression. (Bally 1909: 1, our translation, original italics)[8]

Bally's project was largely overlooked by Saussure (see Curea 2015: 27) and criticised at the time by many prominent linguists. Antoine Meillet (1910), for example, considered the project too context-dependent to allow for realistic generalisations. Indeed, it's probably true to say that, sadly, Bally's approach began and ended with his own work. But elements of his project live on insofar as a number of his assumptions resonate particularly strongly with what would appear much later under the label of pragmatics. And although it is true that many of his claims might be termed over-general, and the technical apparatus of his analysis is perhaps open to criticism, the intuitions in the *Traité* are of interest and, arguably, importance to anyone interested in uniting rather than separating the domains of reason and affect.

In *Le Langage et la Vie* (1926) he proposed his general framework: 'a language exists only in the brains of those who speak it, and it is the laws of the human mind and of society that explain linguistic facts' (Bally 1926: 14).[9] In this claim, he followed Saussure's notion of *langue* as a mental, psychological entity, suggesting that the laws governing language use are not necessarily those of idealised formal logic, or as he terms it 'pure reason':

> Natural language, which we all speak, is at the service not of pure reason nor of art; it doesn't aim at a logical ideal, nor at a literary ideal; its primordial and permanent function is not to build syllogisms, to round periods, to obey the rules of the Alexandrine verse. It is simply at the service of life. (Bally (1926: 14))

Here, Bally means 'life' in a very particular sense: 'the consciousness of living, the will to live, the vital sense that we carry inside us' (1926: 15). This, he says, is comprised of phenomena such as emotions, desires, will and ultimately 'all spontaneous and natural forms of "psychic life"' (1926: 15) or as he also termed it, 'lived thoughts' (1926: 14).[10]

---

[8] For a comprehensive review of Bally's approach, see Curea (2015) (in French).

[9] First edition 1913 (also published by Payot of Paris). We refer in this section to the second, revised and augmented edition of 1926. All quotes in this section are our translations.

[10] 'Mes pensées "vécues" sont d'une tout autre étoffe que celle des idées pures': 'My "lived" thoughts are of a completely other make than that of pure ideas' (1926: 15). Bally is clearly influenced by Bergson's vitalistic notion of 'vital momentum' distinct from intellectual thought.

Bally contrasted the notion of 'lived thoughts' with abstract propositional thought (or ideas, or pure reason) and proposed that they greatly dominate our need to communicate with language. The affective involvement of speakers, which has a crucial bearing on the ideas that we convey propositionally, is what motivates us and our interlocutors in most of our linguistic exchanges. Of course, a proposition might be informative, and hence interesting in itself, but in most communicative exchanges our utterances also carry an affective meaning (crucially non-propositional), and it is that which endows an utterance with (for want of better words) real meaningfulness. This affective dimension connects with the reality in which our own lived lives are anchored, and with the personal appraisals we have about it in the circumstances. Such elements are inextricably intertwined with affect: with feelings, emotions, desires and so on.

He asks us to consider the statement 'Life is short':

If someone tells me that life is short, that axiom is not interesting to me in itself as long as I don't feel it, as long as it is not lived; that general idea only really penetrates in me by a *subjective* modification accompanied by an *affective* vibration, mild as it may be, and this is possible only if, by simple or complex associations, I think of *my* life, or that of other persons involved in *my* existence. (Bally 1926: 15, original italics)

For Bally, ordinary thoughts of the kind expressed in language are never solely concerned with pure reason. They are always charged to at least some degree with emotion. These emotional elements produce epiphanies, frustrations, desires and a range of vital, sometimes visceral impulses, which lead ultimately to courses of action. From his perspective, rational intelligence is only the instrument with which these emotions are conceptualised: yes, it allows us to move unconscious emotional life towards consciousness, but it is this emotional life that is the real driving force.

At this point we pause to draw two parallels: first between Bally's view of the relationship between reason and passions and the Humean conception of reasons as a 'slave of the passions'; second, with particular attention to his conception of affective states as preparatory to action, to those ideas often found in modern theories of emotions (see, for example, Fontaine and Scherer 2013; Moors et al. 2013). The domains of reason and affect merge in acts of speech and Bally's work is largely an attempt to reconcile the two, to see each as serving the other.

The theory of *parole* also anticipates a number of classical claims in pragmatics: even, to some extent, in contemporary cognitive pragmatics. The notions that utterances have a bearing on practical life, involve situations and lead to forms of implications (while admittedly not framed as precisely as they are by later philosophers such as Grice) are all present in his work. For Bally, sensorial stimuli are translated in impressions and judgements of value which are not simply axiological but relate to all sorts of appraisals. These judgements of

4.3 Bally's *Parole*

value are distinct from logical judgements in two respects. First, they aim at a 'subjective' finality (which is to be understood as concerning the individual's own mental life), not at an abstract causal–theoretical level, and they are always to some degree affective. Second, the practical implications of an utterance depend upon external factors that determine its meaningfulness, and these involve affective meanings. Bally asks us to consider an utterance of 'It's hot'. He goes on:

[This] can mean, depending on cases: 'This heat is pleasant to me, or unpleasant; it's good or bad to me; it's favourable or contrary to my interests; I will be able to dispose my winter clothes; I will feel oppressed; my plants will grow or dry up, etc.' (Bally 1926: 2)

To the contemporary pragmatist, these things all look like forms of implicit meaning. What Bally termed judgements of value resemble very much what we now call pragmatic meaning. Such observations may be trivial at first sight, but the link between these elements and utterance meaning is certainly not.

Bally notes that a judgement of value can be expressed just as factually as an objective judgement on a state of affairs (such as 'life is short'). However, even though he doesn't state it explicitly, it transpires that according to him language is underspecified and that many of those extra meanings derived from utterances are added by resorting to forms of subjective judgements and affects. Typically, we make sense of tautologies this way. A sentence such as 'A father is always a father', Bally says, 'would be simply absurd, if sticking to the material interpretation', noting that such an utterance is completed by notions of qualities and values ordinarily attributed to fathers (1926: 18).

Of course, what Bally's approach lacks is a proper theory of linguistic processing to explain how and why hearers interpret utterances. Nonetheless, the notion that a material interpretation might not be informative (that it is 'absurd'), and, moreover, that it might be further developed through affect in order to get rid of that lack of informativeness, appears thoroughly modern to us. We might add that it also seems thoroughly Gricean.

The distinction between expression of pure ideas and expression of lived thoughts is not only impressively novel but is also founded on a rich anthropological conception. As well as being influenced by Saussure, Bally was also probably inspired by the English Egyptologist Alan Gardiner, whom we have mentioned before. Gardiner's conception of language use was also largely based in action (1932: 17):

[I]magine an angry traveller hurling words of abuse at an incomprehending porter, or a judge pronouncing sentence of death upon a murderer. Shall we say that these persons are expressing thought?

Bally gives a further example. Standing in front of a painting by Rembrandt, he says, an individual may give in to their affective state – in this case joy and admiration – and exclaim 'How beautiful!' In this case, the individual's subjectivity is displayed with spontaneous affective force. But this affective force can be filtered out. It can be intellectualised, and the individual might utter 'This is a masterpiece!', thus expressing a judgement of value.[11] Both are loaded with affectivity and subjectivity, but only the second involves mediation by intellectualisation. The distinction between indirect description and direct expression comes to mind here.

And, as it transpires, 'expressivity' is a term that appears in Bally's work. His idea was that propositional forms – which he called the *dictum* (the proposition expressed or 'what is said') – were subjected to particular embeddings and modifications that manifest affectivity by the *modus* (or 'way of phrasing'). The latter might include 'intonation and mimesis by the speaker [which] will show, at least weakly, the affectivity of his thought' (Bally 1926: 17), or 'gestures, face expression' (1926: 19).[12] This, he claims, remains true in virtually all utterances in ordinary conversation. Bally develops a pragmatic theory within which the different layers of meaning are driven not only by rationality but also, quite fundamentally, by affect.

Our aims, while acknowledging that a balance is important, are similar.

Without wanting to make this section overly exegetical or, indeed, take us too far away from the important points, there are further interesting parallels between Bally's notion of *dictum* and ordinary language philosopher R. M. Hare's notion of *dictor*, a term he coined for propositional content. Indeed, this may be more evidence that there were links between the Geneva school and those working in mid-twentieth-century Oxford. Grice was clearly aware of Hare's work at Oxford, and 'dictive meaning', his alternative term for 'what is said', undoubtedly had its roots in Hare's terminology (Wharton 2001). In his 1989 anthology, Grice refers to 'philosophers ... who, in one way or another, have drawn a distinction between *phrastics* and *neustics*' (Grice 1989: 367). Indeed, in the typescript of Lecture VII of the 1967 William James Lectures, he replaces his well-known term 'what is said' with the alternative 'dictive meaning' (see Arundale 1991).[13]

While he is arguing for a particular analysis of imperatives, Hare (1971: 1) does appear to be making a stronger point, one that arguably harks back to Bally rather than meaningfully prefiguring Grice, when he writes:

The sort of sentences which are to be admitted into the logical fold are variously referred to as 'scientific', 'cognitive', 'informative', 'fact-stating', 'true-or-false', 'theoretical', 'referential', 'symbolic', etc.; and the sort of sentences which are to be excluded are

---

[11] This example resonates nicely with the painting appreciation example in Chomsky's 1959 rebuttal of behaviourism.
[12] Nerlich and Clark point out that the terms *modus* and *dictum* were used in the Middle Ages (1996: 10).
[13] Hare's theoretical distinctions – *dictors, phrastics, neustics, tropics* – are incredibly complex, but highly rewarding and equally highly recommended.

called 'emotive', 'evocative', 'non-fact-stating', etc. The latter are held not to state genuine propositions, and therefore, since propositions are the bricks out of which a logical system is built, to be altogether beyond the pale of such a system. They are sometimes even said to be 'literally senseless'.

For Bally, the underlying reason why affectivity, defined as preparing for action, is omnipresent in language use is that not only are humans social organisms by instinct, but they are social in a very particular way. According to him, humans' individual instincts are not subordinated to the social instinct. As a result, an individual entering into contact with other people is at the same time entering into a situation that may be hostile, for the reason that 'there can't be between them a total adaptation and perfect harmony of mentalities' (Bally 1926: 20). This situation is in no way incompatible with love and sympathy and has to be understood at another, deeper, level, as the result of the continuous conflict between the self and its social instinct. For that reason, conversation manifests all sorts of devices aimed at managing the balance of power, from blunt orders to subtle forms which aim at politeness and the preservation of emotional and affective well-being. Here Bally's ideas strikingly resemble Goffman's theory of interaction and face (1964, 1981), Brown and Levinson's famous work on politeness (1987) and also recent work on epistemic and emotional vigilance.

According to Bally's theory of *parole*, usages of language that depart from informational standards are filled with extra meanings, and most of the time also with feelings and affective attitudes. Many truisms or tautologies such as 'I saw him with my own eyes!' are not only filled with extra meanings (parallel to the example 'a father is a father') but are understood as carrying an affective dimension which combines with and enhances the propositional meaning. Hyperboles are exaggerations, and exaggerations aim at conveying impressions. The same holds with metaphors, rhetorical questions and all other similar devices. To analyse them without recourse to affect, as some modern theories do, is to miss something fairly central about them.

We agree. In many ways, this is what this book is all about.

4.4 Speech Acts: How to Do Things with Words (and Emotional Expressions)

As we saw in Chapter 2, Classical philosophers paid little attention to the communication of emotion (apart from the role appeals to affect might play in argumentation). Actually, one could go further, for the communication of *anything* was also only a peripheral concern of the work of the formalised 'ideal' language philosophy of Gottlob Frege, Bertrand Russell and Alfred Tarski, all of whom aimed to show how insights from the languages of logic might be applied to theories of meaning in natural language.

It was this approach which a group of Oxford philosophers we have mentioned several times now began to question in the 1940s and 1950s. They maintained that the truth conditions of sentences exist only in virtue of the linguistic act, or *speech act*, the sentence is used to perform. The group became known as the ordinary language philosophers (though see fn. 5 in Chapter 1), and among them we can single out John Austin, Peter Strawson and Paul Grice. Their work evolved into an alternative approach to the study of language use, which laid the foundations not only for a more action-oriented account but also the more psychological view of pragmatics endorsed in this volume.

The central tenet of speech-act theory is that while logical formulae can tell you all sorts of things about sentence meaning, they overlook entirely the fact that when we speak, we are performing actions. While Carnap's logical positivists suggested that a sentence that was incapable of being proven true or false was in essence meaningless, Austin responded that you can't reduce meaning to truth because many sentences both in the language of philosophy and in everyday language are not intended to be true or false: approaching them from the perspective of truth is to misunderstand completely what they're doing:

'ideal' language ... is in many ways a most inadequate model of an actual language: its careful separation of syntactics from semantics, its list of explicitly formulated rules and conventions, and its careful delimitation of their spheres of operation – are all misleading. An actual language has few, if any explicit conventions, no sharp limits to the spheres of operation of rules, no rigid separation of what is syntactical and what semantical. Austin (1962: 13)

The natural mediator between the positivists of the Vienna Circle and the speech-act theorists, of course, was Ludwig Wittgenstein, whose two major works pay homage to each of the two, very different, sides of the debate.

The most obvious candidates for the kind of thing Austin and the speech-act theorists had in mind are non-declarative sentences such as the interrogative in (9) and the imperative in (10). However, Austin identified a range of other sentence types (see (11) and (12)), none of which lend themselves to being analysed in terms of truth and falsity. Intuitively, none of the following can be said to be true or false:

(9) Does John speak French?

(10) Pass the mint sauce please.

(11) I warn you that a rainstorm is approaching.

(12) I now declare the 2022 Qatar World Cup open!

Austin called sentences such as those in (11) and (12) *performative* utterances, which, rather than describing the world, perform a social act. These he

4.4 Speech Acts: How to Do Things with Words

contrasted with sentences/ utterances that describe states of affairs in the world and can be dealt with in terms of truth and falsity, which he called *constatives*.

Austin proposed and defended his theory in his posthumously published *How to Do Things with Words*. The argumentation is well known. For the first two thirds of the book, Austin enumerates different ways in which his constative–performative distinction might be maintained and proposes various grammatical and morphological criteria to do so. Towards the end of the book, having used his constative–performative distinction as an argument against ideal language philosophy, he decides that – actually – there is *no* systematic way to maintain it. Indeed, he proposes that the search for criteria to maintain the distinction should be abandoned! Once the distinction is abandoned, however, it becomes clear that Austin's real claim is that *all* utterances, not just the ones that he has called performatives, are used to perform speech acts.

Austin distinguishes three main types of speech act that are performed when someone says something: the first of these is the *locutionary act*, the act of saying something (or expressing a proposition); the second is the *illocutionary act*, the act performed *in* saying something – so an utterance might be intended as a warning, or an assertion, or a complaint, apology, etc.); the third is the *perlocutionary act*, the one that results in an actual effect on the hearer. Searle (1969) picked up where Austin left off and carried out perhaps the most developed and sustained work in speech-act theory. Since linguistic acts are understood in virtue of the intentions behind them, a theory of language (and language use) – according to him – should form part of a larger theory of action.

Searle's main concern was with the notion of illocutionary acts. He asked what it is it to question, command or promise them something (see the quote from Thomas Reid quoted in Schumann and Smith 1990: 47). Plainly, speech-act information can be linguistically encoded. So, in (11), the truth-conditional state of affairs *described* is that a storm is approaching. The performative verb 'warn' is a non-truth-conditional *indicator* which embeds the described content in speech-act information. In the same way, the word order in (9) encodes the fact that the utterance is in interrogative mood and effectively embeds the proposition 'John speaks French' under an interrogative indicator.

When it comes to the expression of emotions, Searle adapted the class of speech acts which Austin had called 'behabitives' and renamed them 'expressives'. These were speech acts of which the illocutionary function was to express (indicate) a particular psychological state (defined in the felicity conditions of the speech act) to the proposition expressed. On the face of it, the approach looks promising. However, as we shall see, the spectre of propositions still loomed large. The class of expressives depends not only on the presence of the appropriate psychological state (the emotional attitude), but an embedded proposition. So an example such as (13) would work perfectly well as an expressive since the attitude of delight is directed at the embedded proposition.

(13) *Wow*! The food is delicious!

However, we are left with no account at all of examples such as (2abc) from Chapter 2 (repeated below as 14a–c) since there is no propositional content to embed.

(14a) *Yay*!

(14b) *Wow*!

(14c) *Yugh*!

This argument goes back at least as far as Hume (1739 Book II. Part 3. Section 3: 415):[14]

> A passion is an original existence, or, if you will, modification of existence, and contains not any representative quality, which renders it a copy of any other existence or modification. When I am angry, I am actually possest with the passion, and in that emotion have no more a reference to any other object, than when I am thirsty, or sick, or more than five foot high.

Arguably, the main contribution of speech-act theory lies not so much in the fact that it provided answers to the classical questions of language study, but rather that it enabled philosophers to ask new questions. One radical interpretation of the work of Austin and his colleagues was that the study of meaning cannot be divorced from the study of language use at all. As Recanati puts it (1998: 620):

> [S]entences do not express propositions *in vacuo*, but only in the context of a speech act. Given that the same sentence can be used to make different speech acts with different contents, the 'proposition' which is the content of the speech act must be distinguished from the linguistic meaning of the sentence qua unit of the language ('sentence meaning'). It must also be distinguished from the contextually determined meaning of a particular utterance of the sentence ('utterance meaning'), for the latter includes much more than merely the propositional content of the speech act performed in uttering the sentence.

According to this interpretation, speech-act theory is an alternative to the kind of formal approach advocated by ideal-language philosophers. A more moderate approach, and one which is perhaps closer to the position adopted by many, would be to see speech-act theory as a way of supplementing formal semantics: of bringing language use into the picture. In the late 1960s, Grice

---

[14] Cited from https://davidhume.org/texts/t/2/3/3.

4.4 Speech Acts: How to Do Things with Words

suggested ways in which the work of the formalists and the speech-act theorists might finally be reconciled.[15]

As for speech acts themselves, the notion of such acts is of course a fascinating one. Aside from the notion of a speech act, the theory has also provided insightful concepts such as 'contextual implication' and forced people to pay attention to aspects of *linguistic* meaning that are non-truth-conditional. But in many ways, the generalisations people assume simply follow from the theory simply do not. Both of the authors of this book have attended conference presentations which began: 'We assume a broadly speech-act account of pragmatics.' However, we have yet to see a 'broadly speech-act' account that delivers on its promises.

The main problem is the absence of criteria through which hearers actually choose the intended interpretation (indeed, speech-act theory relies on what is essentially a code model of communication). To our eyes at least, the speech-act account functions as little more than a placeholder for one which might finally be capable of answering all the questions asked of it. It is certainly true that any theory of utterance interpretation requires a developed and systematic account of the interpretation of non-declarative utterances, but acts such as promising, commanding, naming, dubbing and so on are social phenomena, governed by sociocultural conventions that fall outside the domain of pragmatics (or at least are not central to it). It is also worth adding that the most widely accepted speech act account of non-declarative utterances, in which semantic mood equals illocutionary force (see Bach and Harnish 1979, Searle 1965) is problematic (see Wilson and Sperber 1981).

There have been more recent attempts to integrate emotions into a theory based around speech-act pragmatics. In an interesting set of experiments on the perception of speech acts, Holtgraves (2005) demonstrated that when raising the similarities and differences between scenarios, people tend to characterise them not in terms of their illocutionary force but rather in terms of the kind of emotional reaction they caused: so, their perlocutionary rather than their illocutionary force. Liu (2011) replicated Holtgraves' results with speakers of Mandarin. To us, this is more evidence to suggest that there is nothing primitive about the kinds of taxonomies speech-act theorists propose. They are highly context-dependent, sociocultural phenomena.

In the next chapter we present relevance theory and will dwell a short while on the contribution of Grice, whose work was so important not only in the development of modern pragmatics but also as the inspiration for relevance theory. But before we do that, it would be remiss of us not to offer a brief critique of one modern-day attempt to apply the intuitions of speech-act theory to the study of expressive communication. Andrea Scarantino's theory of

---

[15] H. P. Grice's 1967 William James Lectures I–VII, published as chapters 1–7 in Grice 1989.

affective pragmatics (TAP) (2017a) proposes that 'it is possible to engage in analogues of speech acts without using language at all' and that 'there are important and so far largely unexplored similarities between what we can "do" with words and what we can "do" with emotional expressions' (2017a: 165). Scarantino has certainly identified a theoretical gap in the study of emotional communication: speech-act theory has not thus far been carried across wholesale to the study of emotional expressions. It is not clear to us, however, that the theoretical gap he identifies is not one that is actually needed. While some of the analogues work, the fact that they do is of only minor significance, and we submit that there is good reason why the putative similarities he identifies have thus far been unexplored. Actually, we are admirers of Scarantino's work. In particular, his genuinely interdisciplinary perspective has proved hugely insightful and those working in the philosophy of affect and affective science owe him a great deal. Genuine cross-disciplinary study is not easy, and Scarantino has managed it with apparent ease. However, as a comprehensive, explanatorily adequate theory of utterance interpretation, speech-act theory is, as we have pointed out, problematic to say the least. That it won't work for emotional expressions either seems to us to be fairly obvious. In what follows we offer a few brief comments on the theory from the perspective of pragmatics. For the view from the perspective of affective science, we direct readers to Fischer and Sauter (2017), Fridlund (2017) and others who contributed commentaries to the target article in which Scarantino presents TAP.

In his abstract, Scarantino summarises the programme he is embarking on as follows: 'as linguistic pragmatics focuses on what utterances mean in a context, affective pragmatics focuses on what emotional expressions mean in a context' (2017a: 165). We are confused from the outset. One thing that everyone agrees on is that 'utterances' have non-linguistic properties. They involve many different types of information – linguistic and non-linguistic, propositional and non-propositional, explicit and implicit, and much of the information these non-linguistic properties communicate is emotional. The question, then, is how we can realistically have one theory for utterances and another for the affective content of those utterances?

When Marie puts her head in her hands, utters 'It's late again!' in an exasperated tone of voice, her face contorted in frustration, which theory are we to apply? Presumably, we require our theory of linguistic pragmatics to account for the implicatures she is communicating: that the train has, yet again, failed to arrive on time; that she will be late for her rendezvous. And then we need a theory of affective pragmatics to account for the fact that she is expressing her exasperation that the train has failed to arrive on time, and that she will miss her appointment. The numerous parts of any given communicative complex are surely inextricably intertwined. Is not Maria's exasperation directed at the proposition she is implicating? This provides something of

4.4 Speech Acts: How to Do Things with Words

a conundrum for TAP: the fact that most speech acts are parasitic on described, propositional context. We fail to see how these two things – Maria's exasperation and the implicated proposition – are best dealt with by separate theories.

The theory of affective pragmatics is riven through with these kinds of problems: 'The theory aims to unveil both similarities and differences between non-verbal and verbal communication' (2017a: 165), but nowhere in TAP can we find a definition of those terms. The boundary is a very difficult one to draw, or at least is one that is drawn differently by different people. And how does the verbal/non-verbal distinction relate to the linguistic/affective pragmatic one? Is natural tone of voice, one of the principal indicators of emotional expression, non-verbal?

Even Scarantino's main claim, that 'it is possible to engage in analogs of speech acts without using language at all' (165), does not really stand up to scrutiny. When he presents the four true 'emotional expression' ($_{EE}$) analogues of Austin's speech acts, we learn that, actually, *most* of those speech acts, curated and taxonomised by Searle (1965, 1969, 1979) – uniting in matrimony, baptising, firing and so on – do not have analogues$_{EE}$ at all. We're not really surprised. The majority of speech acts are heavily culturally constrained. The whole speech-act enterprise is built around taxonomising cultural acts and, when it is applied to the only truly important ones – *saying, telling* and *asking* – it doesn't work.

During the course of his response to some critical commentary on his article (primarily Fischer and Sauter 2017, Fridlund 2017), Scarantino (2017b) admits to missing one of the authors of this volume entirely from his bibliography (Wharton 2003a, b, 2006, 2008, 2009, 2015). Given that those publications represent a fairly sustained account over the last fifteen-to-twenty years of how pragmatics, emotion and non-linguistic expressions might interact, this is a little disappointing. Scarantino gives his reasons, but points out that there is a big difference between TAP and the approach proposed and defended in, say, Wharton 2009 (and indeed the approach proposed and defended in these pages): 'He [TW] nowhere argues that natural information allows non-verbal information to perform analogues of illocutionary acts' (Scarantino 2017b: 219).

That would be a big difference and, indeed, would indicate a fairly huge oversight on the part of Wharton (2009) (and us as writers of this book). But it's not true. *Of course* natural behaviours can function to perform analogues of illocutionary acts. Wharton (2009) is full of examples of non-verbal behaviours being used to perform illocutionary acts: requests – someone shivering deliberately to signal they want to go inside to the warmth; complaints – someone uttering the interjection '*yuk*!' to complain; warnings – someone saying 'you're late' in an angry tone of voice to indicate to someone else that they don't want them to be late again ... Demonstrating the communicative richness of non-linguistic behaviours is pretty much the whole point of Wharton 2009. And the only reason that book doesn't dwell on the particular speech act performed in any given context is that (as the author of that book says) while the performance of speech acts represents an interesting sideline to an adequate pragmatic theory, it is, equally, relatively unimportant: it is an epiphenomenon at best.

As if all that wasn't enough, another thing missing entirely from TAP is any kind of criterion or procedure through which, or by which, the intended speech acts might successfully be identified by the hearer. The same criticism can be levelled (and frequently has been) by inferential theorists against speech-act theory, which is effectively based on a code model of communication.

We wonder why this is. It might be because Scarantino claims not to be engaged in *Gricean* pragmatics at all. (Wharton is, it appears, and we presume we are too.) No, he contends. He is engaged in *Carnapian* pragmatics. So instead of being concerned with 'reflexive intentions' or 'inferential processes' he is concerned purely with 'context':

[TAP] aims to capture how the meaning of emotional expressions depends on their context of production, not how the meaning of emotional expressions depends on the reflexive intentions of their producers. (2017a: 176)

Once more, we are surprised. Much of Wharton (2009) is devoted to proposing an account of that subset of natural, non-linguistic behaviours that are analysed as natural codes, and therefore interpreted without reference to reflexive intentions at all. As well as which, much of that book is highly critical of Gricean pragmatics.

But, more importantly, and finally, in order for the 'context of production' to play any role in the interpretive process, the people involved in the process of production surely need to be aware of it. The time and location of a conversation (so often presumed to be a 'given' part of context) cannot possibly be a part of the context unless that time and location are known to the interlocutors in the conversation. The previously uttered discourse (another element of context that is often regarded as somehow given) cannot form part of the context if, for some reason, neither interlocutor is able to recall it. Context is not about the time or the place of an utterance, or the content of that utterance; it's about *awareness* of the time and places of an utterance and awareness of the content of that utterance. The context of production is not given; it is a product of the psychological states of interlocutors and, as a natural consequence, whatever context interlocutors *intend*.

4.5 Alternatives

In Chapter 2 we mentioned briefly the more formal approach to the expressive dimension taken by David Kaplan and Christopher Potts. This work is not really 'pragmatic' in the sense we mean it here and, in any case, there is no attempt in that kind of work to build the types of bridges we are attempting to build to span the divide between linguistics and affective science. Rather, the

4.5 Alternatives

aim is to include expressivity in a very philosophical account of language use. There have been other interdisciplinary projects, though, and while some of these are not really pragmatic either, a book on language use and emotion would be incomplete without them.

One attempt at building bridges between linguistics and psychology in particular is Caffi and Janney's (1994) *Towards a Pragmatics of Emotive Communication*. The authors are influenced by many of the same people as we are: notably Charles Bally. It's true, as Vergis (in press: 24) remarks, that this approach 'never became part of mainstream pragmatic theories' and, like Vergis, we are unsure why. To us, the most likely reason is that despite the fact that there were many mainstream theoretical frameworks around at the time (including relevance theory), Caffi and Janney do not really align their work with any particular one. As well as which, the paper is highly programmatic, as can be seen from the following quote (1994: 325):

> This paper outlines some areas in which more work could be done to help coordinate present linguistic research. After briefly reviewing some pioneering historical work on language and affect, the paper discusses ... 'emotive meaning', 'involvement', 'emotive markedness', 'degree of emotive divergence', 'objects of emotive choice', 'loci of emotive choice', and 'outer vs. inner deixis'. ... Finally, some distinctions between potential perspectives, units, and loci of emotive analysis are proposed, and the paper concludes with a call for increased discussion of how research on language and affect might be better coordinated in the future.

Indeed, the Vergis paper we reference here is a useful source of insights into further attempts to accommodate emotions within linguistic theories. He mentions two more 'pragmatic' approaches to language use. The first of these is van Berkum's (2018) Affective Language Comprehension model. This is a quantitative, experimental project, designed to explore the non-verbal modalities communicators use to express referential and social intentions, along with epistemic and affective orientation to the object of their orientation. The second revolves around theories of politeness and the notion of face (Brown and Levinson 1987, Culpeper 1996, Goffman 1964, Spencer-Oatey 2011). Vergis points out numerous ways in which the theories might be finessed in order to move forward, but we note that the latter in particular relies very much on some model of speech-act pragmatics. We remain as sceptical about the possibilities offered by the speech-act approach generally as we do about TAP, as we discussed earlier in this subsection. In the next chapter we present an approach to pragmatics that we think can rise to the challenge.

5 Relevance Theory, Non-propositional Content and Ineffability

> There is a point where too much information and too much information processing can hurt. Cognition is the art of focusing on the relevant and deliberately ignoring the rest.
>
> (Gigerenzer and Todd 1999: 21)

5.1 Introduction

We live, we are told, in the Information Age. Modern-day personal computing, whether it be on phones, tablets or even watches, affords us the ability to create and process frighteningly large amounts of information.[1] But 'information' is not a uniquely human concept. All living organisms exist in an environment, and the challenge of surviving within that environment (and reproducing to ensure the survival of the species) depends on how those organisms respond to changes in that environment. While in the case of very simple organisms, many of us are intuitively reluctant to refer to these environmental changes as 'information' per se (Dusenbery 1992 prefers the term 'causal input'), essentially, that is what they are. Despite the fact that it has no true nervous system, a simple animal such as a sea sponge is able to detect extremes of temperature and dilution of particles in the water. The sponge responds to these conditions by contracting its body in order to protect the tissue from becoming damaged (Bergquist 1974). This mapping of sensory information (or causal input) to the appropriate motor response forms a part of one of the simplest 'cognitive' systems. Heliotropic plants, such as the sunflower, 'perceive' sunlight and respond by slowly turning towards it. While there is debate as to whether such mechanistic responses are truly cognitive in nature, there is a burgeoning literature in plant cognition or (as it is also called) gnosophysiology (Alpi et al. 2007, Baluska and Mancuso 2020, Garzon and Keijzer 2011).

In humans, and other more complex cognitive organisms, the systems for detecting information and responding to it are more highly developed. This

---

[1] We use the word 'process' for convenience and do not in any away endorse the brain-as-a-computer metaphor. See McBeath et al. (1995) for discussion.

5.1 Introduction

reflects the fact that the goals such organisms need to meet involve much more than perceiving whether environmental conditions are DESIRABLE or UNDESIRABLE (as in the case of the sea sponge) or merely turning towards the sunlight (as in the case of the sunflower). In order to establish its location, a bat must somehow process the information it receives in the form of the echoes it receives from its calls. To locate predators or prey, snakes must process information they receive in the form of the infrared radiation they receive from warm bodies that are nearby. To locate small mammals for food, electro-receptors on the bill of the duck-billed platypus track minute electrical signals its prey produces when it contracts its muscles.

Humans are bombarded with a huge amount of information by their perceptual systems (and have been since well before the Information Age). The problem, of course, is that only some of this information is worth processing. This raises the question of whether, given this constant bombardment, there is an alternative to simply sifting through the vast amount of information we have at our disposal and deciding which of it is relevant. As Gigerenzer and Todd (1999) suggest in this chapter's epigraph, the ability to focus on relevant information is central to human cognition.

The concept of 'relevance' has appeared in various forms, in a number of different disciplines. It has played, and continues to play, a key role in a wide range of fields (for a few examples, see Saracevic (1975) for the discussion of notion in information science, Long (2014) in social psychology, di Nanni et al. (2020) in genetics, etc.). In linguistic pragmatics, the notion of relevance is, more often than not, associated with relevance theory (Sperber and Wilson 1986/1995). In this chapter, we present that theory and show how it is ideally placed to rise to the challenges associated with accommodating affect and emotion within a theory of theoretical pragmatics. We begin with an outline of the theory itself and present the two principles of relevance that lie at its heart.

We then turn to two theoretical developments which we feel give relevance theory the advantage over competing pragmatic frameworks. The first of these is the notion of non-conceptual (or *procedural*) meaning, which we present in §5.2.2. This, we believe, is capable of dealing with the problems associated with the challenge of describing versus expressing. The second development involves two key innovations in relevance theory which mean that it diverges in key regards from traditional Gricean and Neo-Gricean approaches. These innovations result in the theory's being able to accommodate extremely vague types of communication and, further, mean that communicated information – whether clock-like or cloud-like – can be *shown* rather than merely meant$_{NN}$, in the Gricean sense. It offers a unique opportunity to respond to the challenge of propositions and ineffability.

5.2 Relevance

5.2.1 The Theory

The William James Lectures at Harvard in 1967 consisted of a series of talks by Paul Grice entitled 'Logic and Conversation'. In these talks Grice was returning to themes he had explored during his time at Oxford (by 1967 he was teaching at the University of California, Berkeley), and in particular, the philosophical nature of meaning. For Grice, whose 1957 paper 'Meaning' remains hugely influential, the meanings of words reduced to the beliefs, desires and intentions of communicators who uttered them. Communication was a rational, purposive, inferential activity and meaning was to be understood in terms of propositional-attitude psychology.

In the second talk (confusingly, published on its own under the title 'Logic and Conversation' in 1975), Grice presented a framework that situated conversational practice within his theory of rational behaviour and, ultimately, meaning$_{NN}$. Over time, the published version of this talk has become the most widely quoted aspect of his work, finding its way into many school, college and university curricula.[2] Grice's argument was that since communication is a rational activity, it follows that it is by and large also a co-operative one: rational conversational participants work towards a 'common purpose' (Grice 1989: 29). Early in the talk he formulated his co-operative principle – 'Make your conversational contribution such as is required, at the stage at which it occurs, by the accepted purpose or direction of the talk-exchange in which you are engaged' (Grice 1989: 26) – which, other things being equal, communicators are expected to observe.

In presenting what became known as his theory of conversation – often, and mistakenly, regarded as separate to his theory of meaning – one of Grice's main aims was to shed light on some of what he later described regarded as the 'the illegitimate applications' (1989: 3) of certain philosophical 'manoeuvres' by members of those involved in ordinary-language philosophy at Oxford. The key component he added to the relationship between it and ideal-language philosophy was the idea that key insights from both could, in fact, co-exist. Speakers uttered propositions, which were closely tied to the meaning of the words within them (Grice's *what is said*), but could also communicate related propositions, which were entirely unrelated to the words they uttered (*what is implicated*).

But the co-operative principle is terribly vague. After all, what makes a contribution co-operative, and who decides on the purpose of our talk-exchanges? Part of Grice's answer was that the co-operative principle is broken

---

[2] Where it is not always accurately represented.

5.2 Relevance

down into a number of different categories – Quantity, Quality, Relation and Manner – which he expressed via a series of conversational maxims, each glossed with a brief explanation. His idea was that, on the whole, speakers are expected to ensure that their conversational contributions comply with these maxims and, hence, the co-operative principle. Grice glossed the third category – Relation – as follows (1989: 27):

> Under the category of RELATION I place a single maxim, namely, 'Be relevant'. Though the maxim itself is terse, its formulation conceals a number of problems that exercise me a good deal: questions about what different kinds and focuses of relevance there may be, how these shift in the course of a talk exchange, how to allow for the fact that subjects of conversation are legitimately changed, and so on.

In the mid-1970s Deirdre Wilson, a linguist/philosopher who knew Grice well (indeed, it was she who typed out Grice's original handwritten notes of the William James Lectures) and French anthropologist Dan Sperber were exploring separately the implications for their work of the kind of the contextual, pragmatic factors in communication that Grice's work had drawn attention to. In her work on non-truth-conditional meaning, Wilson was showing how various problems that had been examined on a semantic level were, actually, better analysed at a pragmatic level. In his work on symbolism, Sperber was arguing for a pragmatic account of figures of speech. The two of them then formed a plan to co-author in a short time an essay outlining the points of contact between their work. However, as they point out in the first edition of the book that resulted (Sperber and Wilson 1986/1995: vii–viii): 'Work did not proceed according to plan. We got involved in carrying out the programme we had merely intended to outline. The months became years. The projected essay became a series of essays and the present book.' Sperber and Wilson begin *Relevance* by showing how the broadly Gricean inferential model of communication they advocate differs from the traditional code model. According to the latter, which has been around roughly since Aristotle, a linguistic utterance is a signal encoding the message a communicator wishes to communicate. In order for a hearer to retrieve the speaker's meaning, all they need to do is decode the signal the speaker has provided into an identical thought or message. Viewed in this way, linguistic communication works according to broadly the same principles as semaphore, or Morse code. Human communication, Sperber and Wilson contend, does not work like this.

Consider Mary's response to Peter's invitation below:

(15) Peter: Would you like to come to the cinema this evening?
Mary: My project application is due in at 9 a.m. tomorrow morning.

Mary's response is certainly indirect and, on the face of it, rather unclear. An analysis of this exchange using the Gricean maxims would go something like this. Mary's response appears not to be relevant. However, Peter assumes that despite this apparent irrelevance she is still following the co-operative principle. As a result, he will process her utterance in such a way that this assumption is preserved – that is, in a manner which assumes it *is* relevant to his question. His most likely conclusion will be that because Mary has an important deadline to meet in the morning, she would probably prefer not to go out and she therefore cannot go to the cinema with him. Of course, it might not. Peter and Mary might both be aware that Mary hates her project and is planning not to submit it anyway, in which case she may be implicating the affirmative. Equally, it is possible that Mary's remark is a coded signal meaning 'I do want to come to the cinema' (in the manner of the kind of verbal handshake used in military operations – 'What did you see last night?', 'Three pink elephants'[3]) but in general this is not how humans communicate. Rather, Mary has provided evidence that she wishes to communicate something, and Peter must infer what that is, according to the inferential model relevance theory proposes.

Nowadays, most people working on meaning believe that the gap between what is linguistically encoded and what is communicated is bridged not by more coding, but by reasoning, or *inference*. So, yes, hearers do decode words, but they only use the decoded meaning as a point of departure from which to work out what the speakers of those words mean by them.

Cases such as (15), in which speakers say one thing and mean something else entirely, are the clearest illustrations of the gap that needs to be bridged between what is encoded and what is communicated. Indeed, if these were the only cases in which such a gap existed, then it might be argued that inference only plays a role in the interpretive process in exceptional circumstances. However, there is considerably more to the gap between linguistics meaning and speaker meaning than that.

Consider (16) and (17):

(16) He found it here yesterday.

(17) Mary gave Peter a file.

Irrespective of any implicatures the speakers of (16) or (17) may intend, the presence of the four indexicals in (16) and the multiple ambiguities in (17) demonstrates that what is linguistically encoded in these utterances falls short even of being a complete statement or proposition (see (18) and (19)):

(18) $Peter_x$ found his_x phone on the desk in my office at $time_t$.

(19) Mary gave Peter a long thin serrated metal object used to smooth metal edges and remove burrs.

---

[3] This was the code used by the Allied-Norwegian forces in Operation Grouse, October 1942, in a mission to destroy the Vemork heavy water plant in Telemark, Norway.

5.2 Relevance

In short, what is linguistically encoded massively underdetermines even the proposition expressed by an utterance (see Carston 2002 for an extended discussion of the pragmatics of explicit communication). Before the utterances in (16) and (17) can be fleshed out into a proposition, a hearer must assign reference to indexicals and disambiguate any ambiguous structures or expressions. Indeed, there is a wide range of processes of contextual enrichment in addition to reference assignment and disambiguation that are needed to establish what proposition a speaker intended to express. The claim that all these processes involve further levels of coding and decoding is unrealistic (see Sperber and Wilson 1986/1995: chapter 1, §2).

Having introduced the inferential model, Sperber and Wilson turn to a range of other questions: How can Grice's insight that the very act of communication creates expectations in an audience be developed? If speaker meaning really can be dealt with in terms of the beliefs, desires and intentions of communicators, then understanding words must, at some stage, involve attributing mental states to communicators. What does this mean in psychologically realistic terms? What *is* relevance, and what role does the search for relevance play in communication?

They address these questions through their presentation of an entirely new notion of relevance; a notion that is not stipulated as part of a conversational maxim, which is itself dependent on a co-operative principle, but rather one that draws from a fundamental claim Sperber and Wilson make about human cognition. While relevance theory (Blakemore 2002, Carston 2002, Sperber and Wilson 1986/1995, Wilson and Sperber 2002) builds on the foundations laid by Grice (and, arguably, others in the Oxford movement) it is a theory with its roots very much in the cognitive revolution of the 1960s rather than in the ordinary-language philosophy of Grice and others of his time. Jerry Fodor, another leading player in the cognitive revolution, has also gone on record as saying that these centralised processes are not amenable to scientific study (Fodor 1983). In many ways, as Carston (2002: 2) puts it 'the relevance-theoretic framework ... can be seen as a response to the challenge presented by these sceptics'. Time will tell how successful the challenge has been, but work within relevance theory has led many people now to question some of the key tenets of, for example, Fodorian modularity of mind and, indeed, the very nature of the central cognitive processes Fodor thought were out of the reach of cognitive scientists.

The theory is built around two principles. According to the cognitive principle of relevance, the human cognitive system is geared to look out for relevant information, which will interact with information that is already mentally represented and lead to positive cognitive effects (in the form of true implications, warranted strengthenings or contradictions of existing assumptions). That the search for relevance plays a central role in human cognition is now widely accepted in cognitive science. Relevant information is information that improves an individual's representation of the world. Indeed, the tendency towards cognitive efficiency is one that is seen in all living things. As we shall see in Chapter 7, even relatively simple organisms 'tag' stimuli as either desirable or undesirable (so-called affective marking) which in time allows them to sort through the array of mostly non-useful information successfully. The tendency towards cognitive efficiency is a natural evolutionary step for all cognitive beings.

This disposition to search for relevance is routinely exploited in human communication. It is a disposition we all share, and speakers know that listeners will pay attention only to stimuli that are relevant enough. Therefore, in order to attract and hold an audience's attention, speakers should make their communicative stimuli appear at least relevant enough to be worth processing. More precisely, according to the communicative principle of relevance, by overtly displaying an intention to inform (through producing an utterance or other intentional (or, *ostensive*) stimulus), a communicator creates a presumption that the stimulus is at least relevant enough to be worth processing, and moreover, the most relevant one compatible with her own abilities and preferences. The reason that Peter is motivated to process Mary's response in (15) the way he does is that, in replying, she has created in her audience an expectation that there is something worth their while to infer. Relevance theory is an attempt to flesh out the notion of what makes communicated information worthwhile.

The interpretive process is underpinned by 'fast and frugal heuristics' of the kind described in Gigerenzer, Todd and The ABC Research Group (1999). The claim that humans are equipped with such heuristics involves an acceptance that we do not have an 'unbounded' form of all-seeing, all-knowing rationality. Rather, evolution has left us with economical rules of thumb that enable us to make the most of our finite cognitive capacity. Utterances are relevant because they give rise to what relevance theory terms 'cognitive effects'. These are effects that are beneficial to an individual's cognitive system insofar as they improve aspects of one's representation of the world. Relevance itself is a property of all inputs to cognitive processes and is defined in terms of both those positive cognitive effects gained *and the* processing effort expended: other things being equal, the more positive cognitive effects gained, and the less processing effort expended in gaining those effects, the greater the relevance of the input to the individual who processes it.

Let us illustrate this with an example. Marie is staying in a chalet in the mountains and wakes early in the morning in her room. The following thoughts come to her mind. These thoughts represent the context in which new inputs to her cognitive processes will be processed.

5.2 Relevance

(20) I'll (probably) go for a hike today.

(21) If the sun is shining, I'll go for a hike today.

(22) If it's raining, I won't go for a hike today.

As she opens the shutters of her bedroom, Marie might become aware of a whole range of things: the snowy peaks in the distance, dogs barking in a nearby farmyard, the ringing of cowbells in the distance. But none of these things are directly relevant to her in the context of the thoughts that she is entertaining. Some things are available to her consciousness and she knows she is aware of them, while others, such as the dogs barking, though still accessible among the things she knows, are not strongly activated in her consciousness: indeed, she may not even be aware that she knows them. For example, it's highly likely that there is some form of heater (or fan) in the room in which you are currently reading this. But while you know that, you may well be unaware of that thing at this moment. (Indeed, it may be turned on, and making a noise, but you can still be unaware of it.) Elements of knowledge that are highly accessible to consciousness are more manifest and things that are not are less manifest. Cognitive effects are all about giving manifestness to pieces of information that were not manifest to the interlocutor, or more manifestness to those which are less manifest than the speaker wishes.

In Examples (20)–(22), what she does attend to is the fact that the sun is rising in a clear sky. This new information is highly manifest; it strengthens the assumption in (20) and interacts with assumption (21) in order to yield the implication 'I'll (definitely) go for a hike'. If, by contrast, she had noticed that the sky was dark with clouds, this information would have interacted with the assumption in (22) and yielded the implication 'I won't go for a hike'. Notice, also that assumption (21) is therefore contradicted. Relevance, then, is a property of inputs to cognitive processes and is defined in terms of cognitive effects gained and processing effort expended: the more positive cognitive effects gained, and the less processing effort expended in gaining those effects, the greater the relevance of the input to the individual who processes it.

As a linguistic illustration of the communicative principle in action, consider an utterance of (23), made by someone opening a door to a room full of people. We choose this well-worn example because, for one of us, it was our introduction to relevance theory, all those years ago in lectures by Deirdre Wilson.

(23) Ladies and gentlemen, *the building*'s on fire.

Definite descriptions such as the italicised phrase above are highly context dependent. Since the speaker of (23) could, in principle, be using the description to refer to any building in the world, to which building should the hearers take the speaker to be referring? According to relevance theory, the answer is the building that would best satisfy their expectations of relevance, which would be the most salient and accessible to them and give them the most cognitive effects for minimal processing effort. Fairly obviously, this is the building they are in. That is the first interpretation – that is, the first cost-effective interpretation – that would be relevant to the individuals in the room in the expected way.

This criterion applies to the interpretation of *all* ostensive stimuli and is powerful enough to rule out all but one interpretation (or a small number of very closely related interpretations). Analysed in this way, and contra-Grice, even explicit communication is a massively inferential affair. The processes of reference assignment and disambiguation and the adjustment of conceptual content are all driven by the search for relevance.

This kind of context-driven adjustment of conceptual content is seen as one of the principal processes in explicit communication. Consider the word 'shark', the meaning of which might be narrowed in (24) to denote a subset of sharks (e.g., a member of one of the (very few) species of sharks that are remotely dangerous to humans), or loosened in (25) to include objects which are not strictly speaking sharks at all, but exhibit, for example, behaviour that might be considered predatory (in a loose sense):

(24) A shark has been terrorising Sydney's north shore beaches over the past few weeks.

(25) I refuse to do business with Mary: she's a shark.

This adjustment of conceptual content is a feature of relevance-theoretic lexical pragmatics. The explicit and implicit content are developed in parallel, with the explicit content being adjusted or 'finetuned' in various ways to yield the implicatures required to satisfy the audience's expectations of relevance. In addition to the types of pragmatic inference illustrated in (24) and (25), the encoded content of individual lexical items occurring in an utterance may have to be narrowed or loosened (assigned a narrower or broader denotation) in context to yield the expected level of implicatures. In the framework of relevance theory, there is a straightforward 'fast and frugal heuristic' which hearers can use to determine the appropriate degree of narrowing or loosening, and more generally, to identify the speaker's meaning (Sperber and Wilson 2002: 13).[4]

---

[4] In recent years there has been a huge amount of work done on precisely what word meanings are, both by relevance theorists (see, for example, Allott and Textor 2017, Carston 2002) and those working from different perspectives (Barsalou 2005, Rayo 2013). Our use of the term 'conceptual content' is intended to be neutral on the issue of whether words' meanings are *actually* concepts. They might equally be simulators, grab-bags or non-conceptual in other ways.

5.2 Relevance

Relevance-Theoretic Comprehension Heuristic

(a) Follow a path of least effort in computing cognitive effects:
   Test interpretive hypotheses (disambiguations, reference resolutions, implicatures, etc.) in order of accessibility.
(b) Stop when your expectations of relevance are satisfied.

Equally, this view depends very much on a particular view of the relationship between words and concepts. According to relevance theory, there are many more concepts than words, because ad hoc concepts can be created and used in the interpretation of almost any word (Sperber and Wilson 1998). Just as we are capable of perceiving new shades of green or red, so – as we remarked in Chapter 3 – are we able to *conceive* such shades temporarily, and in the absence of a stable, lexicalised expression to encode we simply construct a temporary and potentially transient ad hoc concept. It is for this reason we claim that non-German speakers are perfectly capable of reflecting on *Schadenfreude*, and the lack of a word for 'fear' in Tahitian has little to no consequence on the emotional life of the inhabitants of Tahiti.

5.2.2 Non-conceptual Meaning

When asked what a word such as 'shark' means, most people will respond with a definition: 'a kind of fish'; 'an animal with a particular form of dorsal fin', 'a carnivorous predator'. But while words such as 'shark', 'table', 'distributor cap' and so on are entirely amenable to introspection, as indeed word meanings tend to be, there is a small but notable range of words that are not. Consider the word 'so', for example; what does that mean? Providing definitions is very difficult, and rather than provide one we tend to turn to a description of how the word is used. This intuition is behind Kaplan's *Semantics of Use*,[5] which he contrasts with a *Semantics of Meaning* (and which we discussed briefly in Chapter 2). The same kind of intuition lay behind Jakobson (1957/1971) and Benveniste's (1966) work on indexicals or 'shifters', words that are defined purely by the relationship they hold to the utterance in which they occur.

Interestingly, the same problem arises with words that we use to express emotion directly, such as 'shit'. We have already discussed Potts' (2007) attempt to deal with expressive meaning as conventional implicatures. In his survey, he reports that over a large number of interviews and surveys only one person defined the word 'bastard' as a 'vile, contemptible person': most people were happy to say; the word was used to express or vent emotions; pinning down exactly what they meant was impossible.

---

[5] D. Kaplan, 'What is meaning? Explorations in the theory of *Meaning as Use*' (unpublished manuscript, 1997).

82   5 Relevance Theory, Non-propositional Content and Ineffability

In Chapter 2 we also pointed out the two problems associated with accommodating expressives into a framework that is built only to account for propositions. Kent Bach, Neo-Gricean and critic of relevance theory, recognises this and is surely right when he writes:[6]

> To implicate something entails meaning it, that is, intending to convey it to one's audience. Presumably what is meant is a proposition, something that anybody can entertain or believe. But ... if I say, *'That blasted TV isn't working'*, what do I mean in addition to the TV isn't working? Is it something that my audience can agree with? ... I do not mean anything in using *blasted*, although I can express a certain negative feeling towards my TV. Although my audience can recognize that I am expressing this feeling, in using *blasted* I do not mean that I have this feeling. I am expressing that feeling, not implicating it.

However, without a characterisation of precisely what 'expressing a feeling' is, and how expressing a feeling is different from meaning$_{NN}$ that *p*, the account remains incomplete. We propose that two key developments within relevance theory suggest an answer. The first key development is the notion of procedural meaning. We turn to the second in §5.2.3.

Blakemore (1987, 2002) reassesses Grice's account of discourse connectives by introducing a distinction between *conceptual* and *procedural* encoding. Most words encode concepts, constituents of conceptual representations. Most of these contribute to the truth conditions of an utterance; they have logical properties, can act as input to inference rules and are used to describe the world. Some words, however, do not map onto concepts. This is one reason we find it hard to say what they mean. Rather than encoding the constituents of conceptual representations, the function of such words is to constrain the inferential processes involved in constructing or manipulating these representations. They guide the comprehension process by indicating the general direction in which the intended meaning is to be sought, by narrowing the hearer's search space.

To illustrate, consider Blakemore's analysis of the discourse connectives 'so' and 'after all':

(26)   She's merciless in business. She's known as the shark.

(27)   She's merciless in business. So she's known as the shark.

(28)   She's merciless in business. After all, she's known as the shark.

On Blakemore's account, the word 'so' encodes a procedure which leads the hearer to interpret the first of the two propositions as a premise from which the second follows as a conclusion. In (28) the expression 'after all' encodes

---

[6] This quote comes from a 2006 review of Christopher Potts' book *The Expressive Dimension* (Bach 2006: 492).

5.2 Relevance

a procedure which leads the hearer to treat the second proposition as providing evidence for the first. In both cases, the discourse connective is seen as encoding a procedural constraint on the derivation of intended implications (or implicatures). The notion of procedural constraint was, arguably, prefigured by Benveniste's work and also Ducrot's work on *mais* in French (Anscombre and Ducrot 1983; Ducrot 1972, 1973).

Other linguistic expressions which have been analysed in procedural terms include mood indicators and discourse particles (cf. Blakemore 1987, 2002; Hall 2007; König 1991; Wilson and Sperber 1993). So mood indicators – for example, imperative morphosyntax – encode procedures which facilitate the retrieval of a range of speech-act or propositional-attitude descriptions associated with imperatives; discourse particles such as 'please' encode a procedure which facilitates the retrieval of a range of speech-act or propositional-attitude descriptions associated with requests. Properly linguistic prosodic signals (e.g., lexical stress, lexical tone and fully grammaticalised aspects of prosody – perhaps nuclear tones) might be analysed on similar lines, as facilitating the retrieval of certain types of syntactic, semantic or conceptual representation. Thus, the notion of procedural encoding applies straightforwardly to properly linguistic prosodic elements.

Following on from this work, Wharton (2003a, 2009) argues that interjections share with discourse connectives and discourse particles the property of encoding procedural rather than conceptual information. On this approach, the function of an interjection such as *wow* might be to facilitate the retrieval of a range of speech-act or propositional-attitude descriptions associated with expressions of surprise or delight, which might be narrowed in context by information derived from prosody, facial expressions, background assumptions, discourse context and so on, and contribute to the speaker's meaning in the regular way, by falling under the relevance-theoretic comprehension procedure.

Consider the following examples:

(29) Happily, they all passed the exams.

(30) *Wow!* They all passed the exams!

(31) *Wow!*

In *Relevance*, non-truth-conditional expressions, which, after all, cannot contribute at the level of the proposition expressed (in relevance-theoretic terms, the basic *explicature*), are analysed as communicating *higher-level explicatures*. These explicatures embed the basic explicature within a propositional-attitude descriptor. So in an utterance of (29), the hearer will derive the basic-level explicature – 'they all passed the exam' – and embed it under the descriptor 'The speaker is happy that ... ', which together with the proposition expressed forms a higher-level explicature. The distinction between basic-level and higher-level explicatures in many ways reflects the speech-act distinction between describing and indicating discussed in the previous chapter. Note here that there are good reasons to believe that the word 'happily' is a concept, HAPPILY, rather than a procedure: for one, it has a truth-conditional counterpart ('They sang the song happily'); moreover, it is morphologically productive. The conceptual-procedural distinction therefore cross-cuts the distinction between truth-conditional and non-truth-conditional meaning,

The interjection *wow* in (30), however, does not encode a concept. Firstly, it is non-truth-conditional; secondly, it has no truth-conditional counterpart (unlike 'happily'); thirdly, it is not linguistically productive (unlike 'happily'). Rather, we argue, it encodes a procedure which facilitates the retrieval of a range of speech-act or propositional-attitude descriptions associated with expressions of surprise or delight. In the conclusion to the next chapter, we suggest this account solves the problem of describing versus expressing and provides an alternative to the conceptualist account sketched in Chapter 2.

Wharton (2009) takes the idea further and proposes that smiles and other natural, spontaneous facial expressions are *natural codes*, which should be analysed as encoding procedural rather than conceptual information. On this approach, the function of facial expressions of surprise or delight would be to facilitate the retrieval of similar, strongly communicated propositional-attitude descriptions to those activated by the interjection 'wow!'

The use of the word 'natural' here harks back to the Gricean (1957) notion of natural meaning (or meaning$_N$) mentioned in Chapter 2. Grice begins this paper by drawing a distinction between two senses of the word 'mean'. These he calls natural meaning (meaning$_N$) and non-natural meaning (meaning$_{NN}$), where the former is the kind of 'meaning' where a conclusion can be drawn simply on the basis of observable evidence, and the latter is the kind of 'meaning' typical of intentional communication. The two types of meaning are exemplified in (32) and (33) respectively:

(32) That black smoke means$_N$ the tyre factory is on fire.

(33) That white smoke means$_{NN}$ the Vatican Conclave has elected a new Pontiff.

Grice (1957) developed a series of tests to distinguish between the two. He then proposed a variety of ways in which the two types of meaning might be distinguished. The tests are outlined to make a similar point in Wharton (2009), and we repeat them here. The first test was based on the idea that cases of meaning$_N$ are factive, in the sense that x means$_N$ p or x meant$_{NN}$ p entails p. By contrast, cases of meaning$_{NN}$ are non-factive. (We discuss this in intuitive terms in Chapter 2 when we introduce the notion of a semiotic relationship.) An utterance such as 'his remark means$_{NN}$ it is raining' does

5.2 Relevance

not entail that it is raining at all. If our utterance of (32) is true, then, it will indeed always follow that the tyre factory is actually on fire. If it is not, and the black smoke is emanating from a bonfire formed of damp wood, then the smoke does not mean the tyre factory is on fire at all. Rather it means that someone has lit a bonfire formed of damp wood.

The difference between factive and non-factive uses of 'mean' underlay a further series of tests which Grice used to contrast the results of paraphrasing utterances containing the two different uses of the word 'mean'. Here we return to a sentence Grice used to draw the distinction in the original paper: (34) and a parallel one (35) (1957: 377):

(34) Those spots mean (meant) measles.

(35) That remark means (meant) he has measles.

While (36) is a plausible paraphrase of utterance (34), (37) is not a plausible paraphrase of utterance (35). It may be true, but it does not convey the same sense of 'means' as that in the original utterance. (It may, in fact, paraphrase a parallel case of *natural* meaning.)

(36) The fact that he had those spots means he had measles

(37) ??The fact that he made that remark means he has measles.

This test confirms (34) is a case of meaning$_N$ and (35) is not.

A further test, this time for recognising meaning$_{NN}$, involved paraphrases directly quoting the meaning in question. Example (38) below is not a satisfactory paraphrase of (34), but (39) *is* a satisfactory paraphrase of (35).

(38) ??Those spots mean 'he has measles'.

(39) That remark means 'he has measles'.

This confirms that (34) is a case of meaning$_{NN}$, and (35) is not.

In another test, Grice argued that while no conclusion about *what is (was) meant by (something)* can be drawn from an utterance that describes a case of meaning$_N$, such a conclusion can legitimately be drawn from an utterance that describes a case of meaning$_{NN}$ (see (40–1)):

(40) ??What was meant by those spots was that he has measles.

(41) What was meant by that remark was that he has measles.

This test supports the view that (34) is a case of meaning$_N$, while (35) is a case of meaning$_{NN}$. We find Grice's intuitions on this, as in all things, to be reliable. However, Wharton (2009) goes on to point out that certain non-human and human behaviours also pass the factivity test, even though they are inherently communicative.

The American bullfrog (*Lithobates catesbeianus*) has a small range of calls which serve different functions (primarily alarm calls, territorial calls and mating calls). There is, as far as we know, no evidence to suggest that American bullfrogs are capable of entertaining the kind of higher-order meta-psychological states necessary for non-natural meaning. Would we, then, want to characterise the American bullfrog's calls as meaning$_N$ or meaning$_{NN}$?

In light of these tests, it seems fair to suggest that the bullfrog's call is factive. As far as know, there is no evidence that bullfrogs engage in pretence, or irony, or any activity where the meaning of their calls might vary. So from the fact that the bullfrog has emitted the call it follows that the frog is warning other bullfrogs, or staking a claim to territory or searching for a mate. As we have said, there is no evidence that the interpretation of the calls relies on the deployment and attribution of intentions. This suggests that the calls mean naturally.

Nonetheless, there is plainly a sense in which it is unsatisfactory to see the meaning of the bullfrog calls as entirely parallel to paradigmatic examples of Gricean meaning$_N$ such as 'those black clouds mean rain'. There is nothing coincidental about the fact that a bullfrog's call has meaning: the function of the calls is to communicate. It is not the function of black clouds to convey the information that it is going to rain. This observation is confirmed by applying some of Grice's tests for meaning$_{NN}$ to the calls of bullfrogs. The results, which confirm Grice's view that there was a 'reasonably clear intuitive distinction' between the two types of meaning, become strangely unintuitive (42), (43):

(42) The fact that the bullfrog made that call is a warning to other frogs.

(43) The bullfrog call means 'danger'.

According to Grice, these paraphrases should be acceptable only if the type of meaning involved is *non*-natural. Wharton (2009) suggests that the most plausible explanation is that our intuitions reflect the fact, as we said above, that bullfrog calls are inherently communicative: they are coded signals. Bullfrogs don't mean intentionally (in our sense), but something is surely meant (in one sense of the word) by their calls. Grice's dichotomy does not capture this, and the category of natural meaning appears to devolve into two further subcategories: natural codes (or signals), which are inherently communicative, and natural signs, which carry information, but are not inherently communicative (in the sense that the fact that they carry information owes nothing to their continued existence).[7]

Wilson and Wharton (2006) apply these distinctions to the analysis of prosodic phenomena, noting that one consequence of a given behaviour

---

[7] The sign/signal distinction is a distinction used in ethology. Hauser (1996: 54) credits cognitive ethologist Peter Marler as the first to recognise and apply it.

5.2 Relevance

being a natural code is that this will lead to the development of its own proprietary interpretive mechanism. Note, however, that it is not the case that behaviours that are natural codes lead to the development of such mechanisms. Gaze direction, for example, is a natural sign of where someone is looking rather than a natural code. However, the potential relevance of this information is such that a relevance-oriented cognitive system might well be improved by the development of a special-purpose inferential mechanism of this type. (Indeed, Baron-Cohen's (1995) Eye Direction Detector may be just such a mechanism.) Indeed, inferences drawn from the gaze direction subprogram are just the kind of inferences that may be prioritised in a dangerous situation where a person is experiencing fear (see Chapter 6 for more discussion).

Natural codes, which facilitate the production and interpretation of affective facial expressions or tones of voice in terms of underlying mental states, are automatic emotion-reading mechanisms of a coded rather than an inferential nature, dedicated to the interpretation of natural emotional signals rather than natural emotional signs. What distinguishes a special-purpose inferential mechanism from a coding mechanism is, firstly, that the inferential mechanism applies to natural signs rather than signals; secondly, that it is genuinely inferential (i.e., it draws warranted conclusions on the basis of evidence); thirdly, that it is not part of a signalling system with corresponding encoding mechanisms at the production end.

In an important paper from 2011, Deirdre Wilson (2011a) returns to the notion of procedural meaning, and how it has developed over the years. She proposes some interesting changes. Originally, as we have seen, it was thought that the procedural meaning in a word such as 'but' existed to guide the hearer's path more easily to the intended interpretation. Building on Sperber et al.'s (2010) work on 'epistemic vigilance' – those cognitive strategies by which hearers avoid being either accidentally or intentionally misinformed – she proposes an interesting alternative in which the main function of discourse connectives would be not so much to guide the hearer's path as to trigger argumentative procedures which yield intuitions about evidential relations and form part of the capacity for epistemic vigilance (Wilson 2011a: 7):

> The function of the procedural expressions in a language may be to activate [. . .] domain-specific procedures. In principle, these could be of any type at all, although in practice they are likely to be drawn from modules which play a significant role in linguistic communication: these include the modules (or submodules) involved in mindreading (Baron-Cohen 1995), emotion reading (Wharton 2003 [Wharton 2003a], 2009), social cognition (Malle 2004; Fiske and Taylor 2008), parsing and speech production (Levelt 1993), comprehension (Sperber and Wilson 2002) and so on. (Wilson 2011a: 7)

These domain-specific procedures are subattentive and unintentional and help us read emotional states, irrespective of whether those states are conveyed ostensively or non-ostensively. Natural codes are at work *all the time*. Panic does not spread through a crowd by virtue of each person in the crowd acting ostensively, any more than a flu epidemic is caused by everyone in a community deliberately coughing over the person next to them. It is these procedures that emotional communication exploits. the 'patterns of activation' are procedural, and the procedural information encoded by linguistic expressives, interjections, facial expressions or tone of voice puts the user into a state in which emotional procedures are highly activated and are therefore much more likely to give rise to positive emotional effects in another. Notice that these effects are not derived inferentially. In a manner analogous to the way that there is no inferential route between 'so' and the procedure it encodes, so emotional procedures simply 'switch on' other mental states (some of which may be inferential heuristics). Of course, if the hearer infers that a natural behaviour has been deliberately shown, it might even be selected by an audience using the relevance-theoretic comprehension procedure, in which case the standard inferential processes apply.

The non-conceptual activation view sits nicely with the view of Mark Lieberman, who writes (2000: 111):

At all times, we are communicating information about our emotional state, attitudes, and evaluations of whatever we are currently confronting ... Several of the nonverbal cues that reflect our internal state can be controlled consciously to some degree, but this will only occur if one directs one's conscious attention to the process of nonverbal encoding ... We produce most of our nonverbal cues intuitively, without phenomenological awareness. (Lieberman 2000: 111)

It may, for example, be true that feelings, sensations and affect can impact on the degree of manifestness of propositions – humans, after all, regularly rationalise emotion, as we have seen. However, feelings need not be conscious at all. Nor are feelings represented propositionally. Having a 'feeling' that today is going to be a good day, or that you have performed well in an exam, differs from 'believing', or even in one sense 'thinking' the same thing.[8] As far as we can see, the closest the standard relevance-theory view gets to the notion of feeling that we propose is the notion of an 'impression'. But in relevance theory an impression is characterised as an array of weakly manifest propositions (consciously represented or not) and propositions.

---

[8] Kolaiti (2022) draws a similar distinction to the one we draw here between the purely physiological, the qualitative and the cognitive when she describes the 'sensory' mode, the 'conceptualised or perceptual mode' and the (properly) 'conceptual' mode. In the second of these, she claims that perceptual modes take sensory information as input, and that gives 'a significant/ non-minimal degree of activation to conceptual processes, which apparently have enough expected effects to attract and hold the attention'.

5.2.3 Non-propositional Content and Ineffability

Relevance theory is not just a theory of communication. It is a theory of communication and cognition. So, while a linguistic utterance such as (23) is an excellent example of the kind of input that relevance theory is designed to account for, the set of possible inputs to cognitive processes is far from limited to linguistic utterances. (Indeed, even Grice did not limit instances of his notion of non-natural meaning to linguistic utterances.) Relevance is a property of inputs to cognitive processes, whether ostensively communicated or not. Anything can be relevant: inputs from perception – sights, sounds, smells, natural non-verbal behaviours – inputs from thought processes – implications, deductions, memories – or, of course, inputs from other people. The search for relevance then, is not only a search that underpins verbal interaction or even communicative interaction: it is a search that underpins human cognition.

And while it is true that sights, smells or other perceptual stimuli do not carry presumptions of their own relevance in the same way as ostensive acts, it does not follow from this that they cannot be highly relevant to the individual who becomes aware of them. The sight of smoke seeping between a door and doorframe, or the acrid smell of burning emanating from an unknown source, is as likely (possibly, even more likely) to provide the occupants of a room with the same kind of cognitive effects as the utterance in (23). Of course, as with all aspects of pragmatics, context is everything, and unsurprisingly, relevance theory adopts a resolutely cognitive conception of context, which it structures around the notion of cognitive environment. An individual's cognitive environment includes not only all the facts or assumptions of which they are currently aware but also all the facts or assumptions of which she is capable of becoming aware, given their cognitive abilities and her physical environment – in relevance-theoretic terms, the set of facts or assumptions that are manifest to her (i.e., that she is capable of perceiving or inferring) (Sperber and Wilson, 1986/1995: 38–46). The context of an utterance is represented by the intersection between the cognitive environments of the speaker and the hearer and the fact that this information is mutually manifest co-ordinates communicative acts. So, if a speaker wants to inform a hearer of a particular message, then the speaker needs (a) to produce a piece of behaviour consistent with that message and, crucially, (b) to get the hearer to realise that she has produced that behaviour with the overt intention of making the hearer do precisely that.

It takes very little to make a given act ostensive. Think of two friends walking through a forest on a searing hot summer's day. One of them thinks they detect the faintest smell of smoke in the air. She is not certain, but there has recently been a spate of dangerous forest fires and she feels it important to share this information just in case she is right. What should she do? One alternative would be to tell her friend. But given her lack of certainty it might be more appropriate to adopt another, subtler, method. She simply stops walking and sniffs the air ostensively. This behaviour licenses the expectation that the speaker thinks the message will be relevant to her companion. It will give rise to new thoughts and assumptions, subtly affect her friend's cognitive environment, and – as a result – aspects of the cognitive environment they share.

There are two subtle ways in which the relevance theory view diverges from both traditional Gricean and Neo-Gricean ones. These two divergences – coupled with the notion of procedural meaning discussed in the previous subsection[9]–underpin perhaps the most important claim of this book: that, among pragmatic theories, relevance theory is uniquely capable of rising to the problems inherent in accommodating emotions into a theory of pragmatics. The innovations are very closely linked and, together, represent the second of the two key developments within relevance theory that allow us to accommodate emotions into a pragmatic analysis.

As well as making what is being communicated impossible to put into words, the descriptive ineffability of the communication of affect means it is also hard to fit within the model of inferential processes relevance theory employs. As Sperber and Wilson (1986/1995: 57) succinctly put it: 'No one has any clear idea how inference might operate over non-propositional objects: say, over images, impressions or emotions'. We share this doubt. Indeed, we do not believe that inference can 'operate over' emotions at all. But we will argue that it does not follow from this that they play no role in inference: if Hume is right that emotional states motivate acts of inference, then it is but a small step to propose they *influence* them too.

The first divergence is that, contrary to Gricean and Neo-Gricean accounts, the relevance-theoretic informative intention need not always consist in an intention to communicate a single proposition and propositional attitude. Indeed, Sperber and Wilson suggest that, sometimes, whatever that intention is 'cannot be rendered as a proposition at all' (2015: 125). In relevance theory the informative intention is construed more broadly than merely an intention to communicate a proposition p: rather, it is an intention 'to make manifest or more manifest to the audience a set of assumptions **I**' (Sperber and Wilson 1986/1995: 58). When communicated content is vague, it typically involves a marginal increase in the manifestness of a very wide range of weakly manifest assumptions, resulting in an increased similarity between what relevance theory terms the 'cognitive environments' of communicator and audience. An individual's cognitive environment includes not only all the facts or assumptions that he is currently aware of, but also all the facts or assumptions

---

[9] And also the recognition we discussed in the previous chapter, that some notion of relevance plays a key role in the elicitation of emotions.

5.2 Relevance

he is capable of becoming aware of given his cognitive abilities and his physical environment – in relevance-theoretic terms, the set of facts or assumptions that are manifest to him (i.e., that he is capable of perceiving or inferring). We will argue later that a degree of further finessing is necessary to capture accurately the direct communication of emotion, but this change at least goes some way to laying the ghost of propositionality to rest.

The second, related innovation concerns the line Grice (1957) famously drew between showing and non-natural meaning (meaning$_{NN}$). It has often been remarked that this line has had a huge influence on the development of pragmatics. Many pragmatists continue to focus on the notion of meaning$_{NN}$ and abstract away from cases of showing. So where, in fact, should the line be drawn? Grice, of course, was not so much interested in explaining what happened during communication but, rather, how the philosophical notion of meaning$_{NN}$ might be characterised. He noticed that in any overt intentional act, one carried out with the intention of revealing an informative intention, there are *two* layers of information to be retrieved. The first basic layer is the information being pointed out, and the second is the information that the first layer is being pointed out intentionally. What makes a certain ostensive act a case of either 'deliberately and openly showing' or 'meaning$_{NN}$' is the precise nature of the evidence provided for the first layer of information. In cases of showing, the evidence provided is relatively direct – as when I inform you of the time by pointing at the station clock. In cases of meaning$_{NN}$, the evidence provided is relatively indirect – a linguistic utterance, for example. Sperber and Wilson (1986/1995: 53) discuss the relationship between the two notions:

Is there a dividing line between instances of ostension which one would be more inclined to describe as 'showing something', and clear cases of communication where the communicator unquestionably 'means something'? ... What we have tried to show ... is that there are not two distinct and well-defined classes, but a continuum of cases of ostension ranging from 'showing', where strong direct evidence for the basic layer of information is provided, to 'saying that', where all the evidence is indirect[.]

Relevance theory, then, argues that the line should not be drawn at all. Cases of both showing and meaning$_{NN}$ qualify as instances of ostensive-inferential communication and instead of there being a cut-off between the two notions, there is a continuum of cases in between. Not only do those who equate the domain of pragmatics with meaning$_{NN}$ miss out on the the non-propositional side of communication, they miss out also on propositional elements that are shown rather than meant$_{NN}$. So not only can the communicative intention be composed of a series of related propositions rather than a single one (perhaps an array of weakly manifest propositions), but this can be *shown* rather than *meant$_{NN}$* in Grice's strict sense.

Wharton (2009) suggests some of the implications of redrawing the domain of pragmatics in this way. One of the most obvious is that focusing on meaning$_{NN}$ has had the effect of excluding from pragmatics the overt showing of spontaneously produced behaviours that are natural indicators. But there seem to be clear cases where openly showing spontaneous natural signs and signals makes a difference to the speaker's meaning. Take, for example, an utterance of (44):

(44) Peter is late.

If the utterer of (44) makes no attempt to conceal the spontaneous anger in her facial expression and tone of voice, and hence deliberately and openly shows it, she would naturally be understood as meaning not only that Peter was late but that she was angry that he was late (which would be higher-level explicature of the type demonstrated above). Grice's framework excludes such spontaneous expressions of emotion from contributing to a speaker's meaning, but expressive meaning is typically communicated in this natural way and relevance theorists have consistently argued that there is a continuum of cases between showing and meaning$_{NN}$, all of which may fall within the domain of pragmatics and contribute to a speaker's meaning,

In other cases, natural behaviours calibrate degree terms. In this case, they feed into the ad hoc concept-construction mechanisms described earlier in this subsection and contribute to the basic explicature, the truth conditions of the utterance. Consider (45), uttered in response to (44), in an absolutely furious tone of voice, with the appropriate facial expression:

(45) I am angry.

Most people working within pragmatics will point to the fact that the nonverbal behaviours here motivate the hearer's search for the implicated meaning the speaker is intending to convey – that this was Peter's last chance, that now he is facing disciplinary action, or losing his job, for example. However, fewer people have commented on the fact that the successful derivation of these implicatures depends on the degree of anger being communicated in the basic explicature.

As a way of uniting the two divergences in one, easily understood diagram, Sperber and Wilson (2015: 123) amend the original figure of the continuum-as-a-straight-line with a second, separate dimension, which effectively, turns the straight line into a square (see Figure 5.1):

The showing–meaning$_{NN}$ continuum (now on a vertical axis) reflects the directness of the evidence presented for the basic layer of information being communicated. Evidence is shown when the ostensive behaviour that demonstrates it is fairly direct: pointing at something is a good example. In a coded response, such as a linguistic utterance, the evidence provided is indirect, and

5.2 Relevance

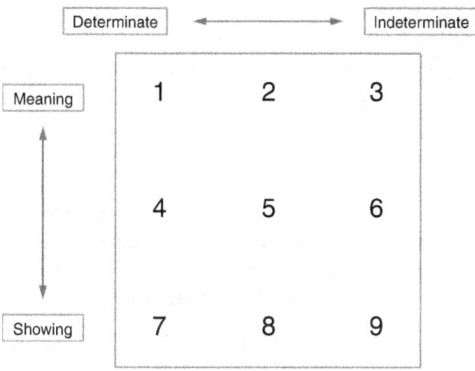

Figure 5.1 The showing–meaning$_{NN}$ continuum

an example of meaning$_{NN}$. Why indirect? Because in order to interpret an utterance the hearer needs to know the code, as well as infer the speaker's intentions. An utterance of 'We're heading towards that peak in the distance' is indirect, and an example of meaning$_{NN}$. (If you don't believe us, have someone say the previous utterance to you in a language you don't know.)

The new dimension of the continuum, the horizontal axis ranging between determinate and indeterminate import, reflects the nature of the information that is being pointed out ostensively, whether that information is being shown or meant$_{NN}$. To return to the distinction we introduced in Chapter 1, determinate information (roughly in the vicinity of 1, 4 and 7) is clock-like; indeterminate information (roughly in the vicinity of 3, 6 and 9) is cloud-like. When someone points to a particularly salient object in the environment or utters the name of that object, what is being shown or meant$_{NN}$ is highly determinate. Think of someone responding to being asked the time that the next train leaves by pointing at a clock. Whether it has been shown or meant$_{NN}$, the intended import in cases such as this is easily paraphrased in propositional terms.

By contrast, a poetic metaphor such as the one in Richardson's poem in our first chapter is a case where what is meant is highly indeterminate: it is too nebulous to be paraphrased at all. Some cases of showing are also indeterminate too. During a hike through the mountains, A might stop and take a deep breath of the fresh air, smile and sigh ostensively. Everything perceivable in their companion B's environment will alter the thoughts that B is entertaining, making it possible for them to infer that A has thoughts, memories and feelings similar to their own. What A intended to convey was merely an impression. They did not mean any one thing. The intended import is not paraphrasable at all.

Many researchers from other disciplines who are interested in relevance theory are critical that the theory tends to concentrate exclusively on epistemic states (see, for example, Wharton et al. 2021). As Deirdre Wilson put it during a workshop held as part of the Balzan Project at St John's College, Oxford, 2011:

relevance theory is a theory of communication, and it defines communication rather narrowly in conceptual terms. Communication involves providing evidence for a range of intended effects, and while this leaves room for images and emotions to play a role as causes or consequences of an appropriate interpretation, they cannot be part of that interpretation unless embedded into a conceptual description. (Wilson 2011b)

But it is simply not true that Sperber and Wilson (2015) ignore non-propositional import. As their way of dealing with the phenomenon, they define 'impressions' as 'arrays of weakly manifest propositions', that is, a more or less indeterminate enumeration or description of propositions, the manifestness of which to a particular individual can't be predicted. If having opened the shutters of her chalet, Marie catches the eye of the person she is sharing her room with and gazes up at the blue sky outside, she does not make manifest any particular proposition, but rather – in relevance theory terms – shares a number of weakly manifest ones. The interpretation of creative metaphors involves a similar process. A metaphor such as 'the swollen tongue of oil' implicates an undetermined array of ideas that relate the slick of oil to the human tongue, probing the 'throat' of the coast.

As we have stressed on numerous occasions in this book, linguists, philosophers and pragmatists have stuck to those areas of meaning illuminated by semantics and logic, and as a result attention has been almost entirely focused on propositional meaning. For reasons we outline in Chapter 2, they have fixated on clocks and avoided clouds completely. Sperber and Wilson (2015: 149) put it beautifully:

Like the proverbial drunkard in the night looking for his glasses under the lamppost not because of any strong reason to believe that they were there, but because at least he could see there, students of language have stayed close to the lampposts of semantics and logic. The drunkard's strategy need not be irrational. But after a while ... especially if there are glimmers of light around ... [.]

The kind of view they are criticising is the one we introduced earlier, in which the domain of pragmatics is exhausted by Gricean non-natural meaning (Levinson 2000). The same kind of view is to be found in the work of Gazdar (1979) (where pragmatics is meaning minus truth conditions) Davidson (1978), Bach (2006) (as we have seen) and more recently Lepore and Stone (2010). Relevance theory proposes a solution to this limiting view. The domain of pragmatics, we argue, needs to be broadened. We develop a framework based around the one in relevance theory (Sperber and Wilson

5.2 Relevance

1986/1995, 2015), and utilising the relevance-theoretic continuum between showing and non-natural meaning (meaning$_{NN}$) first introduced in Sperber and Wilson (1986/1995) and developed in Sperber and Wilson (2015) and Wharton (2009). Emotional communication, we argue, is often not about meaning at all, but about showing. The domain of pragmatic theory needs to be broadened to include cases of showing, if we are to include emotional communication into theories of utterance interpretation.

Indeed, a good deal of what a speaker communicates seems to fall on the 'non-propositional' side: for instance, it is hard to see how the content of moods, emotions and impressions can be reduced to a single determinate proposition (or a small set of such propositions). Many of the interesting explanatory questions concerning the communication of 'non-propositional' effects remain unformulated, and in order to make progress, genuinely interdisciplinary research is needed. Relevance theory's long-standing concern with the vaguer aspects of communication (e.g., Sperber and Wilson 1986/1995; Wharton 2009) is an advantage here.

Relevance theory distinguishes strong from weak communication and strong from weak implicatures. A conclusion is strongly implicated to the extent that it must be derived in the course of constructing a satisfactory interpretation: in this case the array of assumptions {I} contains a single, strongly manifest, assumption. It is weakly implicated if its recovery helps with the construction of a satisfactory interpretation, but is not essential because the array of assumptions {I} contains a wide array of roughly similar conclusions, which are all made weakly manifest (Sperber and Wilson 1986/1995). However, no matter how weakly manifest this array might be, or how unpredictably it may rise in an individual's mind, the elements in the array are still essentially propositional.

In recent work (Carston 2018; Wilson and Carston 2019) intuitions of ineffability and non-propositionality are further described by supplementing this account with some form of 'mental imagery'. The kind of imagery they have in mind is 'consciously experienced' or 'phenomenologically salient', and Wilson and Carston (2019) point out that they are unclear as to how this type of imagery relates to the kind of 'simulations' described in theories of cognition such as those offered by Barsalou 1999; Barsalou 2003; Glenberg 1997, which are typically described as 'embodied'. In support of their claim they cite experimental evidence which demonstrates:

(a) that novel/creative metaphors take longer and are more costly to comprehend than familiar/frozen ones [...] (b) that novel/creative metaphors evoke significantly more and longer activation of sensorimotor areas of the brain than familiar/frozen metaphors [...]. A plausible hypothesis is that the extra time and effort required for understanding a novel/creative metaphor facilitates, and perhaps intrinsically involves, the conscious grasp and manipulation of mental images. The same line of thought applies to non-metaphorical uses of language that induce a hearer/reader to slow down, take more time and expend more effort in reaching an interpretation. (Wilson and Carston 2019: 36)

As an analysis of certain factors involved in the interpretation of poetic metaphors, we see this as a promising direction. We agree that in the kind of cases they describe, imagery and affective states are automatically activated by-products of linguistic and pragmatic processes. However, when it comes to the kind of emotional communication we are trying to characterise, we believe that a stronger stance is necessary.

Firstly, as we saw in Chapter 2, there is clearly something about the expressive dimension that is not conceptual at all: in many ways, it is something better defined not only as in some way procedural or even preconceptual (a term we explain in the next chapter). Secondly, we believe its role is central to human communication rather than merely supplementary: emotion, and the communication of emotion, is hardly an incidental part of human mental life. Finally, we do not think that an account involving mental imagery of the kind Wilson and Carston describe goes anywhere near far enough when it comes to describing the role of the sensorimotor systems in emotional communication.

Firstly, there is no consensus on what these mental images are. Even Carston (2018) and Wilson and Carston (2019) admit mental images are highly 'variable' and 'idiosyncratic'. By way of explication, Carston (2018) discusses in some depth Colin McGinn's view of mental imagery as *Mindsight* (the title of McGinn's 2004 book on the subject). But McGinn's concern is much more with how nebulous notions such as imagination, dreams and creativity might relate to mental imagery rather than the nuts and bolts of what constitutes the images themselves. Indeed, the nuts-and-bolts view that McGinn offers – that we have three eyes, two on the outside and one on the inside – is enigmatic to say the least: firstly, many of the arguments originally raised by Pylyshyn (1973) *against* the notion of a 'mind's eye' hold to this day; secondly, McGinn's notion of what constitutes a 'concept' makes the approach very hard to reconcile with the relevance theory view of cognition. (See Qiu (in press) for discussion.)

The debate on mental imagery itself has generated a great deal more heat than it has shed light, from Pylyshyn's propositional view to Damasio's (1994) view that mental representations are routinely imagistic, and from Rey's (1981) hybrid view to Barsalou's (1999) view that the language of thought is a perceptual symbol system anyway (in sharp contrast with Fodor's (1975) representational theory of mind), as well as Arp's (2008) adaptive notion of scenario visualisation. To our thinking, the clearest exposition of the issues is in Block (1983) and Dennett (1981), and both remain agnostic on whether mental images exist or not.

5.2 Relevance

One possible solution is to appeal, as does Pignocchi (2012), to analogue as opposed to digital mental representations. In the past, we have found this view highly appealing (see Wharton 2009), but we are now unsure. After all, computers produce images that are apparently perfect facsimiles of analogue photographs. However, this analogicity is little more than an illusion since it is built on wholly digital foundations. (We wonder if it is an intuition such as this that lies behind upon Pylyshyn's propositional view of mental images.) By contrast, what most people are happy to refer as 'digital' circuits almost always incorporate analogue transistors.

Secondly, while the notion of a mental image may be a convenient one with which to try to reflect consciously on what is going on when one understands a metaphor (when we can't use words, what *would* we look to but an account based on some form of images?), it doesn't necessarily follow from it that that is in fact what is going on. Having taught courses on the nature of concepts for many years, we can vouch with some degree of certainty that when asked what constitutes the concept BIRD, most people will respond with an image of a bird. But there are many very convincing reasons not to believe this is not, in fact, true. So why, when their very existence is so uncertain, does the relevance theory account of metaphorical interpretation feels the need to appeal to mental images *at all*? Even if mental images do exist, the role of mental imagery is merely the tip of some sensorimotor iceberg. Emotional communication, we claim, exploits a host of other sensorimotor 'images', of varying types, which interact in ways which are synaesthetic in nature. References to this kind of cross-sensory 'imagery' are common: from Dante's region 'where "the sun is silent"' to more commonplace expressions such as 'a sweet sound' or 'a loud shirt'.

Commenting on the standard relevance theory view of poetic effects over twenty years ago, Adrian Pilkington wrote (2000: 190): 'Although this "wide array of minute cognitive effects" may characterise and distinguish poetic effects from other kinds of stylistic effects in terms of propositions, it is not clear that the affective dimension can be reduced to such cognitive effects.' And he went on (2000: 192): 'Although cognitive pragmatics is now in a position to provide a substantive theory of literariness, it is important to be aware of the limits on how far it can go. There is a theory of literariness based on pragmatic theory and there is a beyond.' We agree. The 'beyond' has been ripe for exploration for a long time, and the propositional account, in some ways, is as limiting as one based on non-natural meaning.

A promising direction, we suggest, is offered in the work of Patricia Kolaiti (2019, 2022, in press). Her alternative begins with a view of 'thought' that is perhaps different to the one standardly taken in relevance theory. The answer standardly provided by many philosophers is that thought involves propositions (p) and propositional attitudes such as 'believing that p', 'desiring that p' and so on, an account in which an array of implicatures (propositions) is the traditional way to go. But, she argues, this view is limiting.

Kolaiti argues that thought is a complex state, a mixture of causally interconnected conceptual and perceptual representations and that (for example) the aesthetic effects of literature and art cannot be properly explicated using the traditional relevance-theoretic notion of positive cognitive effect. Rather than supplementing the standard relevance-theory account with mental images, Kolaiti presents the following argument: since thought can be shown to be a mixture of causally interconnected conceptual and perceptual representations, the aesthetic effects of literature and art might not be properly explicated using the traditional relevance-theoretic notion of cognitive effect *at all*. Drawing on findings on the perceptual brain from Ramachandran and Hirstein (1999) as well as work on music and dance (e.g., Calvo-Merino et al. 2005, Tervaniemi et al. 2015), she proposes that the main function of art is not to elicit cognitive effects but, rather, to cause a characteristic type of aesthetic response which is fundamentally sensory or perceptual in nature. The relevance-theoretic notion of cognitive effect, she argues, needs to be supplemented with a new notion of *perceptual effects*. These are subattentive improvements in the mind's perceptual and neural organisation. Effects such as these, we argue, better capture the synaesthetic, cross-sensory nature of the effects of, for example, metaphor.

In the next chapter we argue that in order to fully accommodate emotion within the relevance-theory framework, the notion of cognitive effect needs to be complemented by a notion of *affective effect*. But before that, we return to the notion of relevance itself and compare the one used in relevance theory with the notion as it appears in work in appraisal theory.

5.3 Two Notions of Relevance?

In Chapter 3 (and elsewhere) we have described how, far from being unique to relevance theory, the notion of relevance plays an important role in other disciplines.[10] Given the concerns of this book, however, the most notable place where it plays a central role is in the study of affective science. We remarked that Scherer (1994b) includes the detection of relevance as the first process in his component model of emotion and that Sander et al. (2003) characterise the amygdala as a relevance detector. In appraisal theory, for example, an object will not elicit an emotional episode unless in some way that object is relevant to the person experiencing the emotion. What is the

---

[10] Discussion in this section is based on a section of Wharton et al. (2021). We are grateful to our co-authors Constant Bonard, Danny Dukes, Steve Oswald and David Sander for permission to use some of the ideas in that paper.

5.3 Two Notions of Relevance?

relationship between relevance as it is used in appraisal theory (relevance$_{AFF}$) and relevance as it used in relevance theory (relevance$_{PRAG}$)? Wharton et al. (2021) point to four ways in which the two notions appear to be different.

The first difference is that relevance$_{AFF}$ is characterised in relation to objectives, goals or concerns: typically, it is referred to as 'goal relevance' or 'concern relevance'. Relevance$_{PRAG}$ is not. Rather, it is characterised as a property of inputs to inferential processes: a property of information which will reshape an individual's representation of the world and make it better. Secondly, and relatedly, relevance$_{PRAG}$ appeals directly to the theoretical notions of cognitive effects and processing effort. Just how relevant a particular input is, is a function of these two factors: other things being equal, the more positive cognitive effects gained, and the less processing effort expended in gaining those effects, the greater the relevance of the input to the individual who processes it. Relevance$_{AFF}$, on the other hand, makes no appeal to these notions at all. (Indeed, it is left undefined by affective scientists.)

The third difference concerns the individual's response once an object or information has been appraised as relevant. In appraisal theory (and affective science generally) the response to an object being appraised as, say, goal relevant is the elicitation of a particular emotional episode. If the goal is physical safety, for example, the emotional episode elicited will be fear. In relevance theory, on the other hand, the response to information that is relevant is non-demonstrative inferences, mostly in the form of propositional content. In our previous examples (20)–(22), it was relevant to Marie that the sky was clear and blue. This motivated her to put this new information together with the thoughts she was entertaining at the time and infer that she would, in fact, be able to go out for a hike.

The final difference concerns the nature of the kinds of cognitive processes at play. Relevance theory tends to focus on what we might call 'higher' epistemic processes such as the interpretation of utterances. Affective science tends to be concerned with 'lower' cognitive processes, which might – for example – be shared with neonates or even non-human animals. This distinction reflects the model proposed by LeDoux (1989). Relevance theorists, however, have tended to be interested in verbal communication and have as a result focused on the higher process of the slow, cortical route, while those working in affective science have concentrated on the faster, (mostly) subcortical routes. We turn to the dual-route system once more in Chapter 7, when we consider evolutionary concerns in the light of a little-known work by Paul Grice.

Just how much scrutiny do these differences bear? Regarding the first, it is true that relevance$_{PRAG}$ is not explicitly defined in terms of goals, but we would argue that this has as much to do with the manner in which it is presented in Sperber and Wilson (1986/1995) than it has to do with any of the key details of the actual notion of relevance being presented. Relevance$_{PRAG}$ might just as well have been defined, say, in terms of the twin *goals* of, on the one hand, maximising cognitive effects (in terms of improving one's representation of the world) and, on the other, minimising the amount of processing effort expended in the derivation of effects. And we are playing fast and loose with Sperber and Wilson's thinking here; they are quite explicit that '[e]fficiency can only be defined with respect to a goal' (1986/1995: 46). They go on: 'Resources have to be allocated to the processing of information which is likely to bring about the greatest contribution to the mind's general cognitive goals at the smallest cognitive cost' (1986/1995: 48).

Much of Dan Sperber's work is concerned with evolutionary issues of the kind mentioned in the discussion of Cosmides and Tooby in Chapter 3. Cognition is a biological function, and the mechanisms that mediate cognition are biological adaptations shaped by natural selection. While there is massive variation in the kind of qualitative adaptations that might evolve in response to a particular environment, the selection pressures for *quantitative* improvement are probably relatively stable: the kind of biological mechanisms that endure will tend towards efficiency, whether they are adaptive responses to the challenge of identifying pertinent sensory inputs in the environment, as in the mechanisms that ensure the mind focuses on relevant information, or to the challenge of facilitating successful propulsion through water, as is the case of an anguilliform fish, whose shape maximises speed of propulsion while at the same time minimising processing effort (Lighthill 1970).

Of course, evolution is a complex process and has no goal in itself, but it doesn't seem too presumptuous to suggest that efficient adaptions will tend to be selected ahead of inefficient ones. As we shall see, that all organisms are designed to be efficient is a central claim of current allostatic models (Sterling 2004), besides which, minimising processing effort seems to us to be a special case of a goal that is widespread in the animal kingdom: that of avoiding wasting one's energy.

Moreover, there are instances where relevance$_{AFF}$ and relevance$_{PRAG}$ can be shown to overlap. In the case of so-called 'epistemic' emotions such as interest or curiosity, it turns out that what is relevant$_{AFF}$ meets the criteria for relevance$_{PRAG}$. In an episode of interest, for example, we might appraise a stimulus as relevant to our goal of learning something novel (Silvia 2006), especially if this piece of knowledge is relevant to our current concerns. In this example, the interest has motivated us to improve our representation of the world. As an interesting parallel, affective reactions such as feelings of tiredness or laziness may well prevent you from carrying out otherwise demanding activities, and this motivates you to minimise effort and rest. A classic example is the kind of torpor that for many people has set in after recovering from a Covid infection. Wharton et al. (2021) therefore theorise that relevance$_{AFF}$ and relevance$_{PRAG}$ are actually both subtypes of a much more general notion of

5.3 Two Notions of Relevance?

goal relevance and, indeed, that they intersect at the point where we find epistemic emotions such as interest. They are phenomena which are instantiations of relevance$_{AFF}$ but at the same time also concern the goal of acquiring knowledge (relevance$_{PRAG}$).

The second presumed difference is that while relevance$_{PRAG}$ appeals directly to the theoretical notions of cognitive effects and processing effort, relevance$_{AFF}$ does not. It is true that nowhere do affective scientists explain relevance in this way. But as we have just seen: first, in the case of epistemic emotions a stimulus may well be appraised as relevant$_{AFF}$ when the goal is to maximise cognitive effects; and second, when it comes to our examples of tiredness or laziness, the triggering stimulus may well be appraised as relevant to the goal of minimising processing efforts. If this is correct, then our second theoretical difference dissolves too.

The third difference concerns the course of action an individual undertakes once relevance has been detected. While relevance theory focuses largely on responses as warranted (but, at the same time, non-demonstrative) inferences about propositional, often linguistic contents, the responses of interest in appraisal theory are emotional episodes. But while it is true that the focus of relevance theory thus far has been propositional contents that are ostensively communicated, this is not absolutely essential to relevance$_{PRAG}$. Relevance is a property of inputs to inferential processes, whether they are ostensively communicated or not. Humans are all the time monitoring the environment for clues – perceptual, behavioural, kinaesthetic – which make manifest a wide array of assumptions (and which may form the basis for inferring warranted conclusions). The sight of smoke seeping between a door and doorframe, or the acrid smell of burning emanating from an unknown source, are just as relevant as (possibly more relevant than) a remark someone has made. Yes, it is the case that relevance theory has focused on processes that involve the comprehension of ostensively communicated propositional contents, but this may be considered as a historical contingency and a consequence of the fact that relevance theory originated from research in linguistics (perhaps even a reflection of the kinds of problems we identified in Chapter 2). If we consider once again an epistemic emotion such as interest, we see that both notions of relevance apply.

This is not to deny that events deemed relevant$_{PRAG}$ tend not to lead to an emotional response. And by the same token, when an event is appraised as relevant$_{AFF}$ it typically will not lead to the kind of inferential processes of interest to pragmatists. If we happen upon a large venomous snake as we are walking in the forest, our emotional response will tend to make us recoil from it in fear, rather than trying to start a sophisticated interpretation in order to gain more knowledge about the world (unless we are a herpetologist and it is our *goal* to study this snake). But all that these differences demonstrate is that when stimuli are deemed relevant in the light of differing goals (staying alive vs. studying snakes), different evolutionary responses are elicited. And this does not in any way demonstrate that the notion of relevance itself is different in the two cases. On the contrary, what it demonstrates is that the two cases are relevant *in the same sense*, but just to different things. Indeed, Wharton et al. (2021) suggest that some emotion researchers claim that relevance$_{AFF}$ *can* lead to cognitive effects, and it has been suggested that it is because emotional stimuli are affectively relevant that they have effects on several cognitive mechanisms, such as attention (Maratos and Pessoa 2019; Pool et al. 2016a) or memory (Montagrin et al. 2018).

The fourth and final difference concerns the types of processes that are the focus of the two approaches: the so-called 'higher' epistemic processes which relevance theory tends to concern itself with and the so-called 'lower' processes that are the subject of research into emotion. It is certainly true that relevance$_{PRAG}$ has typically been described in terms of sophisticated cognitive tasks such as inferential comprehension, but we hope we have already shown that it should not be restricted to this territory. Again, the sight of smoke, or the smell of burning, probably will not trigger the 'higher', recently evolved neocortical mechanisms. Nowhere in relevance theory does it state that the mind computes representations of either effect or effort. Instead, the balance of effort and effect in cognitive processes is 'felt': it is less comparable to a mathematical algorithm than it is to those found in bodily processes where, for example, muscular effort is monitored according to effects gained (see Sperber 2005). Relevance$_{PRAG}$, then, may well also operate as a 'low-level' process, one that is present in most animal species. Indeed, in Chapter 7 we show (following Cornell and Wharton 2021) that relevance can be found elsewhere the evolutionary tree (see also for instance Sperber 2019).

Equally, it would be wrong to suggest that relevance$_{AFF}$ is concerned only with 'low-level' cognition. After all, we all react emotionally, all the time, to stimuli that require sophisticated processing: utterances being the paradigm case in point. Indeed, some people working in appraisal theory have proposed that there might exist different levels of appraisal, at a sensory-motor level, involving only 'low-level' cognition, a conceptual level, involving 'higher' cognition and an intermediary schematic level (see Van Reekum and Scherer 1997 for a detailed presentation). It seems, then, that both types of relevance may be concerned with both 'lower-' and 'higher-level' cognition.

We suggest then (following Wharton et al. 2021) that the differences between relevance$_{PRAG}$ and relevance$_{AFF}$ are illusory. Both types of relevance are subsets of a broader category of goal relevance. Notwithstanding that, while affective scientists have made great strides in understanding the processes of emotion elicitation, emotional response and the recognition of emotions in others, the notion of relevance used in that discipline has remained

5.3 Two Notions of Relevance?

underspecified. Wharton et al. (2021) conclude by suggesting that the discussion therein contributes to a debate which will result in a more specific and operational definition, as well as to dedicated experimental research, for instance on the cognitive effects of relevance$_{AFF}$ and affective effects of relevance$_{PRAG}$.

As for relevance-theoretic pragmatics, while the notion of relevance has been precisely defined, its relation to affect – and indeed the role of affect in communication generally – has remained underexplored. Given our aims, this makes the relation an absolutely crucial part of this book. And while the current state of play has it that the domains of relevance$_{AFF}$ and relevance$_{PRAG}$ are subsets of a broader notion of goal relevance and merely intersect, it is to be hoped that as the objects of study of these two disciplines grow closer and closer to each other, the sets in question will cease to differ at all.

One of the aims of this book is to show that emotion is part of cognition, not separate from it. If this is the case, then it seems obvious that the search for relevance will underpin both, where relevance is understood to be a unified concept containing both relevance$_{AFF}$ and relevance$_{PRAG}$.

6   Beyond Propositions

6.1   Introduction

On 10 November 1988, Philipp Jenninger, then Head of the West German parliament in Bonn, rose to speak on the occasion of the fiftieth anniversary of *Kristallnacht*. He began by outlining what he felt were the reasons National Socialism had capture the imagination. The rhetorical style he chose was intended to represent as closely as possible the perspective of an ordinary German of the 1930s who was favourable to the Nazi movement. He would, of course, clearly dissociate himself from the views he was reporting. Adopting free indirect speech and mimicking the tone and stance of early Nazi partisans, Jenninger wondered out loud what it was the ordinary German had found so 'fascinating' (his word) about Nazism. He continued:

> From mass unemployment had come full employment, from mass misery, something like prosperity for the broadest layers of the population. Rather than despair and hopelessness, optimism and self-confidence now ruled. Didn't Hitler make true what Kaiser Wilhelm II had only promised, namely, to lead the Germans toward glorious times? Had he not truly been selected by Providence, a Führer, as Providence grants to a people only once in a thousand years?
>
> And as for the Jews, had they not, in the past, presumptuously assumed a role which they did not deserve? Shouldn't they finally, for once, have to put up with some restrictions? Didn't they perhaps deserve to be put back in their place? (Jenninger 1988)

The response his performance elicited was not what he had hoped for. More than fifty members of the Bundestag promptly walked out. The next day Jenninger was looking for a new job.

Despite the fact that there can have been little doubt about his intentions – Jenninger had been trying to communicate his abhorrence of Nazism and its crimes – the sensitivity of the members of the Bundestag to anyone who even gave the appearance of attempting to legitimise the pro-Nazi vote was hardly unsurprising. For Jenninger, it was obvious he was dissociating himself from the words he had uttered. But his performance was mismanaged and ill-judged in the extreme. His intention to dissociate himself from the content of what he said *wasn't obvious enough.*

6.1 Introduction

Our purpose in presenting this anecdote is to illustrate the impact that the mismanagement of affect in communicative settings can have, even when there is a strong discrepancy between the emotions in question and background assumptions which are well grounded in the audience's cognitive environment. No one present at the event believed Jenninger was a Nazi, or a Nazi sympathiser. They *knew* he wasn't. However, the shock, disgust and revulsion his performance generated was simply impossible to ignore.[1]

Arguably, what we have here is another version of the amygdala hijack we mentioned briefly in Chapter 2 (Goleman 1995). When Robert Badinter wanted to persuade his jury that the lives of those convicts he was defending were worth saving, he did not appeal to their cool, rational side. He appealed to their emotions. Sometimes, somehow, emotions take over. Indeed, Badinter saw the very existence of the death penalty itself as 'la passion et la peur triomphant de la raison et de l'humanité' ('Passion and fear triumphing over reason and humanity', Badinter 1981). It's ironic, therefore, that in order to save people from that fate, it was necessary for him to appeal to the jury's emotional rather than rational side.

In this chapter, we sketch our main set of proposals. Towards the end of the previous chapter, we introduced Patricia Kolaiti's idea of effects that are not cognitive in the current relevance-theory sense. She argues (2019, 2022, in press) that cognition is a mixture of causally interconnected conceptual and perceptual representations and that the aesthetic effects of literature and art cannot be properly explicated using the traditional relevance-theoretic notion of positive cognitive effect at all. She proposes the notion be supplemented with a new notion of positive perceptual effect: partly embodied and, crucially, non-propositional effects, which account for the selective directedness of our mental lives towards art and other objects. (Kolaiti also identifies so-called 'body awareness' – or 'kinaesthesia' – as a candidate for a non-propositional thought process.)

Might the notion of positive perceptual effects be useful in the analysis of the communication of affect and emotion? It seems to us that the answer is no. Perception is a sensory phenomenon and, as we have seen in the previous chapters, emotional states crucially involve the interplay been perception and cognition. In this chapter, then, we augment the existing relevance-theoretic notion of cognitive effect (and Kolaiti's notion of perceptual effect) with the further notion of affective effect (Saussure and Wharton 2020; Wharton and Strey 2019).[2]

---

[1] One year later, Ignatz Bubis, a prominent member of the Jewish community, used several passages verbatim from Jenninger's speech and offended no one. This corroborates the claim that it had not been the words Jenninger used that caused the response; rather, his whole performance. See: Peter Schmalz, 'Keiner hat etwas gemerkt', *Die Welt*, 1 December 1995 (in German).

[2] Wharton and Strey use the term 'emotional effect' in their 2019 paper. The term 'affective effect' was actually originally coined by Sperber and Wilson (1986/1995: 224), and we have already explained why we now prefer that term. The difference, of course, is that we are proposing affective effects are real things in and of themselves and not a subset of cognitive effects.

Sperber and Wilson suggest that one of the main payoffs ostensive communication has is that it enhances the mutual cognitive environments of those engaging in it (in terms of shared thoughts/beliefs, etc.). It does not seem too implausible a claim to suggest that the same may be true of emotional communication. Just as an awareness of the beliefs of others can have important consequences for successful interaction with them, so might an awareness of their emotions be beneficial also. Moreover, it could be argued that representations have little effect without a contribution from one's emotional constitution. But what are affective effects?

We propose they come in two main varieties: the first variety tend to serve as inputs *to* cognitive processing, the second as outputs *from* cognitive processing. For convenience we will refer to these as primary and secondary affective effects, but we add the caveat that this does not mean we endorse a view in which one must occur *before* the other. We prefer a view in which processing is parallel, but want to maintain a distinction whereby some affective effects are, effectively, inputs and others outputs. In the next section we discuss primary affective effects. In §6.2.2 we turn to secondary affective effects by focusing on the literature. In §6.2.3 we return to the Badinter example, with a discussion of the role of affective effects in persuasion.

6.2 Affective Effects

6.2.1 *Primary Affective Effects*

Piskorska (2012; see also Yus 2016) presents an overview of some possible ways in which relevance theory might accommodate emotions. In particular, she explores how they might contribute to cognitive effects. Her view of emotions themselves owes most to the work of Oatley et al. (2006: 260).

Emotions structure perception, direct attention, give preferential access to certain memories and bias judgements; this helps the individual respond to the environment in ways that we recognise as valuable aspects of our humanity. This characterisation is close to that of Cosmides and Tooby (2000), where emotions are seen as superordinate cognitive programmes (in our terms, procedures), functioning to regulate or mobilise the cognitive subprogrammes responsible for perception and attention, goal choice, information-gathering, physiological changes and specialised types of inference. It is also consistent with the componential view of emotion taken by psychologists and affective scientists working in appraisal theory, in which emotions involve cognitive appraisals, action tendencies, expression, subjective feelings and bodily sensations (see, for example, Moors et al. 2013; Scherer 2009), and also the view of emotions as 'quick and dirty' decision-making heuristics (see Greenspan 2002: 206).

6.2 Affective Effects

We agree that emotional communication sometimes works in the way Piskorska suggests; that is, in a way in which the role of emotions is always to facilitate the derivation of cognitive effects. We also agree that the current standard relevance-theory account, under which emotions sometimes result in the communication of arrays of propositions, is partly correct. Interjections, facial expressions and affective tone of voice lead to the construction of higher-level explicatures and these (together with the proposition expressed by an utterance) lead to strong and weak implicatures by either providing strong support for a single, determinate conclusion or marginally altering the manifestness of a wide array of related ones. But both the traditional relevance-theoretic view and Piskorska's view regard all such effects as propositional. We suggest that an account based solely on propositions is problematic, for reasons we have discussed at length already (see the problems of description versus expression and propositions and ineffability described in Chapter 2, §2.2).

Our notion of primary affective effect very much reflects aspects of the characterisations offered by Oatley et al. (2006) and by Cosmides and Tooby (2000) and is consistent with Piskorka's 2012 vision. We illustrate two different types of primary affective effect (thought there may be more) by revisiting an example first described in Wharton and Strey (2016). Andrew and Grace have arrived in a small village in France, late on a summer's evening. They book a room in a small hotel which, aside from the elderly *patrons*, appears to be pretty much deserted. Since it is August, they assume this is because during that month most people are away from the village on holiday. Andrew asks Grace if she thinks they are the only guests staying the hotel. Grace replies:

(46) I can hear footsteps in the room above us.

Grace's response interacts with existing assumptions Andrew is entertaining to yield the contextual implication in (47):

(47) We are probably not the only guests staying in the hotel.

This is a paradigmatic relevance-theory cognitive effect where a new assumption interacts with existing assumptions to communicate an implicature. If Andrew can hear footsteps in the room above, Grace can infer that there is someone there from the assumption that the sound of footsteps indicates the presence of other people. This probably means they are not the only guests there.

Now let us change the context. Andrew and Grace live in a remote part of the countryside. There are no houses for miles around. The nearest building is some distance away, a maximum-security prison. It is a stormy night and shortly before they go to bed they hear on the radio that a dangerous convict has escaped.

In the middle of the night, Grace wakes Andrew and whispers the utterance in (46) in a frightened tone of voice.

Andrew and Grace will now be acutely aware of their own emotional states. They know this is fear, not just excitement and, indeed, are capable of reflecting on that fact consciously. However, there is a great deal that has been going on below the level of consciousness too. Physiological changes over which they have little or no influence have put the two of them in a state of hyper-alertness. Their gaze-direction mechanism will be highly activated and they now automatically pay a high degree of attention to perceptual inputs they may not normally have even noticed: Is that arrhythmic tapping really footsteps? Is there anything else it might be? They are also equipped with a newly defined set of goals, in which safety is suddenly the most important of a range of new informational priorities: Can we get to the phone and call the police? Is there an intruder in the house and, if there is, can we exit the house without them noticing? Where are the bloody car keys?

The elicitation of an emotional episode has many manifestations, and only some of these can be accounted for using extant relevance-theory machinery. In relevance-theory terms, what is happening in this example is not the entertainment of new contextual assumptions but, rather, radical changes in the salience of already existing assumptions (see Wilson and Wharton 2006), or perhaps even a 'shuffling' of assumptions so they are now in a different order (see Maillat and Oswald 2011). The motivation to reason in this particular way comes from the emotional states they are experiencing. This is Cosmides and Tooby's (2000) 'mobilisation of cognitive resources' framed in relevance-theoretic terms. We might call this type of primary affective effect *anticipatory* in the sense that it acts as an input to cognitive processes and anticipates a course of action.

Andrew and Grace will also be communicating information about their emotional states. Their fear will, to a certain extent, be shared. But what they are communicating to each other does not correlate with anything propositional. Indeed, the kind of communication that is occurring may not even be best characterised as ostensive in the relevance-theoretic sense. Our sensitivity to the mental states of others ensures that it takes very little to make a particular act ostensive: in our example, a single glance, lasting less than a fraction of a second, could set off the same of chain of anticipatory effects. But once a certain threshold of affect is reached sometimes even that millisecond-long glance may not be necessary. What is being conveyed here is more a matter of what Sperber and Wilson (2015: 139) call 'patterns of activation', the function of which is to mobilise Tooby and Cosmides' subprogrammes *in each other*. Rather than anticipatory we might call such effects *transfer* effects.[3]

---

[3] The notions of 'anticipatory' and 'transfer' primary affective effects are (we hope) a more worked-out version of the notions of 'environmental' and 'communicative' effects introduced in Wharton (2022).

6.2 Affective Effects

The value of both sorts of effect lies at least partly in the sheer speed at which they allow us to act. According to the 'dual-route' system of cognition we introduced in §1.3.6 (Garrido et al. 2012) and developed in the next chapter, the processing of information through the subcortical pathways of the amygdala – the same amygdala that is sometimes hijacked and is central to emotional experience generally – allows for much faster transmission of information than is possible in the cortical hemispheres responsible for conceptual thought. This increased speed is responsible for the directness of perception and enables us to respond to, for example, dangerous stimuli, well before we have become consciously aware what that stimulus might be and, crucially, attempted to think our way out of it. No one currently alive on the planet has ever seen a sabre-toothed tiger, but we all certainly have ancestors who – if they could – would vouch for the adaptive value of such a response. It is virtually effortless and efficient in the extreme. We see no reason why such processes should be excluded from a theory of utterance interpretation, since the mechanisms for utterance interpretation are built on foundations in which the low, fast route has been highly successful in terms of our survival as a species.

Affective effects involve processes that are not adequately described by the representation and/or management of conceptual information. Neither anticipatory effects nor transfer effects involve a search for relevance in the sense of the derivation of cognitive effects, but they do typically arise as a precursor to them. In some cases, such as the Jenninger case discussed at the start of this chapter, the affective transfer effects pretty much exhausted what there was to retrieve from his performance. At other times, however (and indeed more usually), affective effects serve as a starting point for further processing and better facilitate the search for cognitive effects. In this way, affective effects and cognitive effects interact. Our notion of secondary affective effects (introduced in § 6.2.2) is designed to capture the intuition that, sometimes, thought causes affective effects rather than following on from them.

In support of our claim that affective effects might be regarded as a precursor to conceptual activity, both in real-time cognition and human ontogeny, we cite the case of human neonates. Tye (2004: 225) asks us to consider the reaction of a newborn baby when a cotton bud dipped in liquid sulphur is held under her nose. A baby typically turns up her nose in that universal facial expression of disgust and turns away. The obvious explanation, as Tye goes on, is that this reaction occurs because, to the baby, the cotton bud smells foul. But this reaction does not depend on the activation of a concept FOUL (any more than a frog's reaction to the fly involves entertaining the concept FLY – Lettvin et al. 1959). Indeed, it does not presuppose that the baby even possesses the concept FOUL. The baby's reaction is an entirely affective one, and in developmental terms might be said to be preconceptual.

The capacity, or indeed the need, to produce emotional responses such as these does not end once the concept DISGUST has been acquired, nor indeed does it end with the acquisition of any of the requisite emotion concepts which emerge during a child's conceptual development. Part of a 'mature' person's cognitive ability is precisely to reflect on these spontaneous responses through their conceptualisation. An individual might describe disgust by using an utterance of (1c), repeated here as (48). But they might also express it directly by an utterance of (14c), repeated below as (49):

(48) I'm disgusted.

(49) *Yugh!*

Parallel pairs can easily be constructed for emotions such as joy, anger, surprise and so on. Single-interjection utterances such as (16) 'He found it here yesterday', which are typical of the expressive dimension of language use of interjections, are paradigmatic examples of transfer effects. They feature a mode of activation that bypasses the propositional inferential processes because it utilises the faster of the dual routes. Indeed, part of the explanation for this directness may lie in the fact that they tap into a system of communication which is phylogenetically as well as ontogenetically primitive. We turn to this in Chapter 7. What remains, however, is that pragmatics in general has avoided discussion of these mechanisms, which – as Greenspan says – are 'factors in practical reasoning' (Greenspan 2002: 206) and fundamental to the mental lives of our species.

Transfer-affective effects are inextricably linked with the interpretation of the natural codes we mentioned in the previous chapter: affective prosody, facial expression, gesticulations and so on. To say they are factors in the processes of practical reasoning is not to say they play an active role in propositional, inferential processes. Rather, they constrain the construction of the context against which those processes take place. As a result, they reduce the effort involved in achieving relevance (see also Maillat and Oswald 2013, Saussure 2005). And, crucially, not only do they facilitate the direct transfer of information about affective states, but the affective states themselves are often *caught* by others in a direct and immediate way. This claim is in no way new. There is a vast literature on emotional contagion (see Hatfield et al. 1994) that claims that instances of emotional communication convey not only conceptual information about emotional states, but ultimately and above all, something of the emotional states themselves. In this respect, transfer effects may sometimes have an anticipatory function.

Notice, crucially, that these transfer effects are not derived inferentially (or at least inferentially in the sense we mean it in here). And we admit that it's still not entirely clear to us, for example, what the activation or (for want of a better phrase) the 'switching on' of a non-propositional affective-effect mental state might be, as distinct from causing someone to infer a proposition. We don't have an answer, but would add, firstly, that relevance theorists are perfectly happy to accept that discourse connectives such as 'so' and 'after all' can encode procedural information that activates inferential packages without recourse to any intervening conceptual apparatus. And the directness of natural codes (and the instinctual reaction of the human neonate to sulphur) is strong evidence that conceptualisation can be bypassed, as well as strong evidence that there's much more to the procedural meaning inherent in discourse connectives.

This account not only captures the directness and ineffability of many aspects of the communication of affect but also accommodates the fact that many of the processes associated with it operate below the level of consciousness, without what Lieberman (2000) calls 'phenomenological awareness'. What makes relevance theory the ideal pragmatic approach to shed light on how affect and pragmatics interact is that it is not simply a theory of communication; it is a theory of communication *and cognition*. Wharton (2009) points out that much of the relevance inherent in emotional expression does not come from the fact that it is intentionally communicated at all (though it may be). Relevance is a property of inputs to inferential processes, *whether they are ostensively communicated or not*. Humans are constantly monitoring the environment for clues – perceptual, behavioural, kinaesthetic – which make manifest a wide array of assumptions (and which may form the basis for inferring warranted – and, note, propositional – conclusions). We propose that our notions of anticipatory and transfer primary affective effects will lead us to a deeper understanding of not only the relationship between ostensive and non-ostensive communication but also the relationship between decoding and inference in the way we read the emotions of others.

6.2.2 Secondary Affective Effects

In a famous scene from the Michael Cacoyannis film *Zorba the Greek*, the eponymous hero is working inside the tunnel of a lignite mine that has lain dormant for years. The network of tunnels inside is held up by a set of flimsy, creaking wooden supports. The roof suddenly collapses. There is a deafening noise, and the mouth of the tunnel is quickly shrouded in dust. Mortified, Zorba's friend shouts (50):

(50) Zorba!

The workers outside the tunnel are immediately alerted to the fact that there is a problem. They wait, frozen, prepared for action.

From hearing his friend's tone of voice, Zorba – who is totally unhurt – can immediately sense the speaker's emotional state. Yet this emotional state is ostensively presented, so the easily accessible epistemic proposition – that his friend is terrified he might actually be hurt – occurs to him together with the fact that this was intended by the speaker to be mutually manifest. The proposition may, of course, act as premise to an inference. In the context of the film, it has in particular one consequence, which is that his friend thinks that by failing to properly inspect the flimsy supports, and hence the safety of the roof of the mine, Zorba has been acting recklessly.

Zorba exits the mine safely and responds in a slightly angry tone of voice:

(51) What!?

He pretends *not* to have grasped the primary affective effects, because otherwise he would have to object explicitly to his friend's idea that he was acting recklessly.

In the scene, a stimulus (the collapsing of the mine) triggers an emotional state of fear in Zorba's friend (that Zorba has been hurt), which itself motivates the shouting of 'Zorba'. In turn, this shouting with the emotional tone of voice is straightforwardly interpreted by the hearers around as a signal that the speaker is afraid. It is a primary affective effect. But among the stimuli that can trigger affective effects, linguistic descriptions of situations are deserving of a particular place. Needless to say, the description of particular scenes can give rise to affective effects. The above scene is originally taken from the novel by Nikos Kazantzakis entitled *Alexis Zorba*. A novel is, in a sense, a form of communication directed to an audience of readers, and in this case readers are likely to have affective effects from their own reading of the description of the scene. Notice, however, that such affective effects arise only as a result of the interpretive process. These are *secondary affective effects*, emerging only after the stage of interpreting utterances, as an extra product of the communication.

Emotional episodes are directed towards objects and events, which play a causal role in their elicitation. Primary affective effects are precursors to inference, which takes place over propositions. They are either anticipatory effects or transfer effects in the sense we described in §6.2.1. Secondary affective effects, which we turn to in this section, are caused not by the objects or events responsible for the elicitation of emotional episodes but by thought itself.

Primary and secondary effects often arise together. Returning to example (46), Grace's tone of voice generates anticipatory and transfer effects, but her utterance is also an ostensive stimulus in the traditional relevance-theoretic sense. As such, Andrew will most likely derive a powerful implicature such as (52) or (53):

6.2 Affective Effects

(52) There is someone in the room above us.

(53) We are not alone in the house.

Further affective effects will be generated, but not through tone of voice or non-linguistic indicators. Rather they will emerge as a direct result of the thoughts derived via the slow, cognitive pragmatic route. These are secondary affective effects, prompted by the thoughts a person entertains. The two separate types of effect act in parallel: a primary (tone of voice) and a secondary (description, inference). In terms of the 'dual'-route system of cognition, *both* routes are activated. This, we suggest, is the norm. Again, we remark that pragmatics has focused on the latter at the expense of the former.

Of course, this also happens in a range of quite ordinary cases. When someone utters a descriptive equivalent of an expressive, such as '*It hurts!*', instead of '*Ouch!*', or '*That's amazing!*', instead of '*Wow!*', it's easy to see how secondary affective effects may emerge. But when it happens, they emerge through a very different path: a representation of what it is to be in the condition of saying that it hurts or amazed needs to be construed, which will make sense only insofar as the addressee can find in his memory a trace of what it is to be in a similar condition, or in a condition that resembles that one at least to some extent.

However, there is a third kind of case: a case where there are no non-verbal cues, no facial expressions, no expressives used as such in the deictic moment, but only cognitive effects, that is, propositional information, that serve as cues to generate affective effects. In that case, only secondary affective effects emerge. Literature, we suggest, is the paradigm example of a form that, as well as generating cognitive effects in the traditional relevance theory sense, also generates secondary affective effects.

What is true of descriptions of single states of affairs (such as '*I am in pain*' or '*That's amazing*') is also true of series of propositions describing complex situations, in particular sequences of events. Just as being the witness of a scene can elicit affective reactions, constructing a representation of these situations in our imagination – for example by reading the description of such scenes in a novel – elicits affective effects. We face emotional scenes all the time, and we react to them, in our everyday life, with emotions. Depending upon our own mental, emotional state, but also upon our experience, memories and personality, various affective reactions occur in front of a given scene. At the train station, we might see lovers embracing in joy and feel a little happy smile on our own faces, while other scenes fill us with feelings such as sadness, horror, fear, admiration and so on. Some such scenes fill us with unbearable emotion yet are still propositional descriptions only.

Interestingly, we do label scenes 'happy' or 'sad', as if the happiness or the sadness were in the scene itself, just as when we label landscapes 'lovely' or, again, 'sad'; but of course the loveliness or the sadness is a feeling in the mind of the observer, whose mind is going through a certain process. However, when fellow humans are involved, the joy or the sadness we feel has to do with a sense of sharing something with them, or mentally answering to a prompt of human life. When a communicator uses language to describe scenes – all the more so when she describes a sequence of events where characters are involved – the communicator tells a story. If we are speaking of literature, the communicator writes a novel.

Arguably, the *raison d'être* of novels is to have readers witness – in their own imaginations – scenes and sequences of events involving individuals (characters), and for those readers to take something from this. In some cases, possibly, imagining the scenes will be a source of pleasure and distraction, and in other cases, it will be a source of more subtle emotions. In turn, these emotions lead us to transform aspects of our conceptions, change some of our dispositions or to reflect, with more or less depth depending on the individual, on our own attitudes in life, on the human condition and so on.[4]

These effects depend very much upon the personal history of the reader. The traditional view, according to which there are as many 'interpretations' as there are readers, is nothing more than a way of acknowledging this fact. Wilson (2018: 118) puts it like this:

Not all the import of a literary work may be equally manifest to both writer and reader at a given time, ... different parts of it may become more or less manifest to different readers at different times, and ... some of the responsibility for constructing a satisfactory overall interpretation may lie with the reader as well as the writer.

However, what is meant by 'interpretation' in this quote is something slightly different to 'understanding' in the sense of generating cognitive, propositional effects. The notion of an 'overall interpretation' is about something else, which takes place in parallel with, and is sometimes a consequence of, the realisation of cognitive, propositional effects (i.e., the understanding of the scene itself). It has to do with other psychological effects which, in a way, give a richer psychological import to the literary work. We suggest that this supplement of import, without which a novel would be irrelevant, often resides in the secondary affective effects it provides.

Cognitive effects contribute to relevance insofar as they interact with a particular cognitive environment, that is, a set of pre-existing assumptions: cognitive effects do not arise if the proposition retrieved is trivial or already present with the same epistemic strength in the mind of the addressee or reader. We argue that, similarly, secondary affective effects arise on the basis of pre-existing psychological material. However, we suggest, these pre-existing

---

[4] There is a huge amount of research on how the reading of fiction affects social dispositions, in particular empathy (see, for example, Feagin 2018; Keen 2015; Koopman and Hakemulder 2015; Oatley and Djikic 2018; Pozner 2022).

6.2 Affective Effects

mental elements are not propositions but memorial traces of related affective experiences. More precisely, we suggest that we retrieve dispositions from long-term memory and echo our own past experiences with the situations depicted and imagine what it is to be part of such situations, or to be a direct, real witness of them – and we can't imagine these things without some anchor in our own personal past experience. The relevance of a literary work depends, at least for a central part, upon the reader's capacity to make the descriptions resonate with what they have gone through in their own life and on their capacity for imagination.

Descriptions can be about many different things. Those which may trigger secondary affective effects are, we think, of two main kinds: first, descriptions of situations and sequences of events involving individuals, from which the addressee – the reader in the case of novels – experiences affective effects; second, descriptions of psychological states of individuals. We illustrate these two categories with discussion of themes from two well-known literary works.

The first of these is *Jane Eyre*. As a child, Jane is constantly mistreated by her adoptive family: she is bullied, ordered around, even locked away. Most readers, arguably, are moved by the scenes in which this unjust treatment is described. This emotion can vary from one reader to another: it can be closer to anger, to frustration, to sadness, or to a desire to care for Jane. It might involve various dimensions: our own attitudes towards children, education, social middles, conventions and so on. But what matters to us here is that the reader of this passage will have *some* emotional reaction to the various scenes as they are depicted (and this should be even more so, given the talent of the author). If not, the reader's interest in the novel will fade and disappear. In a way, if certain scenes do not give rise to secondary affective effects for a given reader, the passage would seem to lack meaningfulness, or, simply, relevance. Secondary affective effects, we suggest, make such scenes relevant.

We stress that in order to have these emotional responses, the reader need neither take the perspective of the child (in our discussion of Jane Eyre's mistreatment) nor 'put themselves in the character's shoes'. This is particularly clear in this example, since the child in the story cannot be thought to have the same feelings of frustration and anger as the mature adult reader. After all, mature adults in general know more about not only the story, but about human nature than the character does herself. Actually, these emotions find their source not in the reader's knowledge, in a restricted, propositional, sense of the word, but in a more general notion of knowledge that necessarily includes non-propositional aspects such as the reader's interests, dispositions and personal experience. The reader, we suggest, will derive affective effects in the measure of their capacity to imagine themselves a part of the scene or a real witness of it, of their capacity to set up mentally the components of the scene and to imagine the intentions of the characters from their behaviour, starting from what the author chooses to mention about the characters' behaviour and which will be considered relevant. In so doing, the readers will have made a particular use of the human ability to simulate other perspectives; however the other perspective here is not necessarily that of a particular character but rather the perspective of the reader themselves as a true witness or silent participant in the novel. Having an experience of injustices or a more sophisticated notion of injustice leads to a more complex grasp of what is happening and, possibly, to a higher degree of emotional sensitivity, making the emotional effects stronger. The reactivation, by a description, of the memorial traces of past experiences and imaginative capacities are a key to the generation of secondary emotional effects in stories, and more generally in literature.[5]

When secondary affective effects arise on the basis of descriptions, literary or not, the descriptions that trigger them are processed not only with regard to the reader's own *cognitive* environment, but with regard to the addressee's *psychological* environment, that is, their personal history and experience. The scene will evoke this or that particular emotional context in the mind of the reader (or other addressee) and their imaginative abilities will lead to secondary affective effects. This scheme is, we suggest, parallel to what happens with propositional meaning, which is processed with regard to the addressee's cognitive environment, recruiting cognitive inferential abilities. And when the author chooses to describe not (only) situations but the mental, psychological wanderings of a character, secondary affective effects arise based on the reader's ability to figure out what it is like to be in that psychological situation. Here again, what is key to secondary affective effects is the recovery of *simile* in memory and imaginative capacities.

Let us now introduce a second example, where what is described, is not (only) a scene but the psychological state of a character. A factual description of someone's being sad, nervous, happy, anxious, or the like obviously has the potential to induce affective effects of various kinds in the addressee's mind. However, conceptual items about affects are not the most powerful way to represent the affective, emotional states of individuals and to favour affective effects. This is not very surprising, since the conceptual lexicon is somehow 'flexible' (Escandell-Vidal and Leonetti 2011): generally speaking, a lexical item can refer to indefinitely many concepts depending on the context, circumstances and assumptions available about the speaker's intentions; this holds

---

[5] Note that not all literary works find their relevance in the elicitation of secondary affective effects. For example, La Fontaine's *Fables* are of course literary and tell stories. Yet their aim does not involve affective effects in the sense of what we are discussing in this section. Similarly, Montaigne's *Essays* are certainly literary but again, are about propositional effects rather than affective ones (besides the general feeling of aesthetics and beautiful writing, which may itself cause affective effects).

6.2 Affective Effects

about the vocabulary of emotions, so that 'sad', for example, can mean such a variety of different feelings and degrees of feeling that often authors tend to use other means to evoke the affective mental states of characters. Other ways to represent the affective states of characters include providing more complex psychological descriptions, for example by describing the character's attitudes, from which, in context, the reader may infer a certain psychological state (for example, looking at the sky in a particular context); or the use of metaphors, such as when Shakespeare's Romeo utters 'Juliet is the sun', from which the reader not only gathers a subtle impressionistic meaning (Sperber and Wilson 2015), but, as a consequence, also identifies the loving affective state of Romeo. These are representations which do not necessarily give rise to secondary affective effects, but they may do so, in particular in people who have some real experience of similar, or related, affective states. The adult reader who has felt passionate and romantic love in their life will probably experience an affective effect as a result of Romeo's utterance, but a child with little interest in adult feelings will probably have less relevant elements in their psychological environment to contextualise the representations.

In modern literature, there is another way to talk about the psychological, affective state of a character, which consists in representing the world, and in particular, their thoughts and their flow of consciousness, from their own 'internal', mental, perspective (what the Structuralists call *internal focalisation*: Genette 1983). The typical linguistic device used to achieve this is free indirect speech. In free indirect speech, there is no description of the psychological state of a character but rather an invitation to consider what it is like to be looking at the world through the character's eyes and to be thinking what they are thinking, as represented from within by the cognitive and psychological environment of the character themselves. Our second example is of this kind.

In Flaubert's *Sentimental Education*, the hero, Frédéric, finds himself in anguish when he discovers that the inheritance which he was expecting does not exist. This, he believes, will ruin plans he has made with Mrs Arnoux, with whom he is passionately in love:

[i] Frédéric s'était imaginé que sa fortune paternelle monterait un jour à quinze mille livres de rente, et il l'avait fait savoir, d'une façon indirecte, aux Arnoux. [ii] Il allait donc passer pour un hâbleur, un drôle, un polisson, qui s'était introduit chez eux dans l'espérance d'un profit quelconque! [iii] Et elle, Madame Arnoux, comment la revoir maintenant? (Flaubert, *L'Education sentimentale*)

[i] Frédéric had been under the impression that the fortune coming to him through his father would mount up one day to an income of fifteen thousand livres, and he had so informed the Arnoux in an indirect sort of way. [ii] So then he would be looked upon as a braggart, a rogue, an obscure blackguard, who had introduced himself to them in the

expectation of making some profit out of it! [iii] And as for her – Madame Arnoux – how could he ever see her again now?[6]

Free indirect speech occurs in utterances [ii] and [iii]; they do not express the author's views but the stream of consciousness of the character, reflecting his emotional state. Free indirect speech is traditionally considered a particularly powerful way for the reader to identify with the character; indeed, the reader might well go through some simulation of Frédéric's mental states in the anguishing situations he finds himself dropped into, and free indirect speech is certainly central to such effects. In fact, as argued in Briens and Saussure (2018) and Saussure (2021), the reader will refer to their own experience to simulate what it would be like *for themselves* to be in the position of the character; this, we suggest, achieves the production of secondary affective effects.

Free indirect speech involves a form of meta-representation. In relevance-theoretic terms, it is interpretive use of language. However, it occurs without the explicit linguistic markers of other forms of reported thought or speech (direct and indirect speech). With free indirect speech, the fact that it's an interpretive use of language is only hinted at by elements that find their relevance in the free-indirect-speech interpretation, exclamative forms and interrogatives in particular (Banfield 1973). In this example, what is more, other inferences can be drawn about the author's attitude towards his character's thoughts and emotions; here, perhaps, a subtle form of tender irony about Frédéric's exaggerated reactions.

Free indirect speech is itself a very close relative of irony. Just like ironic utterances, free-indirect-speech utterances are representations of representations and are inferred as such, not explicitly declared as such. A difference between the two is that ironic utterances involve a dissociative attitude on the part of the speaker.

This discussion, incidentally, takes us back to the Jenninger example at the start of this chapter. The source of affective effects in that case was, in essence, mimetic. While the communicator was mimicking the tone and attitude of an individual who sincerely believed the propositional content of their utterances, he completely failed to provide the cues that would have been necessary to indicate adequately his dissociation from this content. Despite objective knowledge that the communicator could not possibly be speaking sincerely, primary affective effects took over (the amygdala hijack again). The audience's feelings of disgust and shame did not emerge as the result of any propositional inferences. Quite the opposite, in fact. Indeed, it is tempting to see parallels between the audience on that night and the baby's response to the smell of sulphur.

---

[6] Flaubert (1885: 137). English translation by Helen Constantine, sourced using freeditorial.com.

6.2 Affective Effects

Jenninger was using free indirect speech in his speech, not irony, but he failed to provide sufficient evidence of a dissociative attitude. This problem was inevitable since it emerged from a double bind: on the one hand, a political leader (particularly a German one) must condemn unambiguously anything near to Nazism. But at the same time, they cannot dismiss or despise or mock ordinary people, even the ordinary people of the past, even the ordinary people who supported such views. Jenninger assumed that his past record of condemning Nazism would suffice and, as a result, allowed the second constraint to prevail over the first. In this particular context – a commemoration of *Kristallnacht* – the affective effects were hardly avoidable. Note that in this case, just as in the example of 'I can hear footsteps in the room above us' (46), both primary and secondary affective effects arise: the former through tone of voice and emotional prosody, the latter through the propositional descriptions made.

According to relevance theory, free indirect speech is a form of the interpretive use of language: that is, language that, on the one hand, is interpretively used – that is, used to represent the thought or utterance of someone other than the speaker – and, on the other, includes the communication of an attitude to the thought or utterance being represented. It is common in literary texts, but it is not specific to literature: it also occurs in speeches (such the example from Jenninger's piece for *Kristallnacht*) and often in everyday conversation. Returning to secondary affective effects, what does appear to be specific to literature is that free indirect speech is used to touch upon issues that will activate experiential, memorial traces in the minds of numerous readers and thus get closer to what it is that the author is expressing. This ability relies on a wide variety of skills, such as the capacity to evoke situations or characters' mental states by means of propositional descriptions but also by means of other, poetic effects, which likewise play with our experiential world.

As we mature, our experiences, which over time turn perhaps into dispositions to feel a certain way, begin to play a key role in our emotional lives. Radcliffe (1999: 113) puts it like this:

Since I am disposed to be fearful of heights ... the representation[7] of standing at the edge of the cliff is associated for me with the idea of discomfort. As a consequence of this association, when I come to the belief that I am actually standing at that location, I feel fear. But if I don't have these tendencies, but others, I might associate the idea of being at the cliff's edge with pleasure, and then I would feel joy at the view or at the sense of freedom I get standing there.

Being angry, moved or passionately in love are largely foreign mental states to individuals who have never experienced them. Young children may understand

---

[7] We leave it open whether this representation is conceptualised or not. (See Fodor 2007.)

love stories in a rational manner, but are not typically very sensitive to them.[8] They might even laugh at the couple embracing passionately at the train station.

Neither is it surprising that they often fail to understand what adults try to communicate to them about the extreme sophistication of and the difficulties that sometimes arise in relationships. However, there comes a point when they begin to be interested in what it is like to be in such circumstances. It could be, for example, that their growing knowledge enables them to grasp some of the more weakly manifest assumptions carried by words such as the following in 'Wild Nights!' by Emily Dickinson (1891), through which she communicates the warmth, safety and all-encompassing security of love:

> Futile the winds
> To a heart in port, –
> Done with the compass,
> Done with the chart[.][9]

However, you can be sure that such lines will be entirely opaque to anyone with no experience of this kind of love at all. This observation sits neatly alongside the notion that only some aspects of knowledge are representational, whereas some sensations, for example, can only be talked about when interlocutors have *experienced* them (or at least similar ones). This is the main property of qualia, and after all, emotions and feelings are qualia. This verse is only truly understood by accessing something like an experience of love. Besides conveying weakly manifest indeterminate assumptions, an extended metaphor such as this – where the speaker is a writer, or a boat, and the loved one a safe harbour – is ineffable because no imaginable explicit counterpart such as an array of propositions, if spelled out, can do the job of exhausting what they convey for an individual. Any attempt to paraphrase 'to a heart in port', be it in one or several sentences, destroys a fundamental element of its expressive power.

We suggest that such creative metaphors evoke intimate experiences about love in a specifically expressive manner, and in so doing elicit affective effects. The metaphor as a whole articulates love in a particular sense of warmth, safety and security and other associated feelings: the recollection of what it was once like to be alone at sea, prey to the winds and storms and an expression of how wonderful it is to feel a sense of belonging in a world where belonging is sometimes so hard. These elements lie beyond any account that relies on

---

[8] Interestingly, small children often have very strong emotional reactions to music. Anecdotally, one of us has a daughter who, between the ages of three and ten, would spontaneously cry at the sound of certain melancholy melodies. The explanation we propose is that music taps into affective resources in a way other art works fail to do, because it creates primary affective effects. (As Tolstoy is famously credited with saying, 'Music is the shorthand of emotion.') The kind of affective effects triggered by literature tend to be secondary.

[9] 'Wild Nights!' was first published in *Poems: Second Series* (Dickinson 1891: 97) The erotic overtones of the image of the heart in a port are equally ineffable (Faris 1967).

propositions. They are also feelings we have when we are experiencing the emotion of joy.

We also suggest that this account is more promising than one which relies on the entertaining of mental images (such as the heart as a boat, imagined in a still harbour surrounded by a harbour wall, which keeps the rough seas at bay). Mental images are so opaquely defined and at least as little understood. In addition, we feel that the appeal to imagery in this way *over-intellectualises* accounts of the interpretation of metaphor and artworks generally. It inflates the relevance-theory account, the strength of which – ironically enough – lies in the fact that it is *de*flationary. It has the effect of making the interpretation of figurative language something different, somehow special. It's not. Our accounts need to be rooted in sensations, feelings and emotion.

If we follow the idea that affective effects somehow activate experiential reactions, then it should follow that the comprehension of a poem, for example, relates whatever is made manifest with equivalents in the reader's experiential memory or imaginings, hence their impact on the reader's affective life. The interpretation of poetry is widely about how to 'make sense' of our intimate experience, and feeling that emotional states similar to our own are shared by others, and that we may be called to share those which we have not yet known directly ourselves. Many poems have this touch of 'expressive maieutics'. Just as some pieces of knowledge appear obvious when they are well formulated and demonstrated, as in Socratic dialogues, the psychological elements brought about by poetry (and the poetic elements in other forms of literature) often appear as fully formed, crystal-clear truths which we might have never thought about before but seem nonetheless familiar to our deep intuitions.

While the processes involved in the derivation of (secondary) affective effects share features with those involved in propositional communication, such as the reliance on Theory of Mind, they also exhibit a number of differences. Sensing someone else's emotional state does not happen through a scheme of inference, nor through logical steps of derivation. As we said earlier, just as there is no inferential route between 'so' and the procedure it encodes, so emotional procedures simply 'switch on' other mental states (some of which may be inferential heuristics). The procedures that are sub-attentive and automatic and emotional states are caught in a direct and immediate way when an individual resorts to the appropriate means: expressives or other linguistic forms, which are loaded with affectivity. We refer the reader again to the literature on emotional contagion (see Hatfield et al. 1994), which claims that in some instances of emotional communication, it is not only conceptual information about emotional states that is conveyed, but something of the states themselves. A theory of utterance interpretation needs to have the machinery to account for such phenomena, and we believe our notion of affective effect is a step in the right direction.

In the Zorba example (50–1), the shouting both immediately attracts the attention of the audience and, as a consequence of the direct expression of the primary affective effect, gives immediate access to an array of propositions about the situation. In that example, the affective effect was reached first with virtually no effort and serves as a pointer to grasp cognitive effects. In the case of secondary affective effects, more needs to be said.

With secondary affective effects, we suggest that cognitive effects are supplemented by affective effects that increase the relevance of the communication and are imperative in order that the threshold at which an utterance is felt to be relevant is reached. In this case, the secondary affective effect activates experiential reactions that provide for a satisfaction of the expectations of relevance. However, in order to accept this theoretical picture one needs to assume that relevance is not achieved only by strictly cognitive, propositional effects, and that the notion that 'relevance has been met' can manage other effects than those that are strictly propositional. This, we suggest, should not be a problem: it's a well-known fact that the mind makes decisions on the basis not only of analytical, propositional working out, but also of emotions and affective states, and there is no reason to think that when it comes to processing language, affective effects do not arise as valid outputs for relevance-oriented checks. We even tend to the view that the notion 'relevance has been met' is perhaps not cognitive in nature, but rather non-propositional. It is a feeling, a feeling of completeness, or achievement, of satisfaction of expectations, and certainly raising affective effects can contribute to the emergence of this feeling of relevance. That a joke is funny is not a strictly cognitive fact: laughing is the manifestation of a feeling, and that feeling is exactly what makes the joke relevant.

Positive affective effects might be said to arise in their own right so long as non-cognitive aspects of the mind are also subject to the principle of relevance, provided, for example, that a notion of affective relevance is integrated into the picture. Consider a case in which affective effects are activated through a process where personal memories and anticipations are compared with the mental states attributed to the communicator, which suddenly appear to make sense in some non-propositional way. That sense could be linked to a mismatch between the normal course of events as anticipated and the affective mental state displayed by the communicator by means of her behaviour.

However, we suggest that in most cases the affective state displayed will impact the cognitive environment of the hearer in a more dramatic way and reduce processing effort drastically while providing cognitive effects in the form of reasons underlying the direct displaying of the affective mental state. Affective effects are therefore linked to attention, as sorts of deictic pointers to those reasons in the circumstances.

Further work will be needed to articulate in detail just how affective effects respond to general principles of interpretation such as those of relevance. As we saw in the previous chapter, while affective scientists do not define affective relevance in terms of effects versus effort, there are good reasons to believe that it is subject to the same general principles as relevance as construed in relevance theory. Emotions, after all, are relevant in the broader sense of being goal-relevant; they are attractors of attention, which can lead to quick cognitive effects and convey forms of information at a low interpretive cost. In the face of principles articulating cognitive effects with cognitive effort, we suggest that similar principles articulate affective effects with processing effort, either in their own right (as with feelings) or as facilitators for cognitive effects themselves. As we have seen, they can be precursors to the search for relevance, or emerge as a consequence of that search. They can (as can standard cognitive effects) be caused by ostensive or non-ostensive behaviours, and (as can standard cognitive effects) rest on our capacity to interpret the mental situations of others or, indeed, rest upon the reactivation of traces of past personal experiences in our memories.

6.2.3 Affective Effects and Persuasion

The various areas of scholarship concerned with the field of argumentation and persuasion – discourse analysis, rhetoric, social psychology, cognitive psychology – have long been interested in the role of emotions in influencing audience's epistemic attitudes, opinion change and 'the manufacture of consent', to use the words of Herman and Chomsky. Klemperer (1947/1998) had already noted how changes in the lexicon can create profound changes in how emotional responses to types of events might be envisaged; Orwell (1946) listed a number of rhetorical devices dealing with emotions which trigger epistemic attitudes and, ultimately, consent. The vast amount of experimental research on heuristics in cognitive psychology since the seminal work by Tversky and Kahneman 1974 (see Petty and Cacioppo 1996 and Gigerenzer and Todd 1999) has established not only the existence of 'cognitive illusions' – whereby people entertain false beliefs and illusory causation schemes – but convincing evolutionary reasons for their existence; see also the whole array of scholarship about the fact that humans generally tend to believe what they 'prefer' to believe, that is, what is emotionally more rewarding, and what is more economical in general for the brain to process. The numerous 'cognitive biases' involved in everyday mental activities point to a preference to believe what is relevant and what does not impact the existing cognitive environment of individuals over a certain level. The general rules seem to be to believe what preserves critical pre-existing assumptions rather than destroying too many of them just because the new piece of information is well grounded analytically. Affect enters this process in many possible ways – for example because some of these rigid pre-existing assumptions are 'dear' to us, with many moral implications and so on – but the manifestation of emotions in communication can be a strong trigger for a form of epistemic contagion.

There is certainly no point in listing all the various ways in which affective effects orient us towards consent or confidence. Showing sympathy, sharing in words the worries or sufferings of a group, or suchlike, are all well-known triggers of open attitudes – unless we spot some warning signs. What matters to us here is something narrower: it's about how affective effects in human interaction orient us towards attitudes of trust in relation with their contribution to relevance. The reason emotion and affect appear to be central contributors to persuasion (see Plantin 2004) is, we suggest, because of the special relationship that exists between affective and cognitive effects in the context of how one achieves relevance in communication.

This perspective raises two important issues. The first is about why *achieving relevance* should enhance persuasiveness at all. The second is about why affective effects should enhance the perceived relevance of a stimulus in the first place.

One could be tempted to suggest that relevance is (taken by humans as) an indicator of truth. This would mean that a particularly relevant utterance is intuitively taken as more likely to be true and thus more believable. However, we suggest that there is no direct relation between being relevant and the epistemic value attributed to the contents communicated in the context. Saussure (2016) claims, on the contrary, that achieving better relevance is taken as an indicator not of saying the truth directly, but of deserving a higher degree of confidence. This is an important point: truth is a matter of propositions matching with the world, whereas confidence is fundamentally a matter of attitude towards the speaker. A central claim in Sperber et al. (2010) is that humans tend to have positive credal attitudes towards individuals that they consider competent (therefore deserving of trust) and benevolent (therefore deserving of confidence). It is clear to us that all things being equal, communication that achieves relevance presents an immediate advantage for the hearer: it is effort-sparing (with regard to the information communicated). And sparing the efforts of others is about preserving their energy, which is ultimately beneficial for their survival. That way, relevant utterances are a valuable gift that orients us towards a form of acknowledgement and, in terms of what concerns us here, a form of confidence, not necessarily about the content (or truth) of the information communicated but about the general reliability of the speaker. The speaker who achieves better relevance exhibits better pragmatic performance, which is beneficial very generally; in sum, relevance itself is taken as an indicator of reliability.

The analysis of the (intentional, delusive) straw-man fallacy in Saussure (2016) suggests that that argumentative move is a winner for the essential reason that the author of an intentional, delusive, straw-man fallacy pretends to

6.2 Affective Effects

unveil a hidden thought – detrimental to the community, or simply ridiculous – on the part of his target simply by interpreting pragmatically some pieces of evidence, usually an utterance. For example, in the US presidential debate between Trump and Clinton, at some point the discussion revolved around the energy grid across Mexico and the United States, and Clinton explained that she wants 'open borders'. Even though everyone was expected at this stage to be aware that the open borders in question were only about electricity, Donald Trump exclaimed: 'She wants open borders, you'll have a disaster with her open borders', hinting, of course, at immigration (Lee and Tanfani 2016). The assumption in Saussure (2016) is that for a significant proportion of the audience, his high pragmatic skills – the ability to derive relevant interpretations – are more likely to encourage confidence than his bad faith (the falsity of his claim) is to discourage it. Such things are tied to how affect is managed in the flow of a debate: among the most successful tools of persuasiveness is the delivering to others of feelings that are simply agreeable.

Taking emotions as indicators of truth is somewhat 'easier' than relying on analytical processing. This is, we suggest, for two kinds of different reasons, depending on whether we are looking at primary, or secondary affective effects. Primary affective effects have a strong impact on processing effort and attract attention to the most relevant element in the environment. Secondary effects will activate, at a lesser cost, a whole array of surplus imports which complement the propositional meaning already delivered.

For Badinter (1981), persuasiveness relies entirely on the affective dimension. This is not, of course, to say that the propositional meanings are irrelevant. But the propositional meanings themselves, the arguments, are not enough to trigger an epistemic decision on the part of the audience. The true function of influence is borne by the affective effects elicited by the non-linguistic means: tone of voice and attitude.

None of this is to claim that the style of Gorgias, the Sophist, is naturally more efficient in triggering consent than the style of the Stoics. But it is a fact that affective effects in communication are often the decisive factor in whether what is stated is to be believed.

7 Emotion and Evolution

> I came to a point where I needed solitude and just stop the machine of 'thinking' ... I just wanted to lie in the grass and look at the clouds –[.]
>
> Jack Kerouac 1960/1977: 116

7.1 Introduction

We remarked in Chapter 2 (p. 25, fn. 9) that continued speculation about the evolutionary origins of language led in 1865 to the Société de Linguistique de Paris's banning all communication on the subject.* We also remarked, perhaps unkindly, that much of the work on the evolution of language in the present day retains the air of speculation that blighted work in the nineteenth century. After all, it's true that the usual methods used to test evolutionary claims – the fossil record, the analysis of homologues of other species within the cline in question – are notably absent in the case of language. The same, of course, can be said (and, indeed, has been said) about the whole project of evolutionary psychology. However, language, which – after all – is so unlike anything else in the natural world, seems to us to be a special case. We therefore endorse the kind of reticence expressed by Chomsky (1995: 18), who said that the issue is 'beyond serious enquiry for the time being, along with many similar questions about cognition generally ... one must be wary of many pitfalls'.

Among the many pitfalls is the fact that for many people the evolution of language and the evolution of communication are the same thing. To take one example, Scott-Phillips (2015) is, by a comfortable margin, one of the better books on the evolution of intentional communication. Aside from worries of testability we find very little to disagree with. He ties together aspects of evolutionary biology and pragmatic theory (in particular, relevance theory) to demonstrate convincingly how human communication might have evolved. Scott-Phillips's book does, however, also claim to be a book about the evolution of *language*. In this respect we find it less successful. Scott-Phillips exapts two pieces of terminology

---

* Parts of this chapter are based on ideas introduced in Cornell and Wharton (2021). The authors are grateful to Louis Cornell for his permission to use thoughts from that paper.

7.1 Introduction

previously used in Wharton (2003b, 2009) – 'natural codes' and 'conventional codes' – and, while he admits to adapting them to suit his own purposes, the definitions he offers are in pretty much the same spirit. Natural codes are codes such as those used in communication that rely on strict coding and decoding (bullfrog calls, bee-dancing, etc.). In the class of natural codes described in these pages we have included human behaviours such as smiling, with the proviso that these can be recruited for use in ostensive-inferential communication by being either deliberately shown (ostensive, in the relevance theory sense) or even faked. Conventional codes, on the other hand, are those regularities perpetuated by tacit agreement between members of a particular community or culture. There are many: driving on the left-hand side of the road (or, inexplicably, the right ...); Morse code; the agreed provision of a percentage of the total bill as a gratuity for waiting staff in a restaurant, or a taxi driver; the tacit agreement that, in the eventuality you are somehow disconnected, the person who initiated the phone call will call back first. Many people include human language on this list, and Scott-Phillips then goes on to define language as 'the rich, structured collection of conventional codes that augment ostensive-inferential communication within a given community' (2015: 20).

This is where we begin to diverge from his view. The notions of 'natural' and 'conventional' codes presented in Wharton (2003b, 2009) were certainly *not* introduced with the intention of accommodating language as an example of the latter. The point, rather, was that the human linguistic code is, at least in the way those two types of codes are defined, *neither natural nor conventional*. As we remarked above, human language is a special case. It's different. Scott-Phillips describes admirably how the kind of system that humans use to put language to use might have evolved (as do Strawson, Grice, Sperber and others), but that's not the same thing as accounting for the evolution of language.

In Chapter 2 we stressed how the cognitive revolution of the 1960s led to huge advances in our understanding of what language is and the unique, sometimes mysterious, properties it exhibits. These properties are totally perplexing. To take three examples, consider (i) the 'headedness' of phrases, (ii) the fact that dependencies are local and (iii) so-called 'island effects'. This is not a book about the evolution of language, and time prevents us from dwelling on the nature of these properties, but they are perplexing because they are properties we only know exist because of the extensive research of generative grammarians. They are also perplexing because these are properties which – despite the fact they can only be identified on the basis of detailed research – we all possess a deep subconscious understanding or knowledge of. If language is *just* a conventional code, how is it that children, who are not only never explicitly taught these rules and, moreover, are never explicitly told what the rules *are not*, induce complex knowledge of such perplexities? Acquiring any knowledge in the absence of any negative evidence is very hard to explain.

For these, and myriad other reasons, we find ourselves convinced that the human neonate is born with a rich innate linguistic endowment (a broadly Chomskyan Universal Grammar – UG) and that it is the maturation of this initial state that is responsible for the *growth* of language. The persistence of (i), (ii) and (iii) in young grammars strongly suggests that it cannot be induced from available data. (See the brief discussion of conceptual development in Chapter 3, which parallels the nativist stance towards language.)

The problem is neatly put by William Lycan (1991: 84): 'most sentences of a language are never tokened at all; since hearers instantly understand novel sentences, this cannot be in virtue of pre-established conventions or expectations directed on those sentences individually'. The notion of language as just another conventional code does not fit with the notion of language as explained by the myriad advances made by generative linguists, where it is viewed from an internalist, modular perspective. Equally, for that matter, we wonder where it fits with the notion of language used in relevance theory, within which Scott-Phillips situates his account. Let's not forget, relevance theory was conceived as a framework intended very much to complement the domain-specific view of language. We are huge admirers of Sperber's (1996) notion of a 'cultural attractor' as a driving force in cultural evolution, and an equally powerful explanatory tool also, but to what extent is it really, as Scott-Phillips (2015: 136) suggests, an alternative to UG?

We do agree that the evolution of conventions may well be part of the story, but it is not the whole one. Mats Furberg, who we quoted in Chapter 1, fn. 6 (Furberg 2010), describes the following description of non-natural meaning as it might have existed at an earlier evolutionary stage. It is from a talk given by Peter Strawson in Sweden in 1963:[1]

S and ... A do not speak the same language. One day when A is out, a lion appears at his hut. Its traces are washed away by the rain. S wishes to warn A. He possesses a lion's paw which he can use for making traces in the sand. If he does so when A is not there, he has not *told* him a lion has been there, since A will take the indentations as signs, possible forged ones, that a lion has been there, *of* a lion, rather than as a message that a lion has been there. Since S wants to get in touch with A, he makes the traces in A's presence, accompanying his performance with an exaggerated facial expression of fear. Then S has, in a single performance, told A there are lions about and also warned him of them. Here is the germ of language. (Furberg 2010: n.p.)

We agree that this example clearly represents the germ of non-natural meaning, However, a lot more is required for it to be an example of the germ of language.

In this chapter we turn to evolutionary concerns that are that are more directly relevant to this book than accounts of evolution of non-natural meaning. Grice is

---

[1] Shared at a meeting of the research group Filosofika föreningen in Gothenburg, April 1963.

famous for what became known as his theory of conversation, which included work on the co-operative principle and maxims but formed only one part of a much larger programme. This famously included his theory of meaning, which we have also mentioned a great deal, and also reason and rationality (see Grice 1982; Neale 1992). One thing that many people overlook about his work on meaning is that while Grice began his famous 1957 paper by introducing meaning$_N$ and saying it was the kind of meaning he was *not* interested in (and effectively dismissed it for the remainder of the paper), Grice was clear that meaning$_N$ and meaning$_{NN}$ were intimately related. Indeed, a central part of his work on meaning was devoted to the task of trying to characterise meaning$_{NN}$ *in terms of* meaning$_N$. Grice suggested that the two forms could be understood as operating under a shared fundamental principle of processing, which he articulated as 'on some interpretation of the notion of consequence, y's being the case is a consequence of x' (1989: 292). As he put it elsewhere, '[i]n natural meaning, consequences are states of affairs; in non-natural meaning consequences are conceptions or complexes which involve conceptions' (Grice 1989: 350).

Grice (1982) addresses this connection and presents us with a 'myth' about how human cognitive capacities might have spiralled in such a way that meaning$_{NN}$ emerged from meaning$_N$. The myth is reminiscent of the Strawson lion example. He asks us to imagine a creature which, when in pain, involuntarily emits a noise – for the sake of argument, a groan. At this stage, the groan means$_N$ that the creature is in pain. Grice then moves through a succession of four further stages designed to show what needs to be added to this scenario in order to arrive at a full-fledged case of meaning$_{NN}$. Grice's (1975) thought experiment is a more highly detailed and nuanced presentation than the one in Grice (1982).

Cornell and Wharton's (2021) exploration of this thought experiment (which we summarise in § 7.2) ends at the stage at which the capacity for recursive meta-representational states of the kind necessary for intentional communication has evolved. They make no claims regarding the evolution of language (see Cornell and Wharton 2021: 179, fn. 1). But Grice was more ambitious than Strawson. He was working towards an account of which the end goal was not just non-natural meaning, or, intentional communication, but *every sense* of meaning$_{NN}$: a capacity for *linguistic* features such as connectives, modal-operators and mood-indicators, as well as certain psychological states such as 'willing' and 'judging' (Grice 1975: 41). Grice was interested not only in the germ of language, but also in its full fruition.

We will say very little more about the evolution of language here, but respectfully suggest that this kind of approach seems to us to be more promising than one in which language is treated as not much more than just another conventional code. Conventional codes are artificial; they are totally *un*-natural. Language is neither.

130   7 Emotion and Evolution

7.2 Creature Construction

7.2.1 Pirot #1: The Sea Sponge

Beginning with simple organisms, Grice (1975) examines how an organism's psychological processes work to construct representations of the surrounding environment in such a way that those representations can be utilised for survival. The more complex the organism, the more nuanced are the processes that have developed to aid it in this task. At first glance it may appear that the experiment is just a phylogenetic study of evolutionary psychology, but Grice does not set out to mirror the evolutionary tree. If it therefore transpires that 'creature construction' does in fact do that, then there is all the more reason to take it seriously. And for Grice, a demonstration of a convincing natural progression would greatly support his claims concerning the relationship which he regards as holding between meaning$_N$ and meaning$_{NN}$.

Grice proposed we consider ourselves as God-like creators – *genitors* – whose role it is to design a series of creatures – *pirots* – which gradually demonstrate increasing cognitive complexity. Our *pirots* must necessarily be oriented towards survival, and any psychological processes we design for them must reflect, in behavioural terms, that orientation for survival. The final *pirot* in our series should possess complex psychological processes characteristic of a higher-order intelligence, but these must always be accountable for in terms of the simpler, lower-order psychological processes preceding them.

By accounting for the evolution of these processes on an incremental basis, Grice sought to ensure that he would be able to reflect upon the interaction between the primitive, simpler cognitive mechanisms and the later, more sophisticated ones. His method stresses a level of consistency, with the notion of organisms evolving over millennia, gradually evolving more and more sophisticated psychological processes, which must all ultimately orient around self-preservation and reproduction. Since Grice's publication, an increasing body of empirical work has grown in different disciplines which examines how evolutionarily more recent circuits are built on top of older circuits and modulate and improve pre-existing functions (Anderson 2010). While, in these pages, we have spoken more about the mind than the brain, study of the ontogenetic and phylogenetic development of the brain has become essential in order to account for how more recent circuits establish more complex patterns of behaviours in the organism by augmenting the core operations carried out by older circuitry. We will therefore remark here and there on brain structures, rather than mind structures, while claiming no expertise on either.

It should be possible to retrace the thought experiment using examples of actual organisms in place of mythical *pirots*, and this is the approach taken in Cornell and Wharton (2021). In the paper, they take the most basic *pirot* to be the sea sponge. Not much turns on this choice; all that matters is that we have some precursory sense of natural meaning, as construed along Grice's general definition 'on some interpretation of the notion of consequence, *y*'s being the case is a consequence of *x*' (1989: 292), and of the fact that that sense of meaning, rather than being a mere fact about the relationship between, say, black clouds and rain, is procedurally embodied in the structure of the organism. Despite lacking a true nervous system (Leys 2015) (or any internal organs) this organism possesses a very basic ability to map sensory information to a motor response. It is able to detect extremes of temperature and dilution of particles in the water and to respond to these conditions by contracting its body in order to protect tissue damage (Bergquist 1974).

At this level of complexity (or perhaps simplicity), the animal possesses no mechanism for conscious experience. However, the kind of mapping it demonstrates between a behavioural response and an environmental condition still provides the basis for an interactive relationship between, on the one hand, the internal and (for want of a better word) 'rational' structures that make up the creature and, on the other, everything that is external to those structures. Since the only variables are the surrounding water conditions and the sea sponge's own capacity for contraction, its experiential states are exhausted by a singular binary pair of meanings: [DESIRABLE] and [UNDESIRABLE]. When the water conditions are [DESIRABLE], no contraction is necessary; it is as a consequence of the water conditions being in this state that the sponge does not need to contract. In a sense, then, the sort of psychological meaning that we are ultimately after can be found emerging as a property of animal–environment interaction the moment a sensory input becomes mapped to a behavioural output. The sea sponge's contractions are certainly meaningful$_N$ (if only in the sense that the actions of set of cells A mean something to set of cells B).

This kind of analogue is useful in demonstrating how our current level of *pirot* complexity might be instantiated within its own meaningful world, but the story of how a capacity to entertain non-natural meaning emerges can be interpreted both phylogenetically and ontogenetically. Another roughly analogous instantiation of the same *pirot* complexity level can observed in human neonates, whose discernment of meanings in the environment and ability to respond to them are similarly collapsed into something resembling a singular pairing of input to output: when reality feels unpleasant, which it often does, it communicates that to its mother. Pause to reconsider the foul smell presented to the neonate.

7.2.2 Towards a Sensorium and a Direct Route

When all is said and done, a sea sponge has a rather easy life. The trade-off is that it also has a rather dull experience of life's meanings. Once, however, the lineage of a psychologically simple organism begins drifting into a more behaviourally demanding environment, the successive generations of its descendants accumulate adaptive changes to pre-existing structures to better cope with the new pressures. A self-propelling organism, on the other hand, interacts with its surrounding environment in a much more complex manner, as it proactively moves itself towards the targets of its biological needs (and away from potential danger). Distinct needs related to eating, drinking, resting, defence and reproduction now require the capacity to instantiate behavioural solutions that are unique to each problem. Anticipating each of these needs *before* their absence becomes critical, and allocating available resources in an attempt to satisfy each of them simultaneously, presents something of a balancing act. This balancing act is termed 'allostasis' (Sterling 2012). Indeed, one of the central principles that underlies an allostatic model is that all organisms, in a sense, are designed to be efficient (Sterling 2004).

An organism capable of self-propulsion naturally interacts with its surrounding environment in a much more involved manner. It is now in a position to move proactively towards the targets of its biological needs. When there is only one goal to pursue, and only one means of pursuing it, our *pirot* can afford to pursue it in a structurally decentralised manner. Now, executive decisions need to be made to determine which subgoal should be prioritised from moment to moment. Cosmides and Tooby's (2000) 'crowded zoo' comes to mind: a basic sensory-motor feedback mechanism, which is all that is needed to perpetuate the integrity of the sponge's bodily structure, now becomes the precursor to a more centralised decision-making process, capable of choosing and sequencing distinct behaviours. But once that goal breaks down into subgoals, executive decisions need to be made – on a moment-by-moment basis – to determine which subgoal should be prioritised. The rudimentary sensory-motor feedback which is adequate to maintain the integrity of the sponge's bodily structure now no longer suffices. What is required is a more centralised decision-making process, capable of choosing and sequencing distinct behaviours. This necessitates the emergence of what is, to all intents and purposes, a sensorium: an internalised map of the surrounding environment, devoted to the fulfilment of allostatic goals.

According to the neurological literature, this moment-to-moment evaluation of allostatic needs takes place in the hypothalamus. Lesions in analogous areas of the rat and human hypothalamus have, for example, been implicated in the development of obesity. When the lesioned circuitry is unable to indicate satiation of its ingestive needs, the organism is unable to detect when it is no longer necessary to eat. This in turn leads to chronic overeating (Swanson 2000). The hypothalamus carries out its function by evaluating and prioritising competing needs, and then initiating the associated behavioural strategy by sending signals to the brain stem, which is responsible for hierarchically organised motor patterns. The execution of this function provides the *pirot* with a level of autonomous agency that it previously lacked. Indeed, having developed *animacy* through its self-initiated behaviour, it begins to resemble something we would consider an 'animal'. (Most people tend to think a sea sponge is closer to a cactus than a cat, but the opposite is true.)

However, the hypothalamus is just one component module that emerges to solve the problem of survival, and despite a recognisable pre-eminence in its phylogenetic emergence, it is not accurate to characterise the hypothalamus (as often happens) as a 'reptilian' layer constituting in itself an earlier stage of evolutionary development (Cesario et al. 2020). Rather, the functionality provided by the hypothalamus has to be complemented by other subsystems.

An increase in the logistical demands of the co-ordination of allostasis requires a more developed capacity to predict and perceive the environment (Clark 2016). To achieve this, associations of encountered sensory experience are stored as distributed patterns of activation across the sensory-motor cortices, where neuronal features are specialised for the storage of different sensory modalities. High-connectivity convergence zones then allow for the information contained in these disparate sensory modalities to be reconstructed as holistic representations of salience encountered in the past (Damasio 1989). Another area of the brain, the hippocampus, acts as a comparator circuit, which assesses incoming sensory inputs against such stored patterns of sensory experience (Gray 1995: 1168). By juxtaposing structural similarities in past experiences with the still-unfolding structures of the present, the hippocampus outputs a predictive stream continually aimed at capturing the next successor state to the present (Stachenfield et al. 2017). This future-predicting perceptual process can now be recruited by the hypothalamus to direct the sensorium into unfolding towards the end-targets of its allostatic goals.

When an interruption to the predictability of unfolding experience is detected by the hippocampal comparator, it sends signals to the densely interconnected circuitry of the amygdala, inducing a physiological alert response (LeDoux 1992). This area of the brain has long been associated with the fear response. However, activity in the amygdala is highest when presented with more ambiguous stimuli; the stimulus of a fearful face, which would indicate a conspecific's detection of a threat but not the threat itself, produces more activity than when the stimulus is an angry face, which would reflect a direct threat (Sander et al. 2003). This suggests the function of the amygdala is not to produce a fearful reaction, but to facilitate the response and processing of uncertainty in the environment. The amygdala is, of course, highly involved in the elicitation of emotional episodes in human.

When an area of the sensorium begins to transform in an unpredicted manner, the amygdala physiologically readies the creature to respond to the unpredicted stimuli, while simultaneously valencing its constituent sensory patterns with affect. Since attention is a finite resource, affective valencing guides the creature to attend to those information structures in its sensorium that are discrepant with its predictions. Since the rest of the perceptual field can be neatly categorised away by predictions, all that is then left to the conscious direction of cognitive attention is relevant stimuli, relevant precisely because they indicate unmapped information with potential allostatic implications. This increases the effectiveness of any deployed response, while also facilitating the integration of the unpredicted experience into the predictive map.[2]

The development of survival circuits such as these eventually result in an internalised model of the environment predicated on a small cluster of psychological processes. The desirability or non-desirability of particular situations – *affect* at a very basic level – is intrinsically entwined with memory. Emotional valences are marked and attached to unpredicted sensory patterns, which facilitates their assimilation into the predictive map of the sensorium. This contextualises their ecological value as primary or secondary reinforcers within a geographic/temporal series of associated reinforcers. The function of memory can only be understood in this context, where it acts as a tool whose purpose is to aid perception and action in the present or future by attaching emotional valences to past experiences (Glenberg 1997). This should demonstrate the weight and importance of the emotional system in terms of behaviour. Emotions are not trifling playthings of self-awareness, there only to enrich and deepen our experience of reality. Emotion, or affect, is intrinsically entwined with memory in the service of survival.

In modern-day humans, it is also, we submit, intrinsically entwined with the processes at play in linguistic communication.

7.2.3   Pirot #2: *The Lizard*

Our next *pirot* must possess all of the psychological processes enabled and instantiated by these neurologically detailed systems and their interactions. It must be capable of goal-directed behaviour, which is initiated by evaluation of allostatic priorities. This evaluation will be facilitated by a predictive sensorium which is capable of, on the one hand, matching its predictions to incoming sensory data, and on the other, integrating the unpredicted experience into the sensorium's predictive map for the future. Any unpredicted inputs will

---

[2] It is observations such as these that are behind Feldman Barrett's (2017a) account in which our traditional categories of emotions are all constructed out of this singular process of affectively valencing unpredicted stimuli. The purpose of possessing a conscious sensorium experience, filled with affective subjectivity, can then be understood as enabling attention to be efficiently directed into the non-overlapping area between prediction and sensory input. We accept the role of affective valencing entirely, but reject the role of concepts in the formation of the emotional states.

7.2 Creature Construction

be affectively marked. This effectively makes the input relevant to the creature. Relevant in what sense? In precisely the sense described in relevance theory. Other things being equal, the greater the effects achieved by processing an input in a context of available assumptions, and the smaller the processing effort required, the greater the relevance of the input to the creature processing it. This cost–benefit analysis dictates the intensity with which any given unpredicted perceptual is affectively marked. Affective relevance has been around for a long time.

Again, the precise nature of the creature we use as our real-life example is unimportant, but let's imagine a lizard, whose hypothalamic circuitry is currently indicating hunger. Following some early period of acquisition, the creature's internal model of the environment contains a map of temporal and geographic associations in sensory-input pattern sequences. The predicted end-targets of goals are optimised for attentive efficiency and the lizard's nervous system is designed to orientate itself towards, and to select between, transformations of the sensory field which it predicts will eventually lead to those end-targets. The result is a predictive map of allostatically desirable behavioural pathways, or corridors, which are projected into the present for the creature to choose from in support of its pursuits.

Consider once again Grice's general definition of meaning (both natural and non-natural): 'on some interpretation of the notion of consequence, y's being the case is a consequence of x' (1989: 292), which underlies these associations between primary and secondary reinforcers. The percept of a lump of meat – seen as the end-target of a strategy aimed at satisfying the hunger it feels – takes on a natural meaning which can be roughly put as 'the imminent satiation of my hunger is a consequence of seeing this percept'. In that respect, a corridor that leads, or potentially leads, to that lump of meat conveys the opportunity for satiation.

Seen this way, percepts are constructed around the way in which an organism perceives their interactive relevance for the completion of goals. James Gibson famously describes these percepts as 'affordances' (1986: 36), which constitute the building blocks of the predictive layer of the sensorium. An object is known when its affordances for interaction have been mapped, because that enables the creature either to interact with the object or ignore it and consequently waste no further cognitive resources on it. Once mastered, the sensory information that gives rise to that object can be ignored, not manifesting in the creature's conscious experience of its sensorium until the corridor specified by goal-directed motor sequences eventually necessitates processing and interaction.

Anything that can result in further updates of the sensorium, such as an unexplored corridor, carries a baseline of relevance, since any unmapped environmental information might ultimately end up being valenced as a goal-target. Once a pattern is discerned from incoming sensory experience which successfully tokens the creature's currently active search category – that is, the percept of the lump of meat – the subgoal *search-for-potential-food-source* is considered accomplished, and the next subgoal in the behavioural sequence, *reduce-distance-from-potential-food-source*, is loaded into the creature's behavioural execution.

For a creature capable of self-directed ambulation, physical objects often present obstacles which require navigation. Let's imagine that our lizard encounters an obstacle: a tree, situated between it and the lump of meat, which has suddenly toppled over and blocked the route. The visual information constituting the percept of a fallen tree blocking its path registers relevance to the creature in conveying the functional implication of *thing-that-cannot-be-moved-through*. In another context, if the creature were pursuing another goal, different affordance qualities of the percept might manifest their relevance – for example, if fallen trees were often home to a particular kind of grub the creature enjoyed, then its relevance would instead manifest as *potential-source-of-food*.

This interruption to the *pirot*'s active goal-directed motor sequence elicits activity in the amygdala, which does two things: first, it sends signals that physiologically prepare the *pirot* for spontaneous movement; second, it affectively marks the stimuli constituting the unpredicted event so that it can be attended to, remembered and integrated into the sensorium's future predictability. The *pirot* now modifies its current active behavioural pattern, from *move-(directly)-towards-the-food-source* to *search-for-a-way-around-the-obstacle (so-that-I-may-continue-moving-towards-the-food-source)*. Perhaps it discovers it can crawl through a gap under the tree. Some of these discoveries might then be marked in the animal's cognitive system as desirable or undesirable (affectively marked), so that successful behaviours can be integrated into the sensorium's predictive capacity. Should the *pirot* find itself in related situations in the future, it will do well to remember what form of behaviour succeeded. For those *pirots* whose behavioural responses were not successful, the opportunity to remember anything no longer presents itself.

By constructing perceptual objects through the lens of their affordances for interaction, a creature's nervous system blinds itself to everything irrelevant to its goals. These affordances are not just implicit properties attached to sensory percepts, but rather shape the form of the percept itself at the point of perception, as supported by neurological evidence. Brain-imaging studies reveal that areas of the premotor cortex associated with tool use are activated when an individual looks at a picture of a hammer (Chao and Martin 2000). Similar effects have also been found for the perception of food (Simmons et al. 2005), as pictures of food activate both the visual cortex and the gustatory processing area. What these results suggest is that the formation of perceptual categories relies on the neural reuse of those areas that are involved in behaviourally interacting with that object.

What a creature perceives when it focuses attention upon any given object in its field of vision, then, are the qualities of that object that have relevance to the goals it is trying to accomplish, with the entire percept being constructed around that relevance. Relevance, situated within a contextualising goal-frame, is therefore a more apt description of what guides a creature's perception, forming the contours of salience in its sensorium, than the objective properties of the entities being represented, since all the creature can see are its goals manifesting through the percepts that compose that goal's movement corridor.

At this stage, none of these representations are embedded into a conceptual description. The creature is simply put into a state in which certain courses of action are activated. Perhaps this is the evolutionary emergence of procedural meaning? Of course, most of the sensory information being taken in by a creature at any given moment has little-to-no bearing on the completion of whichever goal they are currently pursuing. So, in much, much more complex *pirots* – say, the earliest hominins such as an Australopithecines – discoveries that have been affectively marked can be used as relevance detectors in order that incoming stimuli can help restore predictability. At this point, our *pirot* will require a heuristic with which it can sort through the array of mostly useless information successfully, and there will be a strong selective pressure guiding the creature's nervous system to optimise for cognitive efficiency. A tendency towards cognitive efficiency is a natural evolutionary step: a cognitive principle of relevance.

7.2.4   Humean Projection: The Indirect Route

Clearly, an organism with a more developed ability to predict relevant information in the surrounding environment has a much greater chance of success, and one would therefore expect selective pressure towards this predictive capacity to be increased. An expanded capacity to hold, store and compare information might then be turned back towards the individual, with predictions being compared, not with incoming sensory inputs, *but with themselves*. In this way, thoughts might increasingly become a perceptual feature of the environment and the opportunities or affordances they confer on our *pirot* could be explored like any other percept. For social organisms such as primates the internal states of conspecifics become a more and more significant element of the surrounding environment for which a predictive map is developed.

When a *pirot* acquires the degree of complexity afforded by this unconstrained, internalised exploration of sensory pattern associations, the interactive potential it might offer conspecifics greatly increases. For social organisms such as primates, the internal states of our conspecifics form a significant part of the surrounding environment of which we are attempting to develop a predictive map. The Machiavellian intelligence hypothesis (Byrne and Whiten 1988) suggests that dealing with this social complexity presented a particular challenge to early hominids, which led to a kind of 'cognitive arms race', as a result of which human cognitive abilities spiralled. The ability to interpret outward behaviour in terms of the psychological processes giving rise to it would have given an individual strong predictive powers, and it would have been adaptive to become more and more adept at working out the thoughts and feelings of others (Humphrey 1984).

A social *pirot* concerns itself with predicting the internal states of its conspecifics, leading to a basic awareness of their psychological processes and knowledge structures. This produces the means for a sensorium to embed a simulation of itself, perhaps providing a neural substrate for the development of metacognitive processes. The observation of conspecifics, with the aim of reconstructing their internal states in order to better predict their behaviour, may in turn have been the precursor to a creature's capacity to reconstruct its own internal state. A nervous system attempting to produce a definitive abstraction of itself is hindered if notions such as 'self' and 'reality' or 'self' and 'environment' are conflated together. This would prevent the creature from producing a model of itself which is both properly integrated and also differentiated as a singular abstraction.

However, when one *pirot*'s sensorium constructs within itself a speculative map pertaining to the contents of a conspecific's sensorium, it unwittingly embarks on a process of self-discovery, since hiding within the thoughts of any such conspecific will be an objectified perspective of the speculating *pirot*. Determining the internal states of a conspecific necessarily eventually demands accounting for *their* perception of *you* (Rochat 2018). The innate implicit sense of self, reflected in our *pirot*'s perspective of reality, can now be replaced with an explicit self-consciousness derived from an objective perspective with which conspecifics view you, and you view conspecifics.

Pressure to simulate each other's internal states as accurately as possible may, then, have provided the impetus to form categories that internalise psychological processes as manipulable conceptualisations. This is the finalising instance of what Grice called *Humean projection*, our propensity to 'project into the world items which properly (or primitively) considered, are really features of our states of mind' (1975: 41). Psychological processes such as 'knowing that' or 'wanting that' emerge from a place in which they merely support the animal's perspective to one in which they can be actively involved as objectified tools of awareness. Whereas a simple *pirot* might experience a state such as (54):

(54)   want x

A complex *pirot* is capable of experiencing a state such as (55):

(55)   know that [I want x]

7.2 Creature Construction

The introduction of recursion into the *pirot*'s mental representations, allowing it to entertain representations about representations (or meta-representations: Grice 1957, 1982; Sperber 2000), gives rise to an extra magnitude of complexity in the psychological processes that a *pirot* experiences. The unique human disposition to share intentions – in which a meta-representational ability is also implicated – forms the foundations upon which much human interaction (and possibly human culture – see Sperber 1996) is built, being routinely exploited in human communication. On Grice's view, discourse and the recognition of intention operates through rational means; what a speaker means on a given occasion is rationally inferred according to a range of contextual factors.

For Grice, however, rational inferences were by and large, conscious, reflective ones. Relevance theory argues such inferences may be rational, but not necessarily conscious. Speakers know that listeners pay attention only to ostensive acts that are relevant enough, and so in order to attract and hold an audience's attention they should make their linguistic or non-linguistic acts appear at least relevant enough to be worth processing. The communicative principle of relevance claims that by overtly displaying an intention to inform – producing an utterance or other ostensive stimulus – a communicator creates a presumption that the stimulus is at least relevant enough to be worth processing, and moreover, is the most relevant one compatible with her own abilities and preferences.

Our two travelling companions are standing on a train platform. One of them is approached by a stranger, who asks him the time of the next train to Abondance. The decision to respond to this inquiry with the words 'eleven fifty-eight' rather than 'twelve o'clock' is motivated by the communicative principle of relevance. All manner of culturally dependent, encyclopaedic information about trains, how punctual they are in this area and the value that people place on preferring not to miss connections during a journey will inform the speaker's awareness about precisely what kind of information, and to what level of precision, is relevant to the hearer in this context. Had the speaker rounded up the time to 'midday' – a perfectly appropriate thing to do in many other contexts (i.e., when giving the time a train is supposed to arrive) – then it may have resulted in the stranger missing her train.

These considerations over what sort of information might be relevant draw upon certain logical operations, such as conditionals, conjunctives and disjunctives, in determining what needs to be said and what can be left unsaid. However, this rationality is still built on top of the emotional systems that precede it. Antonio Damasio (1994) highlights the problem of considering a rational faculty entirely detached from affect. Inherent in every attempt to arrive directly at an entirely rational analysis of the world is that for every potential hypothesis that may be correct for a given situation or problem, there are infinitely more varieties that could also be considered. For this reason, Damasio suggests, the rational faculty can only operate after emotional valences have worked to constrain our hypothesis-making. On this view, the capacity for rationality emerges relatively late in the *pirot*-building series, as a specialised outgrowth of affect-grounded perception. This is what Ronald de Sousa is getting at when he writes (1987: 195–6): 'The function of emotions is to fill gaps left by "pure reason" in the determination of action: ... it is one of Nature's ways of dealing with the philosophers' frame problem.' Another way Nature found to deal with the philosophers' frame problem is the cognitive principle of relevance.

As an illustration of how rational judgements might amend emotionally valenced perception of environmental affordances, consider the following example. A lower-order *pirot* (P^1) can see a cave as shelter and entertain the thought in (56):

(56) P^1 judges [C = S].

This perception of affordances such as these reflects how, say, the human limbic system constrains the perceptual search space by storing the emotional valences of objects according to their relevance to goals, which are determined by the fundamental drives. With internalised psychological concepts, a higher-order *pirot* can conjoin and embed their own representations, see (57):

(57) P^1 judges [if C = S, & P^2 wills S, then P^2 wills C]

One *pirot* (P^1, or Peter) can determine for himself that if a cave is shelter, and a fellow *pirot* (P^2, or Paul) is searching for shelter, then Paul's search will be satisfied by the discovery of the cave. This draws upon various natural meanings: a cave, including its capacity to provide shelter; a fellow *pirot* and his desire to seek shelter; and the situation of a *pirot* being shown shelter, resulting in a sense of indebtedness. Should P^1 will or desire this situation of indebtedness to occur, then by representing the functional utility of the cave together with P^2 (Paul's) need for shelter, he can perceive the path of behaviour required on his own part to realise the desired situation. *Pirots* of this complexity are in a position to engage in acts of meaning$_{NN}$ (58a–b):

(58a)   Peter utters 'Cave!'

(58b)   Paul judges [Peter judges [if C = S, & Paul wills S, then Paul wills C]]

Given the communicative principle of relevance, Paul searches for the most straightforward way to assimilate the information provided by Peter into the

7.2 Creature Construction 141

contextual frame being set by Paul's current goal – in this case, to find somewhere suitable to shelter. Peter's utterance of the appropriate semantic marker, which causes the activation of Paul's conceptual representation CAVE, leads Paul to explore the manner in which a cave might present those qualities necessary to satisfy the goal of sheltering.

Note that it is not the case that the fact Peter has uttered 'cave' means there is a cave. Instead, what is meant by Peter's utterance is that there is a cave. It means$_{NN}$ 'cave'.

Judgements such as that in (58b) are consistent with a generation of *pirots* who are at such a level of cognitive complexity that evolutionary forces may select for mutations favouring the development of cognitive tools that make these judgements amenable to externalisation. Sperber (2001) suggests that words indicating inferential relationships (e.g., 'since', 'but' and 'nevertheless') might have evolved as tools of persuasion in the cognitive arms race sparked by the communicator's need to demonstrate that an argument is cogent and coherent enough to convince even a hearer who does not have much reason to trust them. As Chomsky has famously suggested: 'Suppose that there was selection for bigger brains ... The brain evolved might have all sorts of special properties ... We have no idea at present how physical laws apply when 10^{10} neurons are placed in an object the size of a basketball' (1975: 321).

Of course, in a rapidly developing cognitive system, in which ever-more-complex embedded syntactic structures are evolving (such as in (58b)), these laws may well result in the kinds of structures that begin to exhibit mysteries such as headedness, local dependency and 'island' effects.[3] And this is our point. When it comes to the evolution of language, non-natural meaning is just the beginning. Grice's thought experiment is so rich in so many regards. Not only is it suggestive in this way, and not only does it show how psychologically complex mental states might emerge from psychologically simple ones, but it also challenges us to carefully consider the relationship between the simpler solutions to evolutionary challenges and the complex ones. Evolution does not dispose of simpler solutions to extant evolutionary problems, particularly if they meet the demands of efficiency. As an example, before the evolution of DNA the earliest life

---

[3] Commenting on Noam Chomsky's now infamous pre–Hauser, Chomsky, and Fitch (2002) views on language evolution, whereby he suggested that language might have emerged in a single genetic mutation, Turner (1998: 72) remarked: 'Imagine a mutant being, genetically gifted to paint like Vermeer born into a culture where no one else can even doodle with a stick. That is the classic Chomskyan view of the origin of language: by genetic accident astounding special language abilities were inserted into the human brain.' The quote misses the point entirely but, in a mind rapidly evolving the type of abilities described in Grice (1975), subtle mutations of the kind through which a novel syntactic ability might evolve (in tandem with a syntax of thought) seem somehow less outlandish.

forms were self-replicating, auto-catalytic ribonucleic acid molecules (RNA); these were the earliest molecules to carry genetic information (they first developed about 4 billion years ago – and one of the largest RNA viruses is SARS-CoV-2, the virus that causes Covid-19). However, although the much more widely known DNA is responsible for the replication and storage of genetic information in modern-day organisms, RNA still acts as an information-transfer system within the human brain. Complex systems augment, rather than replace, simple ones. It is, we submit, entirely reasonable to expect more recently evolved higher-level cognitive processes to be supplemented by more ancient, lower-level ones: a dual-route system is as plausible as it is reasonable.

What distinguishes the two options is that the first involves propositional or conceptual content and the second involves no such content and is entirely non-propositional. Which one do we trust? Anecdotally, our gut feelings tend to have less faith in those who choose to communicate the indirect way than in those who choose the direct way. If we ask someone how they are, someone in whom we somehow sense there is a problem, their cheery response of 'I'm OK, thanks' may well not be believed. In this regard, direct expression seems to take precedence. Perhaps the amygdala hijack is not a 'hijack' at all, but merely a reflection of how humans decisions are actually made. This was knowledge that Robert Badinter knew how to take advantage of.

Grice began by noticing that meaning$_N$ and meaning$_{NN}$ are intimately related: 'on some interpretation of the notion of consequence, y's being the case is a consequence of x' (1989: 292); '[i]n natural meaning, consequences are states of affairs; in non-natural meaning consequences are conceptions or complexes which involve conceptions' (Grice 1989: 350). Cases in which those consequences are incidental to evolutionary function – black clouds, circling vultures – are typically seen as paradigmatic cases of meaning$_N$. But cases which involve an organism possessing a mechanism enabling it to work towards the ultimate evolutionary goal of survival are equally authentic.

What has traditionally been considered the domain of non-natural meaning emerges from the property of conceptualisation which has evolved to isolate, through abstraction of stimulus patterns, functionally salient features of the creature's environment, and which then, in a way we will speculate on no further, somehow develops a system to externalise these conceptualisations for efficient conspecific communication. But as we have said, the simpler processes – sensations, feelings and emotions – enrich and deepen our experience of reality. They are the nuts and bolts of not only the evolutionary game, but also everyday mental life. Without them, an organism's success would be left to incalculably improbable odds, and without

7.2 Creature Construction

them, theories of utterance interpretation are woefully incomplete. What we call language may well be partly, perhaps even mostly, tied in with the evolution of the indirect system: the cortical, clock-like one. But the simpler processes remain, and human mental life and – of course – human linguistic communication is about much more than language: it's about clouds as well as clocks.

It's time we started paying more attention to the clouds.

8 Pragmatics and Emotion
The Challenges Revisited

8.1 Introduction

For reasons we have already outlined, scholars working on utterance interpretation have persisted with the view according to which not only do the mental processes behind cognition and affect exist in two separate domains, but the latter are also somehow less deserving of attention then the former. In some pragmatic accounts, emotion plays no role at all. And even when it does, it plays very much a secondary role to so-called rational and cognitive mechanisms. The view that emotion is somehow antithetical to cognition has its roots deep in the mists of time, in ancient rationalist philosophy. But in the previous chapter we tried to show that emotion and cognition cannot be separated.

When faced with a task of processing information from incoming stimuli, humans have two options: a slow way and a fast way. When faced with the desire to process emotions or to communicate them, these two options are available: the indirect way, in which we conceptualise, and a direct way, in which no such conceptualisation occurs (once more, think of the baby with a phial of sulphur thrust under its nose). Of course, most of the time communicative acts involve *both the indirect and the direct options*, and this is why emotion and cognition are so intertwined. So, we not only hear utterances, but we see and sense and feel them too. Relevance comes in two flavours: affective and cognitive. Communicated effects do too.

In Chapter 2 of this book, we raised two challenges which anyone attempting to accommodate affect into a theory of pragmatics will face. In this closing chapter, and against the backdrop of the discussion in the previous chapter, we revisit those challenges.

8.2 Two Challenges

8.2.1 Description versus Expression

The first challenge we called the challenge of **description versus expression**. One of the principal concepts in the analysis of the meaning of language is its 'aboutness', sometimes called 'intentionality'. Language can be used to describe things in the world. In that sense, sentences and utterances are *about* the world, and in the sense they are about the world, can be judged true or false. Emotions can be described too: an individual might utter '*I am angry*', for example, or '*I am frightened*', and those utterances can be judged true or false. However, this is because those utterances *describe* an emotional state rather than expressing it. But as we have seen throughout the book, emotions can also be expressed directly in such a way that they are not really *about* anything at all (and are most certainly not being rationalised): by shouting '*Aaaaaargh*!' an angry person might express their anger, rather than describe it, and by sitting quaking in a corner with a terrified facial expression, a frightened person might express their fear rather than describe it.

This direct nature of the expression of emotion is a big problem for any attempt to integrate the communication of emotions into a theory of utterance interpretation, whether in everyday human interaction, such as screaming in anger or quaking in fear, or in trying to analyse tropes such as metaphor in the Susan Richardson's 2007 poem 'African Villanelle', which expresses the poet's feelings as well as (or instead of) describing them. The difficulty is, if not an accident of history, certainly a consequence of the way research into language generally has developed and evolved through the years.

8.2.2   Propositions and Ineffability

The second challenge – the challenge of **propositions and ineffability** – is, in essence, the other side of the same coin. This sidelining of emotional communication in modern linguistic pragmatics is very much a consequence of the foundations on which modern theories of semantics and pragmatics are built. Until the nineteenth century, language was almost exclusively studied from either a grammatical or philosophical perspective, and theorists developed theories on how the structure of language reflected the structure of thought, where thought was understood as propositions. Many of the current grammatical and pragmatic notions we have are manifestations of this perspective, which originated in ancient philosophy and continued through to the Port-Royal Grammar. And as a result of this, the vaguer aspects of communication, those descriptively ineffable emotional meanings that are too nebulous to be paraphrased in propositional terms, are not merely overlooked; they are singled out as being unworthy of attention.

8.3   The Challenges: Our Response

In Chapter 5 we proposed that one way to face these challenges, and part of the solution to the problems of exploring the interaction between pragmatics and emotion, is to adopt a relevance-theoretic framework. We begin our response by outlining two theoretical advances which form the basis of our belief that this theory is uniquely positioned to accommodate the communication of affect and emotion. The first of these is the notion of non-conceptual or *procedural* meaning (Blakemore 1987, 2002). This, we believe, is capable of dealing with the problems associated with the first challenge. The intuitions behind procedural meaning have a long history – Ducrot (1972) and Benveniste (1966), among others, have suggested that some linguistic meaning functions to constrain context, rather than provide conceptual information. But the relevance-theory view of procedures is a resolutely cognitive one and has its roots in the distinction between representation and computation made in cognitive science. Moreover, it is not a phenomenon that occurs only in language: interjections and prosody also function to constrain the context, and that can also encode procedural meaning; and what is more, the activation caused by cognitive procedures is not the kind of activation caused by words that encode concepts. Wharton (2009) proposes that non-verbal codes encode procedural rather than conceptual meaning (see the earlier discussion of signals versus signs in §5.2.2).

Our response to the second challenge begins with the second theoretical advance, which devolves into two key innovations in relevance theory. These result in theoretical divergences from the work of Grice and other post-Gricean and neo-Gricean approaches. In the first of these, and in contrast to broadly Gricean approaches, the relevance-theoretic informative intention is not characterised as an intention to modify the hearer's thoughts directly. This move sheds new light on how to better analyse some of the weaker, vaguer aspects of communication, including the communication of impressions, emotions, attitudes, feelings and sensations. In the second, and again in contrast with Gricean approaches, relevance theory does not attempt to draw the line Grice drew between showing and meaning$_{NN}$ and recognises both as instances of overt intentional communication. These two innovations result in the theory's being able to accommodate extremely vague types of communication and, further, demonstrate that communicated information – whether clock-like or cloud-like – can be *shown* rather than merely meant$_{NN}$, in the Gricean sense. It offers a unique opportunity to respond to the challenge of propositions and ineffability presented in Chapter 2. Just as the two challenges are inextricably intertwined, so are these two theoretical developments closely linked.

But, we have argued, more needs to be done. The extant relevance-theory account, in which ineffable content is accounted for in terms of arrays of weakly manifest propositions, is only a preliminary step in addressing the interlinked challenges. We have argued that we need to free ourselves not only from the view under which communication involves a single, or small group of propositions (relevance theory already does this), but also from a view where propositions are always necessary. To this end, we have introduced our

8.3 The Challenges: Our Response

notion of affective effect, designed to complement the relevance-theory notion of cognitive effect.

Affective effects involve processes that are not adequately described by the representation and/or management of conceptual information. Primary affective effects (whether anticipatory effects or transfer effects) do not involve a search for relevance in the sense of the derivation of cognitive effects, but they do typically arise as a precursor to them. The value of these sorts of effects lies in the speed at which they allow us to act. In the previous chapter we have sketched a 'dual-route' system of cognition, similar to the one proposed by Garrido et al. (2012). The increased speed is responsible for the directness we perceive and enables humans to respond to, for example, dangerous stimuli, well before we have become consciously aware what that stimulus might be and, crucially, attempted to think our way out of it.

Secondary affective effects are caused not by the objects or events responsible for the elicitation of emotional episodes, but by thought itself. Literature, we have suggested, is *the* paradigm example of a form in which, as well as generating cognitive effects in the traditional relevance-theory sense, secondary affective effects are also generated. Just as witnessing a particular scene might elicit affective reactions, so constructing a representation of these situations in our imagination – as a result of, say, reading the description of such scenes in a novel – will elicit affective effects. At the train station, we might see lovers embracing in joy, and feel a smile form on our faces. A scene such this will resonate with scenes witnessed within one's own life experiences. Sometimes, a scene is intentionally shown as part of a film, or depicted in a novel, or put in words in a poem. At this point, the aim of the author is to have the reader experience mental states in a particular way, and that experience is again achieved by resonating with memories of the viewer/reader that are familiar. Sometimes, something is felt to be familiar even though we wouldn't have supposed it would be. A feeling of revelation, or epiphany, is then enjoyed. Fabb (2022) explores how such thrills, or strong experiences interact with physical sensations and emotional states.[1]

---

[1] Fabb (2022) presents a fascinating account of the experience of ineffable significance, utilising aspects of the relevance-theoretic framework as well as Dan Sperber's early work on symbolism (Sperber 1975). He also uses elements of Huron's (2006) account of the chills (and sometimes tears) caused by music. In the main, however, Fabb is interested in cognitive effects which, since they rely on meta-representational scaffolding must, by their very nature, be fully propositional. Our hunch is that the non-propositional 'something else' we are getting at may also be involved in poetic effects, but the 'something else' we are searching for is subtly different to the one he is interested in. His views on word meanings as 'schemata' and on the representational nature of perception, are also somewhat at odds with the views of word meaning and perception offered in these pages.

8.4 Pragmatics and Emotion: Closing Remarks

In writing this book we have attempted to be clear about not only what we mean by emotion, but what we mean by pragmatics also. (As well as related topics, such language, communication etc.) This seems to us to be an important thing. As well as the relief one feels at completing a monograph, we also feel considerable excitement about the prospects of future work in this area. One of the most interesting discoveries we have made in the last few years is the extent to which the concept of relevance used in relevance theory bears interesting comparison to the notion of goal relevance as used by those working in appraisal theory. The existence of this parallel, we suggest, is another reason to believe that relevance theory is uniquely equipped to accommodate the emotional dimension of communication. But whether you care to appeal to relevance theory or not, the fact that affective scientists are interested in notions such as context, and how context is determined, should chime with everyone working in utterance interpretation.

We have suggested that the view that reason and affect exist in separate domains is easily understood. It is a hangover from ancient rationalist philosophy. However, it is time to rid ourselves of such outdated biases. Indeed, one of the main aims of our book is to show not only that emotion and cognition work together, but that *the former is a part of the latter*. Indeed, we have argued that the search for relevance underpins both, where relevance is understood to be a unified concept containing both what is called in this book (following Wharton et al. 2021) affective relevance and pragmatic relevance. One of the ways we have tried to achieve this is through the development of the new theoretical notions. Some relevance theorists, we know, will argue that these complicate the relevance-theory picture unnecessarily. (Some already have.) But our actual hope is that there will come a time in the future where people will call what we are now calling 'affective' effects a type of, albeit non-propositional, 'cognitive' effect. Since emotion is a part of cognition, that, after all, is ultimately what they are.

That kind of view depends on a degree of theoretical unity which, at the moment, does not exist. We believe, however, that it is a degree of theoretical unity worth fighting for.

References

Adger, D. (2015a). More misrepresentation: A response to Behme and Evans 2015. *Lingua* 162: 160–6. DOI: https://doi.org/10.1016/j.lingua.2015.05.005.
Adger, D. (2015b). Mythical myths: Comments on Vyvyan Evans' *The Language Myth*. *Lingua* 158: 76–80.
Allott, N. and M. Textor. (2017). Lexical modulation without concepts. *Dialectica* 71(3): 399–424.
Alpi A, N. Amrhein, A. Bertl et al. (2007). Plant neurobiology: No brain, no gain? *Trends in Plant Science* 12(4): 135–6.
Ameka, F. (1992). Interjections: The universal yet neglected part of speech. *Journal of Pragmatics* 18; 101–18.
Anderson, M. L. (2010). Neural re-use as a fundamental organizational principle of the brain. *Behavioural Science* 33: 245–66.
Anscombre, J. and O. Ducrot. (1983). *L'Argumentation dans la Langue*. Brussels: Éditions Madarga.
Arnauld, A. and C. Lancelot. (1966). *Grammaire générale et raisonnée, ou La grammaire de Port-Royal*. Volume 2. Stuttgart: Frommann. (Originally published 1665.)
Arnold, M. (1960a). *Emotion and Personality*, Vol. I. *Psychological Aspects*. New York: Columbia University Press.
Arnold, M. (1960b). *Emotion and Personality*, Vol. II. *Neurological and Physiological Aspects*. New York: Columbia University Press.
Arp, R. (2008). *Scenario Visualization: An Evolutionary Account of Creative Problem Solving*. Cambridge, MA: The MIT Press.
Arundale, R. (1991). Studies in the way of words: Grice's new directions in conceptualizing meaning in conversational interaction. Paper presented to the International Communication Association, Chicago, IL, 23–27 May 1991.
Augustine of Hippo. (1922). *St. Augustine's Treatise on the City of God*, edited by F. Hitchcock. London: Society for Promoting Christian Knowledge. (Originally published 426.)
Austin, J. (1962). *How to Do Things with Words*. Oxford: Clarendon Press.
Bach, K. (2006). Review of The Logic of Conventional Implicatures by Christopher Potts. *Journal of Linguistics* 42(2) (July): 490–5.
Bach, K. and R. Harnish. (1979). *Linguistic Communication and Speech Acts*. Cambridge, MA: Harvard University Press.
Badinter, R. (1981). Abolition de la peine de mort. Speech delivered at the Assemblé Nationale, Paris, September 17, 1981.
Baillargeon, R. (1987). Young infants' reasoning about the physical and spatial characteristics of a hidden object. *Cognitive Development* 2: 179–200.

Bally, C. (1905). *Précis de Stylistique*. Geneva: C. Eggimann.
Bally, C. (1909). *Traité de Stylistique Française*. Paris: Librairie C. Klincksieck.
Bally, C. (1910). *L'étude systématique des moyens d'expression*. Geneva: C. Eggimann.
Bally, C. (1926). *La Langage et la Vie*. Paris: Payot.
Baluska, F., and S. Mancuso. (2020). Plants, climates and humans: plant intelligence changes everything. *EMBO Report* 21(3). DOI: https://doi.org/10.15252/embr.202050109.
Banfield, A. (1973). Grammar of quotation, free indirect style, and implications for a theory of narrative. *Foundations of Language* 10(1): 1–39.
Barber, C. (1972). *The Story of Language*. London: Pan.
Baron-Cohen, S. (1995). *Mindblindness: An Essay on Autism and Theory of Mind*. Cambridge, MA: MIT Press.
Barsalou, L. (1999). Perceptual symbol systems. *Behavioral and Brain Sciences* 22: 577–660.
Barsalou, L. (2003). Situated simulation in the human conceptual system. *Language and Cognitive Processes* 18: 513–62.
Barsalou, L. (2005). Situated conceptualisation. In H. Cohen and C. Lefebvre (eds.), *Handbook of Categorisation in Cognitive Science*, 619–50. Amsterdam: Elsevier.
Benveniste, E. (1966). De la subjectivité dans la langue. In *Problèmes de linguistique générale*, vol. 1, 259–60. Paris: Gallimard.
Bergquist, P. (1974). Phylum porifera. In A. J. Marshall, and W. D. Williams (eds.), *Textbook of Zoology Invertebrates*, 7th ed., 76–103. Basingstoke: Macmillan.
Berkum, J. J. van. (2018). Language comprehension, emotion, and sociality: Aren't we missing something? In S. Rueschemeyer and G. Gaskell (eds.), *The Oxford Handbook of Psycholinguistics*, 644–70. Oxford: Oxford University Press.
Berlin, B., and P. Kay. (1969). *Basic Color Terms*. Berkeley: University of California Press.
Bickerton, D. (2009). *Adam's Tongue: How Humans Made Language, How Language Made Humans*. New York: Hill & Wang.
Blakemore, D. (1987). *Semantic Constraints on Relevance*. Oxford: Blackwell.
Blakemore, D. (2002). *Relevance and Linguistic Meaning: The Semantics and Pragmatics of Discourse Markers*. Cambridge: Cambridge University Press.
Blakemore, D. (2011). On the descriptive ineffability of expressive meaning. *Journal of Pragmatics* 43(14): 3537–50.
Block, N. (1983). Mental pictures and cognitive science. *The Philosophical Review* 93(4): 499–541.
Bohnemeyer, J. (2020). Linguistic relativity: From Whorf to now. In D. Gutzmann, L. Matthewson, C. Meier, H. Rullmann and T. Zimmermann (eds.), *The Wiley Blackwell Companion to Semantics*, 1st ed., 1–33. New York: Wiley.
Boroditsky, L. (2006). Linguistic relativity. *Wiley Online Encyclopedia of Cognitive Science*. https://onlinelibrary.wiley.com/doi/abs/10.1002/0470018860.s00567.
Briens, S. and Saussure, L. de. (2018). Littérature, émotion et expressivité: Pour un nouveau champ de recherche en littérature. *Revue de littérature compare* 365: 67–82. DOI: https://doi.org/10.3917/rlc.365.0067.
Brody, B. (1969). Introduction. In T. Reid, *Reid's Essays on the Intellectual Powers of Man*, xxvi. Cambridge, MA: The MIT Press.
Brown, G., and S. Levinson. (1987). *Politeness: Some Universals in Language Usage*. Cambridge: Cambridge University Press.

Budanovic, N. (2017). 'For sale: baby shoes, never worn': Tracing the history of the shortest story ever told. *Vintage News*, 24 September. www.thevintagenews.com/20 17/09/24/for-sale-baby-shoes-never-worn-tracing-the-history-of-the-shortest-story-ever-told/?chrome=1.

Bühler, K. (1933). Die Axiomatik der Sprachwissenschaften. *Kant Studien* 38(1–2): 19–90.

Buridant, C. (2006). L'interjection: jeux et enjeux. *Langages* 161: 3–9.

Byrne, R. and A. Whiten (eds.) (1988). *Machiavellian Intelligence: Social Expertise and the Evolution of Intellect in Monkeys, Apes and Humans*. Oxford: Clarendon Press.

Caffi, C. and Janney, R. W. (1994). Toward a pragmatics of emotive communication. *Journal of Pragmatics* 22(3–4): 325–73.

Calvo-Merino, B., D. Glaser, J. Grèzes, R. Passingham and P. Haggard. (2005). Action, observation and acquired motor skills: An fMRI study with expert dancers. *Cerebral Cortex* 15(8): 1243–9.

Carston, R. (2002). *Thoughts and Utterances: The Pragmatics of Explicit Communication*. Oxford: Blackwell.

Carston, R. (2018). Figurative language, mental imagery and pragmatics. *Metaphor and Symbol* 33(3): 198–217.

Cave, T. and D. Wilson. (2018). *Reading Beyond the Code: Literature and Relevance Theory*. Oxford: Oxford University Press.

Cesario, J., Johnson, D. J., and Eisthen, H. L. (2020). Your brain is not an onion with a tiny reptile inside. *Current Directions in Psychological Science*, 29(3): 255–60.

Chao, L. L. and A. Martin. (2000). Representation of manipulable man-made objects in the dorsal stream. *Neuroimage* 12: 478–84.

Chomsky, N. (1959). A review of B. F. Skinner's *Verbal Behavior*. *Language* 35(1): 26–58.

Chomsky, N. (1975). *Reflections on Language*. New York: Pantheon.

Chomsky, N. (1995). *The Minimalist Program*. Cambridge, MA: MIT Press.

Chomsky, N. (2000). *New Horizons in the Study of Language and Mind*. Cambridge: Cambridge University Press.

Chomsky, N. (2014). Science, mind, and limits of understanding. Talk at the Science and Faith Foundation (STOQ), The Vatican, January 2014. https://chomsky.info/201401–/.

Cicero, M. (1914). *On Ends*. Translated by H. Rackham. Loeb Classical Library 40, Book III. Cambridge, MA: Harvard University Press.

Cicero, M. T. (1883). *De Finibus Bonorum et Malorum Libri Quinque*. Cambridge: Cambridge University Press.

Clark, A. (2016). *Surfing Uncertainty*. New York: Oxford University Press.

Clough, P. and J. Halley. (2007). *The Affective Turn: Theorising the Social*. Durham, NC: Duke University Press.

Cooper, J. (1999). *Reason and Emotion: Essays on Ancient Moral Psychology and Ethical Theory*. Princeton, NJ: Princeton University Press.

Cornell, L. and T. Wharton. (2021). Before meaning: Creature construction, sea-sponges, lizards and human projection. In E. Ifantidou, L. de Saussure and T. Wharton (eds.), *Beyond Meaning*, 177–98. Amsterdam: John Benjamins.

Cosmides, L. (1989). The logic of social exchange: Has natural selection shaped how humans reason? Studies with the Wason selection task. *Cognition* 31(3): 187–276.

Cosmides, L. and J. Tooby. (1987). From evolution to behavior: Evolutionary psychology as the missing link. In J. Dupré (ed.), *The Latest on the Best: Essays on Evolution and Optimality*, 276–306. Cambridge, MA: The MIT Press.
Cosmides, L. and J. Tooby. (2000). Evolutionary psychology and the emotions. In M. Lewis and J. Haviland Jones (eds.), *Handbook of Emotions*, 91–115. New York: Guilford.
Crawford, R., S. Davis, R. Harding et al. (2000). Initial impact of the Treasure oil spill on seabirds off western South Africa. *South African Journal of Marine Science* 22(1): 157–76.
Culpeper, J. (1996). Towards an anatomy of impoliteness. *Journal of Pragmatics* 25(3): 349–67.
Curea, A. (2015). *Entre Expression et Expressivité: L'Ecole Linguistique de Genève de 1900 à 1940: Charles Bally, Albert Sechehaye, Henri Frei*. Lyons: ENS Éditions.
Damasio, A. R. (1989). Time-locked multiregional retroactivation: A systems-level proposal for the neural substrates of recall and recognition. *Cognition* 33(1–2): 25–62.
Damasio, A. (1994). *Descartes' Error*. New York: Harper Perennial.
Darwin, C. (1998). *The Expression of the Emotions in Man and Animals*. Edited with foreword, commentary and afterword by P. Ekman. London: Harper Collins. (Originally published by John Murray in 1872.)
Davidson, D. (1978). What metaphors mean. *Critical Inquiry* (Special issue on Metaphor) 5(1): 31–47.
Dennett, D. (1981). *Brainstorms: Philosophical Aims on Mind and Psychology*. Boston, MA: MIT Press.
Dennett, D. (1995). *Darwin's Dangerous Idea: Evolution and the Meanings of Life*. London: Penguin.
Deonna, J., and F. Teroni. (2012). *The Emotions: A Philosophical Introduction*. London: Routledge.
de Sousa, R. (1987). *The Rationality of Emotion*. Cambridge, MA: MIT Press.
Dezecache, G., H. Mercier and T. Scott-Phillips. (2013). An evolutionary approach to emotional communication. *Journal of Pragmatics*. DOI: http://dx.doi.org/10.1016/j.pragma.2013.06.007.
Dickinson, E. (1891). Wild nights! In *Poems by Emily Dickinson, Second Series*, 97. Edited by T. Higginson and M. Loomis Todd. Boston: Roberts Brothers.
Ducrot, O. (1972). *Dire et ne pas dire*. Paris: Hermann.
Ducrot, O. (1973). *Le preuve et le dire*. Paris: Mame.
Dukes, D., K. Abrams, R. Adolphs et al. (2021). The rise of affectivism. *Nature Human Behaviour* 5: 816–20. DOI: https://doi.org/10.1038/s41562-021-01130-8.
Dusenbery, D. (1992). *Sensory Ecology: How Organisms Acquire and Respond to Information*. New York: W. H. Freeman.
Ekman, P. (1972). Universal and cultural differences in facial expression of emotions. In J. Cole (ed.), *Nebraska Symposium on Motivation*, 207–83. Lincoln: University of Nebraska Press.
Ekman, P. (1989). The argument and evidence about universals in facial expressions of emotion. In H. Wagner and A. Manstead (eds.), *Handbook of Social Psychophysiology*. New York: Wiley, 143–64.
Ekman, P. (1992). An argument for basic emotion. *Cognition and Emotion* 6 (3/4): 169–200.

Ekman, P. (1994). Strong evidence for universals in facial expressions: A reply to Russell's mistaken critique. *Psychological Bulletin* 115(2): 268–87.

Ekman, P. (1999). Emotional and conversational nonverbal signals. In L. Messing and R. Campbell (eds.), *Gesture, Speech and Sign*, 45–57. Oxford: Oxford University Press.

Ekman, P., and W. Friesen. (1971). Constants across cultures in the face and emotion. *Journal of Personality and Social Psychology* 17(2): 124–9.

Ekman P., E. Sorenson and W. Friesen. (1969). Pan-cultural elements in facial displays of emotion. *Science* 4(164) (3875): 86–8.

Elffers, E. (2020). Significs and Jacques van Ginneken. *History and Philosophy of the Language Sciences* (online only). https://hiphilangsci.net/2020/09/14/significs-and-jacques-van-ginneken/.

Ellsworth, P. C. (2013). Appraisal theory: Old and new questions. *Emotion Review* 5(2): 125–31.

Ellsworth, P. C. and K. R. Scherer. (2003). Appraisal processes in emotion. In R. Davidson, K. Scherer and H. Goldsmith (eds.), *Handbook of Affective Sciences*, 572–95. Oxford: Oxford University Press.

Erdman, K. (1900). *Die Bedeutung des Wortes*. Leipzig: Haessel.

Escandell-Vidal, V. and M. Leonetti. (2011). On the rigidity of procedural meaning. In V. Escandell-Vidal, M. Leonetti and A. Ahern (eds.), *Procedural Meaning: Problems and Perspectives*, 81–102. Bingley: Emerald.

Escobar B., C. Velasco, K. Motoki, D. Byrne and Q. Wang. (2021). The temperature of emotions. *PLoS ONE* 16(6): e0252408. DOI: https://doi.org/10.1371/journal.pone.0252408.

Evans, V. (2014). *The Language Myth: Why Language Is Not an Instinct*. Cambridge: Cambridge University Press.

Fabb, N. (2022). *A Theory of Thrills, Sublime and Epiphany in Literature*. London: Anthem Press.

Faris, P. (1967). Eroticism in Emily Dickinson's 'Wild Nights!'. *The New England Quarterly* 40: 269.

Feagin, S. L. (2018). *Reading with Feeling: The Aesthetics of Appreciation*. Ithaca, NY: Cornell University Press. DOI: https://doi.org/10.7591/9781501721465.

Fehr, L. and Russell, J. A. (1984). Concept of emotion viewed from a prototype perspective. *Journal of Experimental Psychology: General* 113: 464–86.

Feldman Barrett, L. (2006). Are emotions natural kinds? *Perspectives on Psychological Science* 1(1): 28–58. DOI: https://doi.org/10.1111/j.1745-6916.2006.00003.x.

Feldman Barrett, L. (2011). Was Darwin wrong about emotional expressions? *Current Directions in Psychological Science* 20: 400–6.

Feldman Barrett, L. (2017a). The theory of constructed emotion: An active inference account of interoception and categorization. *Social Cognitive and Affective Neuroscience* 12(1): 1–23.

Feldman Barrett, L. (2017b). *How Emotions are Made*. Oxford: Macmillan.

Fernández-Dols, J.-M., and M.-A Ruiz-Belda. (1995). Are smiles a sign of happiness? Gold medal winners at the Olympic Games. *Journal of Personality and Social Psychology*, 69(6): 1113–19.

Fischer, A., and D. Sauter. (2017). What the theory of affective pragmatics does and doesn't do. *Psychological Inquiry*. 28: 190–3.

Fiske, S. T. and S. E. Taylor. (2008). *Social Cognition: From Brains to Culture.* New York: McGraw-Hill.
Flaubert, G. (1885). *L'Education sentimentale.* Paris. Quantin.
Fodor, J. (1975). *The Language of Thought.* New York: Crowell.
Fodor, J. (1983). *The Modularity of Mind.* Cambridge, MA: MIT Press.
Fodor, J. (1998). *Concepts: Where Cognitive Science Went Wrong.* Oxford: Clarendon Press.
Fodor, J. (2007). The revenge of the given. In Brian P. McLaughlin and Jonathan D. Cohen (eds.), *Contemporary Debates in Philosophy of Mind*, 105–16. Oxford: Blackwell.
Fodor, J. (2008). *LOT II: The Language of Thought Revisited.* Oxford: Oxford University Press.
Fontaine, J. and K. Scherer. (2013). Emotion is for doing: The action tendency component. In J. Fontaine, K. Scherer and C. Soriano (eds.), *Components of Emotional Meaning: A Sourcebook*, 170–85. Oxford: Oxford University Press.
Foolen, A. (1997). The expressive function of language: Towards a cognitive semantic approach. In S. Niemeier and R. Dirven (eds.), *The Language of Emotions*, 15–31. Amsterdam: John Benjamins.
Fowler, A. (1989). A new theory of communication. *London Review of Books*, 30 March. www.lrb.co.uk/the-paper/v11/n07/alastair-fowler/a-new-theory-of-communication.
Frege, G. (1948). Sense and reference. *The Philosophical Review* 57(3): 209–30.
Freud, S. (1957). The unconscious. In J. Strachey (ed.), *The Standard Edition of the Complete Psychological Works of Sigmund Freud*, Vol. XIV, 159–216. London: Vintage. (Originally published 1915.)
Fridland, E. (2015). Knowing how: Problems and considerations. *European Journal of Philosophy* 23(3): 703–27.
Fridlund, A. (1992). Darwin's anti-Darwinism in the 'Expression of the Emotions in Man and Animals.' In K. T. Strongman (ed.). *International Review of Studies on Emotion* Vol. 2: 117–37. New York: Wiley.
Fridlund, A. (1994). *Human Facial Expression: An Evolutionary View.* San Diego, CA: Academic Press.
Fridlund, A. (2017). On scorched earths and bad births: Scarantino's misbegotten 'theory of affective pragmatics'. *Psychological Inquiry* 28(2–3): 197–205.
Frijda, N. (2007). *The Laws of Emotion.* Mahwah, NJ: Lawrence Erlbaum Associates.
Furberg, M. (1970). An analysis of non-natural meaning. In T. Dahlquist and T. Pauli (eds.), *Logic and Value*, 9–21. Uppsala: Filosofiska Föreningen Och Filosofiska Institutionen Vid Uppsala Universitet.
Furberg, M. (1971). *Saying and Meaning: A Main Theme in J. L. Austin's Philosophy.* Totowa, NJ: Rowman and Littlefield.
Furberg, M. (2010). Ursus Philosophicus. In *Philosophical Communications*, Web Series, No. 32. (Online resource.) Gothenburg: Department of Philosophy, Gothenburg University, Sweden.
Gardiner, A. (1932). *The Theory of Speech and Language.* Oxford: Clarendon Press.
Garrido, M. I., G. R. Barnes, M. Sahani and R. J. Dolan. (2012). Functional evidence for a dual route to amygdala. *Current Biology* 22(2): 129–34. DOI: https://doi.org/10.1016/j.cub.2011.11.056.

Garzon, P. and F. Keijzer. (2011). Plants: Adaptive behavior, root–brains, and minimal cognition. *Adaptive Behavior* 19(3): 155–71.
Gazdar, G. (1979). *Pragmatics: Implicature, Presupposition and Logical Form.* New York: Academic.
Genette, G. (1983). *Narrative Discourse: An Essay in Method.* Ithaca, NY: Cornell University Press.
Gibson, J. (1986). *The Ecological Approach to Visual Perception.* Hove: Psychology Press.
Gigerenzer, G. and P. Todd. (1999). Fast and frugal heuristics: The adaptive toolbox. In G. Gigerenzer, P. Todd and the ABC Research Group (eds.), *Simple Heuristics That Make Us Smart*, 3–34. Oxford: Oxford University Press.
Gigerenzer, G., P. Todd and The ABC Research Group. (1999). *Simple Heuristics that Make Us Smart.* Oxford: Oxford University Press.
Ginneken, J. van. (1907). *Principes de Linguistique Psychologique.* Paris: Rivière.
Ginneken, J. van. (1943). *Het Mysterie der Menschelijke Taal.* Haarlem: Bohn.
Glenberg, A. M. (1997). What memory is for. *Behavioral and Brain Sciences* 20(1): 1–55. DOI: https://doi.org/10.1017/S0140525X97000010.
Goffman, E. (1964). The neglected situation. *American Anthropologist* 66(6): Part 2; 133–6.
Goffman, E. (1981). *Forms of Talk.* Oxford: Blackwell.
Golding, A. (2016). Metaphor in the embodied mind: Beyond the propositionality of figurative language. (PhD thesis, University of Brighton.)
Goleman, D. (1995). *Emotional Intelligence.* New York: Bantam Books.
Graver, M. (2002). *Cicero on the Emotions: Tuscan Disputations III and IV.* Chicago: Chicago University Press.
Gray, J. (1995). A model of the limbic system and basal ganglia. In M. S. Gazzaniga (ed.), *The Cognitive Neurosciences*, 1165–76. Cambridge, MA: The MIT Press.
Greenspan, P. (2002). Practical reasoning and emotion. In A. Mele and P. Rawlings (eds.), *Rationality*, 206–21. New York: Oxford University Press. DOI: https://doi.org/10.1093/0195145399.003.0011.
Grice, H. P. (1957). Meaning. *Philosophical Review* 66: 377–88.
Grice, H. P. (1969). Utterer's meaning and intentions. *Philosophical Review* 78: 147–77.
Grice, H. P. (1975). Method in philosophical psychology (from the banal to the bizarre). *Proceedings and Addresses of the American Philosophical Association* 48: 23–53.
Grice, H. P. (1982). Meaning revisited. In N. Smith (ed.), *Mutual Knowledge*. London: Academic Press.
Grice, H. P. (1989). *Studies in the Way of Words.* Cambridge, MA: Harvard University Press.
Gregg, M. and G. Seigworth (eds.) (2010). *The Affect Theory Reader.* Durham, NC: Duke University Press.
Gutt, E.-A. (2013). How does the affective relate to ostensive-inferential communication? (Unpublished MS.)
Hall, A. (2007). Do discourse connectives encode concepts or procedures? *Lingua* 117 (1): 149–74.
Hardwick, C. S. (ed.). (1977). *Semiotic and Significs: The Correspondence Between Charles S. Peirce and Victoria Lady Welby.* Bloomington: Indiana University Press.
Hare, R. (1949). Imperative sentences. *Mind* 98 (529): 21–38.

Hare, R. (1971). *Practical Inferences*. London: Red Globe Press.
Hatfield, E., J. Cacioppo and R. Rapson. (1994) *Emotional Contagion*. Cambridge: Cambridge University Press.
Hauser, M. (1996). *The Evolution of Communication*. Cambridge, MA: MIT Press.
Hauser, M., N. Chomsky, and T. Fitch. (2002). The faculty of language: What is it? Who has it, and how did it evolve? *Science* 298: 1569–79.
Heine, B. (2023). *The Grammar of Interactives*. Oxford: Oxford University Press.
Herman, E. S. and N. Chomsky. (1988). *Manufacturing Consent*. New York: Pantheon.
Hess, W. R. and K. Akert. (1965). Experimental data on role of hypothalamus in mechanism of emotional behavior. *A.M.A. Archives of Neurology and Psychiatry* 73: 127–9.
Hitchcock, F. R. M. (ed.). (1922). *St. Augustine's Treatise on the City of God*. London: Society for Promoting Christian Knowledge.
Hockett, C. (1960). The origin of speech. *Scientific American* 203: 88–111.
Hoggett, P. and S. Thompson. (2012). Introduction. In S. Thompson and P. Hoggett (eds.), *Politics and the Emotions: The Affective Turn in Contemporary Political Studies*, 1–20. London: Continuum.
Holtgraves, T. (2005). The production and perception of implicit performatives. *Journal of Pragmatics* 37(12): 2024–43.
Humboldt, W. von. (1999). *'On Language': On the Diversity of Human Language Construction and Its Influence on the Mental Development of the Human Species*. Cambridge: Cambridge University Press. (Originally published in 1836.)
Hume, D. (1739). *A Treatise of Human Nature*. Oxford: Clarendon Press.
Humphrey, N. (1984). *Consciousness Regained*. Oxford: Oxford University Press.
Huron, D. (2006). *Sweet Anticipation: Music and the Psychology of Expectation*. Cambridge, MA: MIT Press.
Izard, C. (1971). *The Face of Emotion*. New York: Appleton–Century Crofts.
Jackson J., J. Watts, T. Henry et al. (2019). Emotion semantics show both cultural variation and universal structure. *Science* 20(366) (6472): 1517–22.
Jagoe, C. and T. Wharton. (2012). Meaning non-verbally: The neglected corners of the bi-dimensional continuum communication in people with aphasia. *Journal of Pragmatics* 178: 21–30.
Jakobson, R. (1929). Romantické všeslovanství – nová slavistika. [Romantic pan-Slavism – A new Slavistics.] *Čin* 1(1): 10–12.
Jakobson, R. (1971). Shifters, verbal categories and the Russian verb. In *Selected Writings of Roman Jakobson*, vol. 2, 386–92. Berlin: Mouton. (Original manuscript 1957.)
James, W. (1884). What is an emotion? *Mind* 9: 188–205.
James, W. (1890). *The Principles of Psychology*, vol. 1. New York: Henry Holt and Co.
January, D. and E. Kako. (2007). Re-evaluating evidence for linguistic relativity: Reply to Boroditsky (2001). *Cognition* 104(2): 417–26.
Jenninger, Philip. (1988). Rede am 10. November 1988 im Deutschen Bundestag. Landesmedienzentruzm Baden-Wurtemberg. Online. www.lmz-bw.de/fileadmin/user_upload/Downloads/Handouts/2018-06-13-jenninger-rede.pdf. (Translation ours.)
Jowett, B. (trans.). (n.d.) *Cratylus, by Plato*. The Internet Classics Archive. www.classics.mit.edu/Plato/cratylus.html. (mit.edu).
Kay, P., B. Berlin, L. Maffi, W. R. Merrifield and R. Cook. (2011). *World Colour Survey*. Stanford, CA: CSLI Publications.

References

Keen, S. (2015). Intersectional narratology in the study of narrative empathy. *Narrative Theory Unbound: Queer and Feminist Interventions*, 123–46. Ohio: Ohio State Press.
Keltner, D., K. Oatley and J. Jenkins. (2019). *Understanding Emotions*. Oxford: Blackwell.
Kerouac, J. (1977). Alone on a mountain top. In *Lonesome Traveler*, 116–30. St. Albans: Granada Press. (Originally published 1960.)
Kleiber, G. (2016). Du cri de douleur au signe de douleur: l' interjection 'Aïe'. *Synergies Pays Scandinaves* 11/12: 113–33.
Klemperer, V. (1998). *I Will Bear Witness: A Diary of the Nazi Years – 1933–1941*. London: Random House. (Originally published 1947.)
Kneepkens, C. H. (2015). The collection of grammatical sophismata in MS London, BL, Burney 330. An exploratory study. *Vivarium* 53: 294–321.
Knuuttila, S. (2004). *Emotions in Ancient and Medieval Philosophy*. Oxford: Clarendon Press.
Koerner, K. (1989). Leonard Bloomfield and the cours de linguistique générale. *Cahiers Ferdinand de Saussure* 43: 55–63.
Kolaiti, P. (2015). The poetic mind: A producer-oriented approach to literature and art. *Journal of Literary Semantics* 44(1): 23–44.
Kolaiti, P. (2019). *The Limits of Expression: Language, Literature, Mind*. Cambridge: Cambridge University Press.
Kolaiti, P. (2022).Perceptual relevance and art: Some tentative suggestions. *Journal of Literary Semantics:* 49: 2.
Kolaiti, P. (in press). *From a Poetics of Language to a Poetics of Action: Literature and Art as a Cognitive Object*. Cambridge: Cambridge University Press.
Kolaiti, P., and T. Wharton. (in press). *Language, Literature and Art: The Composite Organism*. Cambridge: Cambridge University Press.
Komatsu, E. and R. Harris. (1993). *Saussure's Third Course in General Linguistics (from the Notebooks of Emile Constantin)*. Oxford: Pergamon.
König, E. (1991). Identical values in conflicting roles: The use of German ausgerechnet, eben, genau and gerade as focus particles. In A. Werner (ed.), *Discourse Particles*, 11–36. Amsterdam: John Benjamins.
Koopman, E. and F. Hakemulder. (2015). Effects of literature on empathy and self-reflection: A theoretical-empirical framework. *Journal of Literary Theory* 9(1): 79–111.
Kraut, R., and R. Johnston. (1979). Social and emotional messages of smiling: An ethological approach. *Journal of Personality and Social Psychology* 42: 1529–53.
Land, S. (1986). *The Philosophy of Language in Britain: Major Theories from Hobbes to Thomas Reid* (AMS Studies in the Seventeenth Century). New York: AMS Press.
Lange, C. and W. James (eds.). (1922). *The Emotions*. Baltimore: Williams and Wilkins Company. (Original *Om Sindsbevægelser, en Psyko-fysiologisk Studie*, 1885.)
Lazarus, R. S. (1966). *Psychological Stress and the Coping Process*. New York: McGraw-Hill.
Lazarus, R. (1991). *Emotion and Adaptation*. Oxford: Oxford University Press.
LeDoux, J. (1989). Cognitive emotional interactions in the brain. In C. Izard (ed.), *Development of Emotion Cognitive Relations*, 267–89. Hillsdale, NY: Lawrence Erlbaum.
LeDoux, J. E. (1992). Emotion and the amygdala. In J. P. Aggleton (ed.), *The Amygdala: Neurobiological Aspects of Emotion, Memory, and Mental Dysfunction*, 339–51. New York: Wiley–Liss.

LeDoux J. (1996). *The Emotional Brain: The Mysterious Underpinnings of Emotional Life*. New York: Simon and Schuster.

Lee, K. and J. Tanfani. (2016). Donald Trump's claim that Hillary Clinton wants 'open borders' doesn't hold up. *Los Angeles Times*, 19 October. www.latimes.com/politics/la-na-pol-open-border-fact-check-20161019-snap-story.html.

Lepore, E. and M. Stone. (2010). Against metaphorical meaning. *Topoi* 29: 165–80.

Leslie, A. (1994). ToMM, ToBY and agency: Core architecture and domain specificity. In L. L. Hirschfeld and S. German (eds.), *Mapping the Mind: Domain-Specificity in Communication and Culture*, 119–48. Cambridge: Cambridge University Press.

Lettvin, J, H. Maturana, W. McCulloch and W. Pitts. (1959). What the frog's eye tells the frog's brain. *Proceedings of the IRE* (September): 1940–51.

Levelt, W. J. M. (1993). Lexical access in speech production. In E. Reuland and W. Abraham (eds.), *Knowledge and Language*, 241–51. Dordrecht: Springer. DOI: https://doi.org/10.1007/978-94-011-1840-8_11.

Levinson, R. (2003). Blood, sweat, and fears: The autonomic architecture of emotion. *Annals of the New York Academy of Sciences* 1000: 348–66. DOI: https://doi.org/10.1196/annals.1280.016.PMID:14766648.

Levinson, S. (2000). *Presumptive Meanings*. Cambridge, MA: MIT Press.

Leys, S. (2015). Elements of a 'nervous system' in sponges. *Journal of Experimental Biology* 218: 581–91.

Lieberman, M. (2000). Intuition: A social-cognitive neuroscience approach. *Psychological Bulletin* 126: 109–37.

Lighthill, M. (1970). Aquatic animal propulsion of high hydromechanical efficiency. *Journal of Fluid Mechanics*, 44(2): 265–301. DOI: https://doi.org/10.1017/S0022112070001830.

Liu, S. (2011). An experimental study of the classification and recognition of Chinese speech acts. *Journal of Pragmatics* 43(6): 1801–17.

Locke, J. and J. Bennett. (1689/2004). *An Essay Concerning Human Understanding*. N.p.: Jonathan Bennett.

Long, W. (2014). Understanding 'relevance' in psychology, *New Ideas in Psychology* 35: 28–35.

Lycan, W. (1991). Review of Avramides, A. (1989) *Meaning and Mind: An Examination of a Gricean Account of Language*. *Mind and Language* 6: 83–6.

Maillat, D., and S. Oswald. (2011). Constraining context: A pragmatic account of cognitive manipulation. In C. Hart (ed.), *Critical Discourse Studies in Context and Cognition*. Amsterdam: John Benjamins.

Maillat, D. and S. Oswald (eds.). (2013). Biases and constraints in communication: argumentation, persuasion and manipulation. Special issue of *Journal of Pragmatics*. Volume 59, Part B. Amsterdam: Elsevier.

Malle, B. (2004). *How the Mind Explains Behavior: Folk Explanations, Meaning, and Social Interaction*. Cambridge, MA: MIT Press.

Maratos, F. and L. Pessoa. (2019). What drives prioritized visual processing? A motivational relevance account. *Progress in Brain Research* 247: 111–48.

Margolis, E. (1998). How to acquire a concept. *Mind and Language* 13: 347–69.

Martinovic, J., G. V. Paramei and W. J. MacInnes. (2020). Russian blues reveal the limits of language influencing colour discrimination. *Cognition*. 201 (August):

104281. DOI: https://doi.org/10.1016/j.cognition.2020.104281.Epub2020Apr7 .PMID:32276236.

Marty, A. (1875). *Ueber den Ursprung der Sprache (On the Origin of Language).* Würzburg: Stuber.

McBeath, M., D. Shaffer and M. Kaiser. (1995). How baseball outfielders determine where to run to catch fly balls. *Science* 268 (5210): 569–73.

McElvenny, J. (2014). Ogden and Richards' *The Meaning of Meaning* and early analytic philosophy. *Language Sciences* Vol. 41, Part B: 212–21.

McGinn, C. (2004). *Mindsight*. Cambridge, MA: Harvard University Press.

McGuinness, B. (1966). The mysticism of the Tractatus. *The Philosophical Review* 75 (3): 305–28.

Meillet, A. (1910). Compte-rendu: Ch. Bally – Traité de stylistique française. *Bulletin de la Société de linguistique de Paris* 16: cxviii–cxxii. http://gallica.bnf.fr/ark:/121 48/bpt6k321579/f125.image.

Melcher, J. and J. Schooler. (2004). Perceptual and conceptual training mediate the verbal overshadowing effect in an unfamiliar domain. *Memory and Cognition* 32: 618–31. DOI: https://doi.org/10.3758/BF03195853.

Montagrin, V., T. Sterpenich, D. Brosch et al. (2018). Goal-relevant situations facilitate memory of neutral faces. *Cognitive, Affective and Behavioral Neuroscience* 18: 1269–82.

Moors, A. (2009). Theories of emotion causation: A review. *Cognition and Emotion* 23 (4): 625–62.

Moors, A. (2014). Flavors of appraisal theories of emotion. *Emotion Review* 6(4). DOI: https://doi.org/10.1177/1754073914534477.

Moors, A., P. Ellsworth, K. R. Scherer and N. H. Frijda. (2013). Appraisal theories of emotion: State of the art and future development. *Emotion Review*, 5, 119–24.

Murphy, C. (1999). Aquinas on our responsibility for our emotions. *Medieval Philosophy and Theology* 8: 163–205. Cambridge: Cambridge University Press.

Naar, H. and F. Teroni. (2018). *The Ontology of Emotions*. Cambridge: Cambridge University Press.

Nanni, N. di, M. Gnocchi, M. Moscatelli, L. Milanesi and E. Mosca. (2020). Gene relevance based on multiple evidences in complex networks. *Bioinformatics* 36(3): 865–71.

Neale, S. (1992). Paul Grice and the philosophy of language. *Linguistics and Philosophy* 15(5): 509–59.

Nerlich, B., and D. Clark. (1996). *Language, Action, and Context: The Early History of Pragmatics in Europe and America*. Amsterdam: John Benjamins.

Oatley, K. and M. Djikic. (2018). Psychology of narrative art. *Review of General Psychology*, 22(2): 161–8. DOI: https://doi.org/10.1037/gpr0000113.

Oatley, K. and P. N. Johnson-Laird. (1987). Towards a cognitive theory of emotions. *Cognition and Emotion*, 1(1): 29–50. DOI: https://doi.org/10.1080/0269993870 8408362.

Oatley, K., D. Keltner and J. Jenkins. (2006). *Understanding Emotions*. Oxford: Blackwell. (Originally published 1996.)

Ogden, C. and I. Richards. (1923). *The Meaning of Meaning: A Study of the Influence of Language upon Thought and of the Science of Symbolism*. New York: Harcourt Brace.

Olteanu, L., S. Golani, B. Eitam and A. Kron. (2019). The effect of relevance appraisal on the emotional response. *Emotion* 19(4): 715–25. DOI: https://doi.org/10.1037/emo0000473.

Orwell, G. (1946). Politics and the English language. *Horizon*, April. www.orwell.ru/library/essays/politics/english/e_polit.

Padilla Cruz, M. (2009a). Might interjections encode concepts? More questions than answers. *Lodz Papers in Pragmatics* 5(2): 241–70.

Padilla Cruz, M. (2009b). Towards an alternative relevance-theoretic approach to interjections. *International Review of Pragmatics* 1(1): 182–206.

Papert, S. (1970). *Teaching Children Thinking* (AI Memo No. 247 and Logo Memo No. 2). Cambridge, MA: MIT Artificial Intelligence Laboratory.

Petrilli, S. (2009). *Signifying and Understanding Reading the Works of Victoria Welby and the Signific Movement*. Semiotics, Communication and Cognition, Vol. 2. Berlin: de Gruyter.

Petty, R. and J. Cacioppo. (1996). *Attitudes and Persuasion: Classic and Contemporary Approaches*. New York: Avalon Publishing.

Piaget, J. (1957). *Construction of Reality in the Child*. London: Routledge & Kegan Paul.

Pignocchi, A. (2012). The intuitive concept of art. *Philosophical Psychology* 27(3): 425–44.

Pilkington, A. (2000). *Poetic Effects*. Amsterdam: John Benjamins.

Piskorska, A. (2012). Cognition and emotions – a joint effort at obtaining positive cognitive effects? In A. Piskorska (ed.), *Relevance Studies in Poland, Vol. 4. Essays on Language and Communication*, 102–11. Warsaw: Warsaw University Press.

Plantin, C. (2004). On the inseparability of emotion and reason in argumentation. In E. Weigand (ed.), *Emotion in Dialogic Interaction (Current Issues in Linguistic Theory 248)*, 265–76. Amsterdam: John Benjamins.

Pool, E., T. Brosch, S. Delplanque and D. Sander. (2016a). Attentional bias for positive emotional stimuli: A meta-analytic investigation. *Psychological Bulletin* 142(1): 79–106.

Pool, E., V. Sennwald, S. Delplanque, T. Brosch and D. Sander. (2016b). Measuring wanting and liking from animals to humans: A systematic review. *Neuroscience and Biobehavoral Reviews* 63(2016): 124–42. DOI: https://doi.org/10.1016/j.neubiorev.2016.01.006.

Popper, K. (1973). *Objective Knowledge*. Oxford: Oxford University Press.

Potts, C. (2005). *The Logic of Conventional Implicatures*. Oxford: Oxford University Press.

Potts, C. (2007). The expressive dimension. *Theoretical Linguistics* 33(2): 165–97.

Pozner, I. (2022). The relevance-affective model: Explaining narrative empathy within relevance theory. (Thesis, University of Neuchatel.)

Premack, D. (1990). The infant's theory of self-propelled objects. *Cognition* 36(1): 1–16.

Premack, D. and A. Premack. (1994). Moral belief: Form versus content. In L. Hirschfeld and S. German (eds.), *Mapping the Mind: Domain-Specificity in Communication and Culture*. Cambridge: Cambridge University Press.

Pylyshyn, Z. (1973). What the mind's eye tells the mind's brain: A critique of mental imagery. *Psychological Bulletin* 80(1): 1–24.

Qiu, M. (In press). Communicating conceptual and perceptual dimensions: Mental imagery and a dual-route processing of metaphor. (PhD thesis, University of Brighton.)
Radcliffe, E. (1999). Hume on the generation of motives: Why beliefs alone never motivate. *Hume Studies* 25(1–2): 101–22.
Ramachandran, V., and W. Hirstein. (1999). The science of art: A neurological theory of aesthetic experience. *Journal of Consciousness Studies* 6(6–7): 15–51.
Rayo, A. (2013). A plea for semantic localism. *Noûs* 47(4): 647–79.
Recanati, F. (1998). Pragmatics. In E. Craig (ed.), *Routledge Encyclopedia of Philosophy*, 620–33. Abingdon: Routledge.
Recanati, F. (2004). *Literal Meaning*. Cambridge: Cambridge University Press.
Reekum, C. van and K. Scherer. (1997). Levels of processing in emotion-antecedent appraisal. *Advances in Psychology* 124: 259–300.
Reid, T. (1774). A brief account of Aristotle's logic, Vol III, Book III, p. 309. In H. Home, Lord Kames (ed.), *Sketches of the History of Man*. Edinburgh:W. Creech.
Reid, T. (1969). *Essays on the Intellectual Powers of Man*, edited by B. Brody. Boston, MA: Harvard University Press. (Originally published 1785.)
Rey, G. (1980). Functionalism and the emotions. In A. Rorty (ed.), *Explaining Emotions*, 163–98. Los Angeles: University of California Press.
Rey, G. (1981). Introduction: What are mental images? In N. Block (ed.), *Readings in the Philosophy of Psychology*: 117–27. Cambridge, MA: Harvard University Press.
Richardson, S. (2007). *Creatures of the Intertidal Zone*. Birmingham, UK: Cinnamon Press.
Rochat, P. (2018). The ontogeny of human self-consciousness. *Current Directions in Psychological Science* 27(5): 345–50.
Roseman, I. (2013). Appraisal in the emotion system: Coherence in strategies for coping. *Emotion Review* 5(2): 141–9.
Rousseau, J.-J. (1986). *On the Origins of Language*. Chicago: University of Chicago Press.
Rousseau, J.-J. (2009). *Essai sur l'Origine des Langues*. Paris: L'Harmattan. (Originally published 1761.)
Russell, B. (1903). *The Principles of Mathematics*. Cambridge: Cambridge University Press.
Russell, J. A. (1991). Culture and the categorization of emotions. *Psychological Bulletin*. Nov. 110(3): 426–50. DOI: https://doi.org/10.1037/0033-2909.110.3.426 . PMID: 1758918.
Russell, J. (1994). Is there universal recognition of emotion from facial expression? A review of cross-cultural studies. *Psychological Bulletin* 115: 102–41.
Russell, J. (2003). Core affect and the psychological construction of emotion. *Psychological Review* 110(1): 145–72.
Russell, J., and L. Feldman Barrett. (1999). Core affect, prototypical emotional episodes, and other things called emotion: Dissecting the elephant. *Journal of Personality and Social Psychology* 76(5): 805–19.
Salazar-López, E., E. Domínguez, V. Juárez Ramos et al. (2015). The mental and subjective skin: Emotion, empathy, feelings and thermography. *Consciousness and Cognition*, 34: 149–62. DOI: https://doi.org/10.1016/j.concog.2015.04.003. Epub 2015 May 4. PMID: 25955182.

Samuel, S., G. Cole and M. Eacott. (2019). Grammatical gender and linguistic relativity: A systematic review. *Psychonomic Bulletin and Review* 26(6): 1767–86.

Sander, D., J. Grafman and T. Zalla. (2003). The human amygdala: An evolved system for relevance detection. *Reviews in the Neurosciences* 14: 303–16.

Sapir, E. (1921). *Language: An Introduction to the Study of Speech*. London: Harvest.

Saracevic, T. (1975). Relevance: A review of and a framework for the thinking on the notion in information science. *Journal of the American Society for Information Science* 26(6): 321–43.

Saussure, F. de. (1916). *Cours de linguistique générale*. Lausanne and Paris:Payot.

Saussure, L. de. (2005). Manipulation and cognitive pragmatics: preliminary hypotheses. In L. de Saussure and P. Schulz (eds.), *Manipulation and Ideologies in the Twentieth Century. Discourse, Language, Mind*, 113–46. Amsterdam: John Benjamins.

Saussure, L. de. (2021). An experiential view on what makes literature relevant. In E. Ifantidou, L. de Saussure and T. Wharton (eds.), *Beyond Meaning*, 99–118. Amsterdam: John Benjamins.

Saussure, L. de and P. Schulz. (2009). Subjectivity out of irony. *Semiotica* 173(1–4): 397–416.

Saussure, L. de and T. Wharton. (2020). Relevance, effect and affect. *International Review of Pragmatics* 12(2): 183–205.

Scarantino, A. (2017a). How to do things with emotional expressions: The theory of affective pragmatics. *Psychological Inquiry* 28(2–3): 165–85.

Scarantino, A. (2017b). Twelve questions for the theory of affective pragmatics. *Psychological Inquiry* 28(2–3): 217–23.

Scarantino, A., and R. de Sousa. (2021). Emotion. In E. Zalta (ed.) *The Stanford Encyclopedia of Philosophy* (Summer 2021 edition). https://plato.stanford.edu/archives/sum2021/entries/emotion.

Scherer, K. (1982). Emotion as a process: Function, origin and regulation. *Social Science Information* 21: 555–70. DOI: https://doi.org/10.1177/053901882021004004.

Scherer, K. (1994a). An emotion's occurrence depends on the relevance of an event to the organism's goal/need hierarchy. In P. Ekman and R. Davidson (eds.), *The Nature of Emotion: Fundamental Questions*, 227–31. New York: Oxford University Press.

Scherer, K. (1994b). Toward a concept of 'modal emotions'. In P. Ekman and R. Davidson (eds.), *The Nature of Emotion: Fundamental Questions*, 25–31. New York: Oxford University Press.

Scherer, K. (2003). Vocal communication of emotion: A review of research paradigms. *Speech Communication* 40(1–2): 227–56.

Scherer, K. (2009). The dynamic architecture of emotion: Evidence for the component process model. *Cognition and Emotion* 23: 1307–51.

Scherer, K. (2013). The nature and dynamics of relevance and valence appraisals: Theoretical advances and recent evidence. *Emotion Review* 5: 150–62. DOI: https://doi.org/10.1177/1754073912468166.

Scherer, K. and A. Moors. (2019). The emotion process: Event appraisal and component differentiation. *Annual Review of Psychology* 70: 719–45. DOI: https://doi.org/10.1146/annurev-psych-122216-011854.

Scherer, K., A. Schorr and T. Johnstone. (2001). *Appraisal Processes in Emotion: Theory, Methods, Research*. Oxford: Oxford University Press.

Schmitter, A. M. (2014). 17th and 18th century theories of emotions. In E. Zalta (ed.), *The Stanford Encyclopedia of Philosophy.* https://plato.stanford.edu/entries/emotions-17th18th/.

Schooler, J., and J. Melcher. (1994). The ineffability of insight. In S. T. W. Smith and R. Finke (eds.), *The Creative Cognition Approach*, 97–133. Cambridge, MA: MIT Press.

Schuhmann, K. and B. Smith. (1990). Elements of speech act theory in the work of Thomas Reid. *History of Philosophy Quarterly* 7: 47–66.

Scott-Phillips, T. C. (2015). *Speaking Our Minds.* London: Palgrave Macmillan.

Searle, J. (1965). What is a speech act? In M. Black (ed.) *Philosophy in America*, 221–39. Melbourne: Allen and Unwin.

Searle, J. (1969). *Speech Acts.* Cambridge: Cambridge University Press.

Searle, J. (1975). A taxonomy of illocutionary acts. In K. Gunderson (ed.) *Language, Mind and Knowledge.* Minnesota Studies in the Philosophy of Science, vol. 7. (Reprinted in Searle 1979: 1–29.)

Searle, J. (1979). *Expression and Meaning.* Cambridge: Cambridge University Press.

Silvia, P. J. (2006). *Exploring the Psychology of Interest.* New York: Oxford University Press. DOI: https://doi.org/10.1093/acprof:oso/9780195158557.001.0001.

Simmons, W. K., A. Martin and L. W. Barsalou. (2005). Pictures of appetizing foods activate gustatory cortices for taste and reward. *Cerebral Cortex* 15: 1602–08.

Soteriou, M. (2018). The ontology of emotion. In H. Naar and F. Teroni (eds.), *The Ontology of Emotions*, 71–89. Cambridge: Cambridge University Press.

Spelke, E. (1990). Principles of object perception. *Cognitive Science: A Multidisciplinary Journal.* 14(1): 29056.

Spencer-Oatey, H. (2011). Conceptualising 'the relational' in pragmatics: Insights from metapragmatic emotion and (im)politeness comments. *Journal of Pragmatics* 43(14): 3565–78. DOI: https://doi.org/10.1016/j.pragma.2011.08.009.

Sperber, D. (1975). Why are perfect animals, hybrids, and monsters food for symbolic thought? *Method & Theory in the Study of Religion* 8(2): 143–69.

Sperber, D. (1996). *Explaining Culture: A Naturalistic Approach.* Oxford: Blackwell.

Sperber, D. (2000). Metarepresentations in an evolutionary perspective. In D. Sperber (ed.), *Metarepresentations: A Multidisciplinary Perspective*, 117–37. Oxford: Oxford University Press.

Sperber, D. (2001). An evolutionary perspective on testimony and argumentation. *Philosophical Topics* 29: 401–13.

Sperber, D. (2005). Modularity and relevance: How can a massively modular mind be flexible and context-sensitive? In P. Carruthers, S. Laurence and S. Stich (eds.), *The Innate Mind: Structure and Content*, 53–68. Oxford: Oxford University Press.

Sperber, D. (2019). Instincts or gadgets? Not the debate we should be having (Commentary on Heyes C. (2019) *Précis of Cognitive Gadgets: The Cultural Evolution of Thinking*). *Behavioral and Brain Sciences* 42: 35–7.

Sperber, D., F. Clément, C. Heintz et al. (2010). Epistemic vigilance. *Mind and Language* 25: 359–93.

Sperber D. and D. Wilson. (1995). *Relevance: Communication and cognition.* Oxford: Basil Blackwell. (Originally published 1986.)

Sperber, D. and D. Wilson. (1998). The mapping between the mental and public lexicon. In P. Carruther and J. Bouchers (eds.) *Language and Thought: Interdisciplinary Themes*, 184–200. Cambridge: Cambridge University Press.

Sperber, D. and D. Wilson. (2002). Pragmatics, modularity and mindreading. *Mind and Language* 17(1&2): 3–23.
Sperber, D. and D. Wilson. (2015). Beyond speaker's meaning. *Croatian Journal of Philosophy* 15(44): 117–49.
Sperber, H. (1914). *Über den Affekt als Ursache der Sprachveränderung*. Halle a.d. Saale: Max Niemeyer.
Sperling, G. (1960). The information available in brief visual presentations. *Psychological Monographs: General and Applied* 74(11): 1.
Stachenfeld, K., M. Botvinick and S. Gershman. (2017). The hippocampus as a predictive map. *Nature Neuroscience* 20: 1643–53.
Stanley, J. (2011). *Know How*. Oxford: Oxford University Press.
Sterling, P. (2004). Principles of allostasis. In J. Schulkin (ed.). *Allostasis, Homeostasis, and the Costs of Physiological Adaptation*, 17–64. Cambridge: Cambridge University Press.
Sterling, P. (2012). Allostasis: A model of predictive regulation. *Physiology and Behavior*, 106(1): 5–15.
Sterling, P. (2020). *What Is Health? Allostasis and the Evolution of Human Design*. Cambridge, MA: The MIT Press.
Stussi, Y., S. Delplanque, S. Coraj, G. Pourtois and D. Sander. (2018). Measuring Pavlovian appetitive conditioning in humans with the postauricular reflex. *Psychophysiology* 55(8): Article e13073. DOI: https://doi.org/10.1111/psyp.13073.
Suppes, P. (1996). The primacy of utterer's meaning. In R. Grandy and R. Warner (eds.), *Philosophical Grounds of Rationality: Intentions, Categories, Ends*, 109–29. Oxford: Clarendon Press.
Swanson, L. (2000). Cerebral hemisphere regulation of motivated behaviour. *Brain Research* 886: 113–64.
Swee, G. and A. Schirmer. (2015). On the importance of being vocal: Saying 'ow!' improves pain tolerance. *Journal of Pain* 16(4): 326–34.
Tarski, A. (1941). *Introduction to Logic and to the Methodology of the Deductive Sciences*. New York: Dover Press.
Tervaniemi, M., L. Janhunen, S. Kruck, V. Putkinen and M. Huotilainen. (2015). Auditory profiles of classical, jazz, and rock musicians: Genre-specific-sensitivity to musical sound features. *Frontiers in Psychology* 6: 1900.
Thompson, S. and P. Hoggett (eds.). (2012). *Politics and the Emotions: The Affective Turn in Contemporary Political Studies*. London: Continuum.
Tomkins, S. (1962). *Affect, Imagery, Consciousness, Vol. 1. The Positive Effects*. New York: Springer.
Tooby, J., and L. Cosmides. (1992). The psychological foundations of culture. In J. H. Barkow, L. Cosmides and J. Tooby (eds.), *The Adapted Mind: Evolutionary Psychology and the Generation of Culture*, 19–136. Oxford: Oxford University Press.
Trotter, D. (1992). Analysing literary prose: The relevance of relevance theory. *Lingua* 87: 11–27.
Turner, M. (1998). Poetry for the newborn brain: A commentary on Terrence Deacon, The Symbolic Species. *Bostonia* Spring (1): 72–3.
Tversky, A., and D. Kahneman. (1974). Judgment under uncertainty: Heuristics and biases. *Science* 185(4157): 1124–31.

Tye, M. (2004). On the non-conceptual content of experience. In M. Reicher and J. Marek (eds.), *Experience and Analysis: Papers of the 27th International Wittgenstein Symposium*, 221–39. Vienna: Austrian Ludwig Wittgenstein Society.

Vergis, N. (In press). Emotion and speaker meaning: A review of experimental research on conversational inference. *Cognition and Emotion*.

Viano, C. (2018). Aristote et la rhétoriques des émotions: Théorie et mode d'emploi. *Revista Ideação*. DOI: https://doi.org/10.13102/ideac.v0i0.3006.

Wałaszeska, E. (2004). What to do with response cries in relevance theory? In E. Mioduszewska (ed.), *Relevance Studies in Poland. Volume I*, 119–29. Warsaw: University of Warsaw.

Weil, H. (1844). *De l'Ordre des Mots dans les Langues Anciennes Comparées aux Langues Modernes*. Paris: Crapelet.

Wharton, T. (2001). *Paul Grice, Saying and Meaning*. UCL Working Papers in Linguistics, 207–48.

Wharton, T. (2003a). Interjections, language and the 'showing'/'saying' continuum. *Pragmatics and Cognition* 11(1) May: 39–91.

Wharton, T. (2003b). Natural pragmatics and natural codes. *Mind and Language*. 18(5): 447–77.

Wharton, T. (2006). The evolution of pragmatics. In K. Brown (ed.), *The Elsevier Encyclopaedia of Language and Linguistics*, 338–45. Amsterdam: Elsevier.

Wharton, T. (2008). Meaning and showing: Gricean intentions and relevance–theoretic intentions. *Intercultural Pragmatics* 5(2): 131–52.

Wharton, T. (2009). *Pragmatics and Non-verbal Communication*. Cambridge: Cambridge University Press.

Wharton, T. (2015). That bloody so-and-so has retired: Expressives revisited. *Lingua* 75–6: 20–35.

Wharton, T. (2022). Relevance: Communication and cognition and . . .? *Pragmatics and Cognition* 28 (2): 321–47.

Wharton, T., D. Dukes, D. Sander, C. Bonard and S. Oswald. (2021). Relevance and emotion. In special issue of *Journal of Pragmatics* 181: 259–69.

Wharton, T. and C. Strey. (2019). Slave of the passions: Making emotions relevant. In K. Scott, B. Clark and R. Carston (eds.), *Relevance: Pragmatics and Interpretation*, 253–66. Cambridge: Cambridge University Press.

Wierzbicka, A. (1992). The semantics of interjection. *Journal of Pragmatics* 18: 159–92.

Wierzbicka, A. (1996). *Semantics: Primes and Universals*. Oxford: Oxford University Press.

Wierzbicka, A. (2000). The semantics of human facial expression. *Pragmatics and Cognition* 8(1): 147–83.

Wilkins, D. (1992). Interjections as deictics. *Journal of Pragmatics* 18: 119–58.

Williams L. and J. Bargh. (2008) Experiencing physical warmth promotes interpersonal warmth. *Science* 24(322) (5901): 606–7. DOI: https://doi.org/10.1126/science.1162548. PMID: 18948544; PMCID: PMC2737341.

Wilson, D. (1991). *Slave of the Passions*. Basingstoke: Picador Press.

Wilson, D. (2011a). The conceptual-procedural distinction: past, present and future. In V. Escandell, M. Leonetti and A. Ahern (eds.), *Procedural Meaning: Problems and Perspectives*, 3–31. Bingley: Emerald.

Wilson, D. (2011b). Literature as an object of knowledge. Talk given at workshop on 'Concepts', part of the Balzan project, St John's College, Oxford, September 2011.

Wilson, D. (2018). Relevance theory and literary interpretation. In T. Cave and D. Wilson (eds.), *Reading Beyond the Code: Literature and Relevance Theory*, 185–204. Oxford: Oxford University Press.

Wilson, D. and R. Carston. (2019). Pragmatics and the challenge of non-propositional effects. *Journal of Pragmatics* 145: 31–8.

Wilson, D., and D. Sperber. (1981). On Grice's theory of conversation. In P. Werth (ed.), *Conversation and Discourse*, 155–78. London: Croom Helm.

Wilson, D., and D. Sperber. (1988). Mood and the analysis of non-declarative sentences. In J. Dancy, J. Moravcsik and C. Taylor (eds.), *Human Agency: Language, Duty and Value*, 77–101. Stanford, CA:Stanford University Press.

Wilson, D. and D. Sperber. (1993). Linguistic form and relevance. *Lingua* 90(1): 1–25.

Wilson, D. and D. Sperber. (2002). Truthfulness and relevance. *Mind* 111(443) (July): 583–632.

Wilson, D. and T. Wharton. (2006). Relevance and prosody. *Journal of Pragmatics* 38: 1559–79.

Yus, F. (2016). Propositional attitude, affective attitude and irony comprehension. *Pragmatics and Cognition* 23(1): 92–116.

Index

affect
    affective effect, 11, 98, 103, 106
    affective language-comprehension
        model, 71
    affective marking, 137
    affective pragmatics (theory of), 9, 68
    affective relevance, 122, 135, 148
    affective science, 8, 27, 28, 36, 38, 41, 43, 48, 51, 68, 70, 98, 99
    affective valencing, 134
    see also primary affective effect, secondary affective effect
affordances, 135, 136, 140
amygdala, 12, 50, 98, 109, 133
    amygdala hijack, 19, 105, 118, 142
appraisal theory, 8, 10, 33, 37, 38, 39, 48, 98, 99, 101, 102, 106, 148
Aquinas, Thomas, 8, 24, 32, 34
apathea, 2, 34
Apollonius, 24
argumentation, 11, 63, 123
Aristotle, 8, 21, 24, 33, 35, 54, 75
Augustine, St., 8, 21, 34
Ausdruck and *Appel* functions of language, 25
Austin, John Langshaw, 9, 13, 53, 55, 64

Bally, Charles, 2, 8, 9, 52, 55, 57, 58, 59, 60, 61, 62, 63, 71
Benveniste, Emile, 57, 81, 83, 146
Bloomfield, Leonard, 58
Bréal, Michel, 8, 53, 56
Bühler, Karl, 25, 55

Chomsky, Noam, 4, 26, 28, 54, 58, 62, 123, 126, 128, 141
Cicero, 2, 33
code
    natural, 11, 70, 84, 86, 87, 88, 110, 111, 127
cognitive effects, 10, 77, 78, 79, 80, 81, 89, 97, 98, 99, 100, 101, 102, 103, 105, 106, 107, 109, 113, 114, 122, 123, 124, 147

cognitive pragmatics, 58, 60, 97
    see also relevance theory
compassio, 21
conceptual information, 11, 83, 84, 109, 110, 121, 146, 147
constructionism, 42, 43, 49
constructivism, 27, 49, *see* constructionism
conventional implicatures, 81

Damasio, Antonio, 96, 133, 139
Darwin, Charles, 8, 32, 35, 36, 38, 39, 40
Descartes, René, 8, 35
deictics/deixis, 24, 71, 113, 122
    see also indexicals
description vs. expression, 13
    descriptive ineffability, 4, 7, 14, 18, 55, 90, 113, 120, 145, 146
    descriptive meaning, 18
dictum, 62
    dictor, 62
    dictive meaning, 62
dual-route system, 99, 110

embodiment, 20, 30, 41, 95, 105, 131
empathy, 3, 114
Epiphany, 147
    see also Eureka moments
ethnomethodology, 27
Eureka moments, 20
    see also Epiphany
experience, 11, 30, 32, 44, 45, 49, 95, 115, 116, 117, 118, 119, 120, 121, 123, 131, 133, 134, 138, 142, 147
    conscious, 131
    emotional, 8, 38, 109
    felt, 24
    religious, 37
    sensory, 133, 135
expressivity, 18, 62, 71, 82
    expressive meaning, 2, 3, 8, 65, 67, 70, 81
    expressive maieutics, 147

facial expression, 6, 11, 36, 38, 39, 40, 83, 84, 87, 88, 92, 107, 109, 110, 113, 128, 145
feelings, 3, 5, 7, 10, 14, 16, 24, 30, 35, 37, 44, 48, 49, 52, 59, 60, 63, 82, 88, 93, 100, 106, 113, 115, 117, 118, 120, 121, 122, 123, 125, 138, 142, 145
Feldman Barrett, Jennifer, 38, 42, 43, 45, 46, 49
Fodor, Jerry, 26, 42, 77, 96
free indirect speech, 11, 104, 117
Frege, Gottlob, 13, 24, 25, 53, 63

Ginneken, Jacobus van, 2, 3, 53
goal relevance, 10, 48, 101, 102, 148
Grice, Herbert Paul, 9, 10, 11, 12, 13, 22, 53, 54, 60, 61, 62, 64, 66, 67, 70, 73, 74, 75, 77, 80, 82, 84, 85, 86, 89, 90, 91, 94, 99, 127, 128, 129, 130, 131, 135, 138, 141, 142, 146
    Gricean intention-based pragmatics, 26, 70
    Gricean maxims, 75, 129

Hare, Richard, 62
Humboldt, Wilhelm von, 25
Hume, David, 1, 8, 32, 33, 35, 52, 55, 60, 66, 90
    Humean projection, 137, 138

illocutionary acts, 55, 65, 69
intuition, 3, 16, 20
impressions, 1, 10, 60, 63, 90, 94, 95, 146
indexicals, 18, 24, 76, 77, 81
    see also deictics/deixis
interjections, 15, 16, 17, 18, 21, 23, 24, 25, 83, 88, 107, 110, 146
interoception, 45

Jenninger affair, 104, 109, 118, 119

knowing how, 20

literature, 11, 27, 98, 106, 113, 116, 117, 119, 121, 147
    literary effects, 11
literary theory, 27
logic–grammar parallelism, 23, 55, 56

meaning
    natural, 22, 74
    non-natural, 10, 23, 74, 82, 84, 85, 89, 91, 92, 95, 97, 128, 129, 130, 131, 140, 142, 146
mental imagery, 96, 97, 98, 121
metaphor, 3, 5, 7, 14, 63, 93, 94, 95, 97, 98, 117, 120, 121, 145
music, 11, 20, 29

Ogden, Charles K., 53, 54

parole (v. *langue*), 9, 52, 55, 58, 59
pathē, *pathos*, 2, 21, 34
perceptual effects, 98, 105
perturbatio, 34
Plato, 2, 21, 24, 30, 32, 33, 34, 35
    Cratylus, 24
    Gorgias, 21
    Republic, 33
poetic effects, 97, 119, 121
    see also metaphor
Popper, Karl, 3, 4, 26
Port-Royal Grammar, 7, 21, 22, 23, 56, 145
primary affective effect, 11, 106
    anticipatory effects, 11, 109, 112, 147
    transfer effects, 11, 108, 109, 112, 147
    see also affect: affective effect
procedural meaning, 10, 82, 83, 87, 88, 90, 111, 137, 146
prosody, 11, 83, 110, 119, 146

relevance theory, 8, 10, 12, 26, 27, 28, 67, 72, 105, 106, 107, 108, 113, 118, 119, 121, 123, 126, 127, 128, 135, 146, 148
Richards, Ivor, 54
Rousseau, Jean-Jacques, 3, 8, 24, 25, 52, 55, 57
Russell, Bertrand A. W., 13, 25, 53

Sapir–Whorf hypothesis, 44, 58
Saussure, Ferdinand de, 8, 52, 55, 56, 57, 58, 61
Scarantino, Andrea, 30, 67, 68, 69, 70
Searle, John, 13, 53, 65, 67, 69
secondary affective effect, 11, 106, 109, 111
    see also effect: affective effect
sensations, 5, 10, 14, 24, 30, 37, 42, 45, 48, 52, 88, 106, 120, 121, 142, 146, 147
sign, 21, 22, 146
    emotional sign, 87
    natural signs, 11, 22, 86, 87
    Saussurean sign, 57
signal (coded), 75, 76, 83, 86, 92, 112, 146
    emotional, 87
    prosodic, 83
Significs movement, 3, 53
simulation, 95, 118, 138
speech acts, 55

Index

Sperber, Dan, 75, 100
Spinoza, Baruch, 32, 35
Stoics, 2, 33, 34, 54, 55
Stylistics, 58
sympathy, 21, 63, 124

Tarski, Alfred, 13, 25, 63
tranquillitas, 34

Varonus, 24
vigilance
   emotional, 12, 63
   epistemic, 63, 87

Welby, Lady Victoria, 53, 54, 56
Wilson, Deirdre, 75
Wittgenstein, Ludwig, 64

For EU product safety concerns, contact us at Calle de José Abascal, 56–1°,
28003 Madrid, Spain or eugpsr@cambridge.org.

www.ingramcontent.com/pod-product-compliance
Lightning Source LLC
LaVergne TN
LVHW020347260326
834688LV00045B/1576